It was not my war. I had just done what my country had asked me to do. After all, John F. Kennedy had said it all:

> "Ask not what your country can do for you,
> but what you can do for your country."

Well, I have just given my country one of the most incredible years of my young life. Thank God I didn't have to give it all. Lots of fine young men did, and I had the privilege of living and fighting with some of them, of saving some of them, of bleeding and crying with some of them, and mine were the last eyes some of them looked into as they laid down their young lives. My life will never be the same because of them.

May God rest their young souls. . . .

VIETNAM
1968–1969
A Battalion Surgeon Journal

Dr. Byron E. Holley

IVY BOOKS · NEW YORK

Ivy Books
Published by Ballantine Books
Copyright © 1993 by Dr. Byron E. Holley

Library of Congress Catalog Card Number: 92-92758

ISBN 0-8041-0934-6

Manufactured in the United States of America

First Edition: April 1993

Acknowledgments

There are so many different people who have contributed to this project that to name them all would be impossible. However, some have been so directly involved that I feel compelled to mention them by name. Even though I mentioned to Sondra in one of my early letters to save them as I might write a book someday, had it not been for Col. David Hackworth, I would never have written it. He was staying in our home while doing some promotional work for his book *About Face*, when he shared with me the tremendous emotional catharsis that writing the book had been for him. "I highly recommend it, Doc!" he had said. It dawned on me that I had been very reluctant to discuss my tour in Vietnam with anyone other than another Vietnam vet and that perhaps I was holding in too much. The tears I shed as I typed the original manuscript bore stark testimony to that fact.

Although I typed the original manuscript over a period of five and a half months of late-night sessions, many times extending into the wee hours of the morning, much credit has to go to Jan Portnoy who typed the final draft and provided a much needed objective critique of the book. My son John and his friends as well as daughter Allison and her friends provided the fresh insight that only youth can provide. As always, Sondra was nearby, and always willing to contribute as needed. Many other friends and family members added to the content, often unknowingly, by a question or comment they made. An obvious expression of gratitude goes to Mr. Owen A. Lock, editor in chief of Del Rey Books, who agreed to read my manuscript and later accepted it for publication.

The greatest word of thanks I have saved for the end. Unlike many less fortunate veterans of the Vietnam conflict, I have two good eyes to see with, and two hands with intact fingers to type with. Some would say fate—I would say *faith* in my Lord and Savior, Jesus Christ, without which I would never have returned intact.

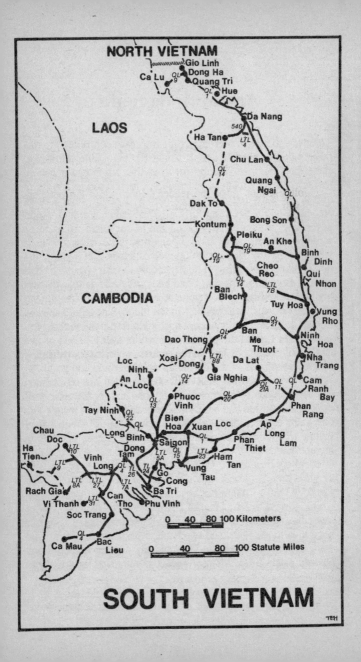

Foreword

Doc Holley's book gives the reader a look inside the butcher shop of war. It's not a pretty picture. In these pages you see how grunts live and die and why the combat medic is the most honored and respected member of the fraternity of the brotherhood of war.

The doc was my battalion surgeon in that mad, bad war in Vietnam. He was a draftee who wore a captain's railroad tracks and didn't give a tinker's damn for all the power and protocol of the system. He cared only for the warriors of the HARDCORE battalion. He was a rebel with a cause. It was his mission to keep the HARDCORE troopers fighting fit and try to keep them alive when a human hunter had done him damage.

Doc Holley told me early in the game that I didn't know much about doctoring and field sanitation, and if I didn't "fuck around" with his medics, he'd keep my troops in fighting shape. He was as good as his word. On the battlefield, the doc was everywhere: on patrol with the troops, patching up the wounded in the center of a nasty minefield, and riding shotgun in my chopper. He was the combat surgeon of combat surgeons. Many HARDCORE troopers are alive today because of his skill, courage to get to the killing field, and strong leadership that made sure his combat medics were well trained and with their platoons, caring for their charges.

In these pages, Holley brilliantly recaptures the battlefield: the waste, the horror, the futility, and the comradeship and love that are the magic glue that keeps warriors sane while wading through the swamp of insanity.

Holley's book doesn't suffer from a foggy memory or the spin that old warriors put on their frequently told war stories. His data base is from the letters he wrote home. So the story is 1969-fresh and has the feel and sound of the battlefield about it. I could smell the swamp stink of Delta water and feel the mud cling to my legs and see the punji stakes, leech bites, and sweat-blackened fatigues of the file of troopers cautiously moving through the hell of the Mekong Delta. It will make you cry, laugh, and rage with anger. It's a moving, gut-wrenching story that explodes like a hand grenade and holds the reader like a minefield.

The doc was everywhere, so his story is not that of an individual platoon, company, or battalion leader. The reader sees the complete big picture. It not only tells the story of the combat medic at war but tells the grunt's story in simple and clear language. It also brought back the terrible casualties the powerful U.S. war machine inflicted on the Vietnamese civilians caught up in the holocaust of war: the women and children blown in half by an ambush patrol who thought they'd snared the Viet Cong, and how this horror affects the kids who triggered the ambush.

This book will become a primer for future combat medics and field surgeons. It will show them how to accomplish their mission of mercy and live through the horror of war.

Since the Vietnam War ended, there has been a carefully managed campaign to rewrite the history of America's involvement in that bloodbath. Retired general William C. Westmoreland and Col. Harry Summers have been the prime movers in this disgusting effort to paint a fresh picture of America's most disastrous war. Both argue that the United States won all the battles but lost the war because of lack of political will at home. Doc Holley's story, written down at the bottom of the killing chain, refutes that lie in spades. His story shows the enemy played the tune, and most American units danced.

He also recaptures the spirit of the heroic combat medic, the most respected of all battlefield players. Elsewhere, I wrote the following words describing this hero and his deeds.

I didn't know what it was about medics. I used to think they joined the Medical Corps because they had a double load of courage, but maybe it was just the title itself that transformed them into the most valiant band of men I ever knew. Medics didn't wait for a miracle to pull the wounded to a safe shelter—they were the miracle that pulled, slid, dragged, and packed shattered bodies out of danger. And they performed miracles: stopping bleeding, stopping shock, relieving pain with morphine, and getting IVs going to pump life into broken fighters. Many packed M-16s along with their forty-pound medical kits, but their job was to save lives, not take them, and they risked their own, again and again, answering calls that took them right into the line of fire—machine gun, mortar, sniper, mines—without hesitation. Their most powerful medicine was their encouragement ("You got it made . . . just a scratch . . . you'll see that girl again"), a never-ending patter to keep minds occupied while deft hands administered aid or tried to sort out a stomach or a chest ripped open by shot. Grievously wounded soldiers were further assisted by the brave pilots who performed medevac missions, but it was the medics who made the difference on the ground, until the choppers could get in. Selfless and serving beyond good sense, countless medics died in the line of duty to save not just their buddies but the life of every man who fell on the battlefield.

This book is a tribute to those mainly unsung heros. From seven wars, it is these men, the medics—the "docs"—who hold the most special place of respect and trust in my infantryman's heart, and I'm sure there are millions of other men in the United States alone who feel the exact same way.

DAVID HACKWORTH
Whitefish, Montana

This book is founded largely on memories and recollections that were rekindled after pouring over hundreds of letters written to my loved ones back home. Most of them were written to my sweetheart, Sondra, now my wife and the mother of two of my fine children. Out of respect for that relationship, little, if any, of the intimacy is related here, but one sentence so struck me that I feel it necessary to share it. In reply to one of her letters in which she was particularly blue, I responded with:

> Love is that relationship between a man and a woman—such that when one sheds a tear, the other tastes salt . . .

With this in mind, I dedicate this book to Sondra, with love and appreciation for her long and patient wait.

Prologue

It is late fall of 1967. I am enjoying an arduous but challenging role as a rotating intern at Baptist Memorial Hospital in Memphis, Tennessee, the largest private hospital in the world. I have heard about Vietnam, but only in newspapers and on television reports. Vietnam is located on the other side of the world, and I am situated very comfortably on the banks of the mighty Mississippi, putting the finishing touches on the skills and knowledge attained in medical school. A friend calls to tell me that our classmate, Dr. Bob Fields, has just been drafted and will be going to Vietnam. Poor guy, I hope he makes it through OK. I think and turn back to the busy routine of another evening shift in the emergency room. I have just met and fallen in love with a wonderful nurse by the name of Sondra Dobbs, a very pretty, green-eyed blond with rosy cheeks and the sweetest southern drawl I have ever heard. She is from Walnut Ridge, Arkansas, and I don't think I can live without her! As soon as I finish my year of internship, we will get married, and I will begin my three years of residency in eye surgery.

Well, it's amazing how one letter from Uncle Sam can change your entire outlook on life! The envelope was white with black print; all I saw was the return address which read Selective Service System, and my heart sank into my stomach. I knew without opening it what the contents of the envelope would say. "Greetings. Your specialized services are required by the U.S. Army Medical Corps. You are hereby directed to maintain direct contact with your local draft board pending further instructions from this agency. You will be allowed to complete your internship, but you are advised not to apply for any further postgraduate clinical training at this time. You can expect to be assigned to the USARV in SE Asia following completion of basic military medical training at Fort Sam Houston." *Damn!* Drafted because I am a doctor! How many guys do you know who are being

1

drafted at age twenty-six and being sent to Vietnam? None! Becoming a doctor has almost been a lifelong dream, and now it may become my death warrant. This is a hard pill to swallow. Will I become another casualty of this insane war on the other side of the world? Will Sondra wait for me to return, knowing full well the risk of my being killed or maimed? If I do survive the war, will I be physically and mentally competent to pursue my chosen field of eye surgery? All these questions bombard my brain as I lay back to reflect on how I came to be a doctor in the first place.

As my great-grandfather, Dr. David E. Saxton, died when I was four years old, I am not sure that I remember him at all. However, the many stories I had heard about his stature as a man and as a physician had made a lasting impression on me. He had been one of Tampa's most highly respected physicians in the early twentieth century, and his son, Jesse J. Saxton, was also a doctor, practicing with his father until his untimely death in an automobile accident shortly before I was born. Many of my great-grandfather's personal possessions were retained in the family, and I had always been especially interested in the medical texts he had studied, one of them dating back to 1823. As a youngster, I had spent many hours examining these materials, pretending that I was a doctor and dreaming of the time when I would enter the field which interested me so much and in which my ancestors had been so successful.

Then there was the fourth of July in 1956 when I had been stung by the bumblebee while out in the woods, and how I had nearly died before my friend, Ronnie McBurney, had brought me to the Palmetto Medical Clinic in Wauchula where a quick-thinking doctor and a nurse had known what to do to sustain my life. I remember the nurse telling me how close I had come to dying and tried to picture my young, healthy body lying in a coffin at my funeral. My admiration for the medical profession took on a new and very realistic dimension.

My thoughts are interrupted by the low sound of a foghorn from a riverboat plying the river below the bluffs of downtown Memphis. In the past I had enjoyed hearing these sounds in the night, but on this particular night, the sound is suddenly very sad and lonely, almost mournful, and I feel the tears begin to well up in my eyes as I contemplate my uncertain future.

Now, it is twenty-two years later, and again I am in Memphis, sitting in a Boeing 727 parked on the tarmac of the same airport where I left for Vietnam so long ago. Now, I feel so different. Now, I'm sitting here reading about myself and many of my friends of the 4/39th Infantry Battalion in Col. David Hackworth's best-selling book, *About Face*. I now have the wonderful knowledge that I did survive my year in Nam with only a couple of scratches. And that Sondra did wait for me and is now my wife and the mother of a fine son and daughter. And that I did realize my dream of becoming an eye surgeon. As I sit here in the cozy security of the jet plane, I feel a slight smirk beginning to form on my face as I think about Hack, the "commie-killer," and how he has almost turned into an antiwar peacenik. My, how times have changed since the sixties!

9 Sep 1968

Fort Sam Houston

Dear Sondra,

Well, here we are. It's kind of hard to believe isn't it? One day you are going along in the routine job of being a rotating intern in a large hospital, and then along comes that fateful letter from Uncle Sam: "Greetings! Your medical services are required in Southeast Asia. Report to Fort Sam Houston in San Antonio NLT than 8 Sep 68 for induction into the U.S. Army Medical Corps."

I sure do miss you, darling, and I've barely gotten started. It's like I'm going away on a little trip and will be back soon. I will be back for a few days in October. We will finish up boot camp on the A.M. of Friday, October 11. I will drive to Tampa and say my good-byes there and will fly to Memphis on the fourteenth. I will have to fly out of Memphis sometime on the sixteenth in order to process in at Travis Air Force Base for my flight to Vietnam.

I am so tired. We have run our butts all over Fort Sam Houston today, and tonight we had to go downtown and buy our uniforms—$255.86 worth, and we still need a few items. Guess what? We bought our uniforms from a private clothing store, the same one where LBJ buys his clothes. In fact, his tailor measured us, and everywhere you looked there were photographs of him fitting the president with different outfits. Bob Flowers was really funny and said, "Well, I never was real impressed with LBJ's clothes anyway!" We all had to agree. LBJ's friend will collect over thirty thousand dollars from our class alone, and there are lots of groups coming through here on a continuous basis all year-round.

On the way downtown, we drove by the Alamo, and I couldn't help thinking about the brave Americans who died there in vain, trying to help a small band of Texans defend against the much larger force of invading Mexicans. Of course, eventually the Texans prevailed, but not without extensive loss of life. "Remember the Alamo" was the battle cry born out of that brave but inglorious defeat. The thought kept racing through my mind: If they remember the Alamo, why are so many young Americans continuing to die in Vietnam, and for what cause? Will we be among the Davy Crocketts of our age who will be remembered only for fighting a good fight enroute to our defeat at the hands of the Viet Cong?

I chose not to share my thoughts with my friends. It hurt too much to talk about it.

12 Sep 68

Today at Fort Sam we spent the entire day studying the ballistics of the different weapons we will be encountering over in Vietnam. They are all very-high-velocity weapons. The M-16 fires a bullet at over 3,250 feet per second. That's over half a mile in the time it takes to snap your fingers! A missile traveling that fast leaves a large zone of tissue destruction surrounding it, from a combination of its tumbling and from the sound waves it generates. They wanted us to visualize some of these and be able to debride them. So we went down to a lab in the basement of one of the buildings, where we could hear muffled gunshots. It soon became apparent what all the shooting was about. We were led into a large laboratory where fifteen or twenty goats were lying on tables with M-16 wounds in their thighs. They were all asleep and in no pain, but it still kind of bothered me. Well, we paired off and started working on debriding their wounds, when our instructor came over and took our minds off the goats! He is a medic, fresh back from Vietnam. He returned on April 13, minus his right hand and forearm. He has a prosthesis with hooks, and it is so pitiful to look at on his otherwise healthy body. He was handing out a bunch of papers, and he dropped them all over the floor. Several guys helped him, and it seemed to embarrass him, but later he told me he thought it was good for him to work with us. He had attended the University of Florida, and we knew several people in common. He is a real neat kid, and it really breaks your heart to see the sacrifice he has made. And I don't mind telling you, I was thinking that he would have a hell of a time learning to perform cataract surgery. He was telling me about a battalion surgeon he knew in Nam who had fallen asleep too near the open door of the aid station bunker. A mortar round landed about eight feet from him and filled him with shrapnel. He was evacuated, patched up, and two months later he was back out in the field with the same unit. Our instructor was also personally aware of two MDs who were killed while he was over there. So, all this bullshit they were feeding us about no doctors being killed is just that—bullshit! He said there are many precautions available to doctors, and he strongly advised that I take full advantage of them. He need not worry—I plan to! He is planning to return to the University of Florida when his two years are up. He was premed, but has decided to go into pharmacy as he knows how most people would react to a doctor with a hook for a hand. Isn't that sad?

We saw a movie on the helicopter and its many uses in Vietnam, with heavy emphasis on air-ambulance missions, referred to as "dust-off" missions. We also saw lots of dead Viet Cong, whom he referred to as "Charlie." Short for "Victor Charlie," which is the radio jargon for VC. The reality of this thing is really beginning to sink in, and it leaves an empty feeling in the pit of my stomach.

13 Sep 1968

Today we had an introductory class in military medicine, contrasting the objectives and goals of this form of medicine with those of civilian medicine, from which we are all coming. Two of the obvious differences are the adverse conditions of war and the fact that under certain tactical situations the care of the patient becomes secondary to the military mission at hand. The success of military medicine in a combat zone depends heavily on intelligent prior planning and training, which anticipates the types of injuries and illnesses that will be encountered as well as the adverse conditions themselves, and how such conditions will affect the treatment and movement of injured troops. It further depends on the organization of teams of medical personnel, trained to provide different levels of care requiring different levels of skill and training at different locations from the fray of battle where the injury has just occurred, to a variety of facilities at varying distances from the front line.

At each level, medical personnel must be well trained and not only willing but capable of accepting responsibility to deliver the care required within their capabilities. The entire system also depends on flexibility on the part of all involved, from the medic in the field, who first applies a pressure dressing to the wound of his fallen comrade, to the neurosurgeon who ends up performing a craniotomy at 3:00 A.M. in the MASH [Mobile Army Surgical Hospital] or evac hospital. The common thread which binds this fabric into a workable garment is the air-ambulance team, affectionately known as the "dust-off."

The helicopter has completely revolutionized the manner in which American and allied troops are evacuated from the field of battle and has reduced fatalities in this conflict by untold thousands. In contrast, the Viet Cong and NVA must rely on the most rudimentary means of evacuation and treatment. The best they can hope for is to survive long enough to be hauled by stretcher to an underground medical facility, where the care will be far below the standards in the American facilities. Many will die for lack of the proper antibiotic, intravenous fluid, blood transfusion, or the availability of a competent surgeon with the skills and capability to save their lives. Some will survive these crude conditions only to have their underground hospital cave in on them from a B-52 raid. The wounded American soldier has an unquestionable advantage in the quest for survival in Vietnam.

The basic concept of wartime medical care involves different echelons of care, provided by persons of increasing levels of skill and expertise at facilities of increasing staff and capabilities, usually at increasing distances from the front line. The dust-off helicopter has shortened this distance significantly since its introduction in the Korean conflict. These echelons can be likened to the rungs of a ladder, with the bottom rung being the medic and his wounded soldier out in the field, and the top of the ladder being the same soldier recovering at an evacuation hospital or even possibly at a general hospital in the Philippines, Japan, or Hawaii.

The first echelon involves the medic in the field with the rifle platoon. He often directs the wounded soldier to the battalion aid station, located near the front line, where the battalion surgeon is waiting to provide emergency care. In cases where the wounds are critical, the medic will usually evacuate the casualty directly to the MASH or evacuation hospital, whichever is closest and able to receive that particular type of injury. In either case, the patient receives essential emergency medical care at this level, aimed at stabilization and preparation for evacuation to the rear. This care may consist of starting intravenous fluids, maintaining an airway, applying tourniquets or pressure dressings, or administration of morphine for pain relief. Primary repair of lacerations and removal of shrapnel may be done at the aid station when life or limb is not threatened.

In the second echelon, the patient is taken to a clearing station (clearing company) where basic hospital and nursing care are available, and if immediate surgery is required, he is sent on to the MASH (Mobile Army Surgical Hospital), usually situated adjacent to the clearing station. Once the surgery has been done and the patient stabilized, transfer to an evacuation hospital is usually the next step.

In this, the third echelon, the patient is moved to a facility which is staffed and equipped to provide wound repair, exploratory and corrective surgery of all types, as well as the necessary postoperative care needed for up to thirty days. Field hospitals serve at this level of care, and many times the choice between an evac or a field hospital will depend on proximity, current caseload, or the requirement for a surgical specialist not available at one or the other location.

If extensive postoperative care or rehabilitation is required beyond thirty days, the patient is sent on to the fourth echelon, a military general hospital located at a remote location away from the war zone.

At all levels of care, triage is carried out. Triage, or sorting of casualties, is based on the principle of accomplishing the greatest good for the greatest number of wounded and injured soldiers. Triage involves decisions concerning the need for resuscitation, the need for emergency surgery, the lack of need for resuscitation or emergency surgery, and the futility of surgery in patients with the most lethal types of wounds. Sorting also involves the establishment of priorities for treatment and evacuation. Triage is one of the most difficult tasks facing the medical corps. The officer responsible for triage has a very heavy responsibility. He must exercise sound surgical judgment as he decides which patients are suitable for transportation and as he weighs the status of nontransportable patients in terms of lifesaving measures immediately at hand against means and speed of transportation. Triage, by the very nature of the echelon system, continues at each level reached, with the preliminary sorting taking place at the battalion aid station or the field, and more careful and detailed sorting occurring at the higher levels. Very little follow-up reporting is possible, so it is unusual for the battalion surgeon to learn of the final disposition of his more seriously injured troops.

Sorting at the aid station or field level involves rapidly classifying casualties into four categories. Category one involves slight injuries which can be managed by the medic on the scene. Category two involves wounds which require more extensive medical care but are not emergent enough to require extended care from a physician or immediate evacuation. Category three contains those with more serious injuries which require surgical attention, either immediately or after resuscitation. Category four is reserved for those who are hopelessly wounded or dead on arrival. An example of a Category four patient would be one with a large portion of brain tissue extruding through a large bony defect in the skull, but who is still breathing on his own and has a normal blood pressure. This patient would of necessity be passed over for one with a gunshot wound of the abdomen, who is bleeding internally and is going into shock.

If this Category three patient doesn't get an intravenous started and stabilized for evacuation, he will surely die. With proper triage, however, he will likely have a full and speedy recovery, which unfortunately will not be the case for the open head injury.

It is a tough business which requires the strictest of discipline in decision making. Also, casualties in categories one and two can be passed on to the medic after a quick assessment by the battalion surgeon. The bottom line states that the saving of a life takes precedence over the saving of a limb, and the preservation of function takes precedence over the correction of an anatomical defect.

Priorities of treatment begin with the need to maintain an open airway to prevent asphyxia and maintain the circulatory system to prevent shock with IV fluids. Second priority wounds would include visceral injuries to include perforating abdominal and perforating chest wounds where the patient is capable of maintaining spontaneous respiration. Vascular injuries which can be controlled with a tourniquet also fall into this category. Closed head injuries, with increasing loss of consciousness, would also qualify as second priority injuries. Third priority wounds would include spinal cord injuries requiring decompression, soft-tissue wounds requiring debridement, fractures and dislocation, and maxillofacial injuries including eye injuries.

15 Sep 1968

Camp Bullis, Texas

We are going to be bivouacked out here for a few weeks, learning our basic infantry training as well as undergoing an intensive conditioning program to help prepare us for the rigors of living in Vietnam without the comforts of air-conditioning, etc. The camp itself is located about forty miles out from San Antonio and is situated in an area of rolling hills covered with lots of mesquite and low trees, which I would characterize as scrub brush. It does provide cover for lots of jackrabbits, deer, and rattlesnakes. "Whatever you do, don't let a snake prevent you from going to Nam!" we all keep telling each other with a hearty laugh. We are housed in some Quonset huts and sleep on cots. We have three hot meals per day, so it could be worse, in fact, it is almost guaranteed to get worse for most, if not all, of us.

Most mornings find us up and out by 0600 hours for a breakfast of powdered eggs, ham, biscuits, with black coffee that you can't stir, it is so thick. With a brief stand-down after chow, we usually spend anywhere from one and a half to two hours doing various sorts of organized exercise programs including push-ups, calisthenics, and running. It has been pretty dry and dusty, so the heat in the mornings has not been unbearable, but it will be where we are going. Most of my classmates are in worse shape than I am. Most are fatter, and I have the feeling that few of them have ever done as much physical work as I did those summers tenting houses for Termitrol in Tampa. Not being a smoker has helped a lot. So has all those years of weight lifting. Lots of guys get sick almost every day and slip off to the side of the formation to vomit in the ditch, but so far I haven't had too much difficulty keeping up with the instructors, most of whom are back from Nam within the past year.

This afternoon, we had a very interesting exercise. They gave us a brief lecture on chemical warfare and told us how it is administered by gas canisters that are either dropped from an airplane like a bomb or are shot out of cannons like an artillery shell. The first protection you have to be familiar with is the gas mask, so they took us in groups of twenty-five into a gas chamber and closed the door. The interior of the chamber was dimly lit by one sixty-watt incandescent bulb, and it very closely resembled a tomb—about twenty by thirty feet with a low seven-foot ceiling. I have never experienced claustrophobia, but I got a real uncomfortable feeling when that door slammed shut. But I kept my cool by looking around the dimly lit room at all the other guys. They had us put on our masks, and then they started popping CS grenades (tear gas). Well, you know how poor my vision is without my glasses, and they won't fit under a gas mask and permit it to seal, so I had taken off my glasses and stuck them in my pocket and hoped for the best. Immediately all the other men became blurred images, barely seen. And as the cloud of gas increased, visibility rapidly dropped to less than three feet. Our NCO instructor had briefed us about the drill before donning his own mask, telling us that he would go around the room, stopping in front of each of us, one at a time, and when he tapped us on the shoulder, we were to remove the mask, call out our name, rank, service, and serial number. Then he would open the door, and we could run out. "Don't try to cheat on me, or I will make you start over," he said. "Whatever you do, don't splash water in your face as it will just make it worse!"

Well, about half of the guys went before me, and it was pitiful listening to each one cough and gag. A few vomited. And later I learned that a number of them went right to the water faucet and splashed water in their faces and eyes, making it worse, just like our instructor had said it would. Finally, it was my turn as I blurted out, "Holley, Byron E., Captain, U.S. Army, 05345559!" and rushed out the door to the now laughing bunch of doctors.

"This is a bunch of shit!" I blurted out as I saw Harold Sexton laughing his head off. Harold, a real nice guy I had interned with at Baptist Memorial Hospital in Memphis, Tennessee, had been drafted despite having useful vision in only one eye, the result of a congenital cataract. Had he not been a doctor, he would never have been allowed to enter the army, but because he was a doctor, they chose to ignore his physical problem. Not that it interfered with his ability to practice medicine; to the contrary, he was one of our finest interns, but the increased risk for a lifetime of total darkness was so much greater for him. I felt very strongly that he should be deferred from serving in a war zone, but I secretly admired his courage for not trying to pull strings to get himself out of our impending trip to Vietnam. He never said a word, good man that he was.

One intern from my group was a good physical specimen, but he had such a shitty attitude, I found myself almost hoping he would buy the farm over there. I don't know if he did, I never heard about him again.

Last night, we had an interesting exercise in "how not to get your ass shot off." They call it "the Pit," but officially it's known as the obstacle course. There are some sections that have various physical obstacles like barbed-wire fences, trenches, walls, simulated land mines and booby traps, camouflaged ditches and holes, and assorted water hazards. Then there is one which is designed to teach you to crawl like a snake across rugged terrain, under crisscrossing strands of barbed wire, while some recent Nam returnee is firing an M-60 or .50-caliber machine gun a few inches above the wire. This course is about seventy-five yards long with a big ditch at one end, which everybody falls into when they complete the course. Apparently you can't get any part of your body above the wire without the risk of getting it shot off, so it really is a sort of introduction to live fire, even though they are trying *not* to hit us, whereas the VC will be trying very hard to hit us. The noise and the grime are almost unbearable, so thank God we only have to complete it twice, once during daylight hours and once again at night.

Well, last night we finally finished our obstacle course training, and was it ever a hoot! The daytime course went pretty well because you could watch the fellow ahead of you and pretty much do what he did. You could see the barbed wire and obstacles, but you couldn't see the bullets. Well, at night all that changed. Now you can see the bullets (tracers), but you can't see the guy ahead of you nor the barbed wire and other obstacles. There was this one huge fat guy who got hung up on the barbed wire until everybody else had finished. When he finally got there and rolled down into the muddy ditch, he looked down the ditch and with a broken Puerto Rican accent said, "Look at that shit, a thousand years of higher education lying in a fucking ditch!" Everybody just rolled with laughter. He is a real funny and likable sort, but he has really had a hard time with the field maneuvers, tripping on every simulated land mine near him and always the last man in. I really feel sorry for him, and I don't know how he will do on the night map course, where we will go on an eight-mile forced march through the woods, trying to sneak through snipers who will be shooting at us with blanks as we try to slip through their positions. The snipers are all graduates of the real school of infantry—Vietnam. I hear it is both difficult and frightening. More on that later.

18 Sep 1968

Fort Sam Houston, Texas

Yesterday, we received our immunizations against typhoid, paratyphoid, and typhus, as well as a tetanus booster and a tine test. Today I am running a fever, and my arm is swollen up like a loaf of bread. I went to bed at 8:30 P.M., but 5:30 A.M. still came early, especially with my red, swollen, and painful arm. Lucky us, we get more shots today. I think they are just trying to see if they can weed out the weak ones early! I have been told that I would have about a ninety percent chance of not going to Vietnam if I would join up with the Airborne, i.e., the paratroopers. They need doctors badly and they pay $110 per month extra, and chances are that after a three-week jump school at Fort Benning, Georgia, I would be assigned to Fort Bragg, North Carolina, for the entire two years. Of course, there would always be the chance of my division being sent to Vietnam, but they seemed to doubt it would happen. I would have to jump at least once every three months to maintain my proficiency, and probably more often than that. It's a lot to think about, but so is going to Vietnam in three weeks.

22 Sep 1968

Camp Bullis, Texas

Well, last night we finished up our stay at Camp Bullis with our forced eight-mile, night map course, and it was quite an experience. It was really exciting, and I now feel pretty good about my chances of surviving out in the jungles of Vietnam with an infantry unit after all that I have learned here. Of course, over there people will be shooting real live ammo at us, but I do feel like we accomplished a lot in the past few weeks. We were ferried out to an isolated area in the bush country and told to plot out a map course to include four checkpoints along the way, where we would get our ticket punched by one of the instructors. One general direction of movement was from the northwest to the southeast across eight miles of hilly, rocky, rattlesnake-infested terrain, with one stream running diagonally across the area we were to traverse.

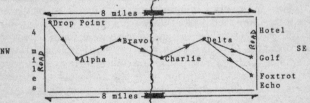

It was a cloudy night, so we got no help from the stars or the moon. We had to depend on our compasses, and used the infrared covers on our flashlights to see them without being detected. Some of the guys thought it was Mickey Mouse, but I'm taking it very seriously, considering where I am heading soon. We were told there were no roads between the one where we were dropped off and the one where the four pickup points were located. So if you reached the road you had either made it or you had gone in a complete circle and had ended back where you'd started. "Don't be that stupid!" our instructor had bellowed at us as he

14

dropped us off at the drop point in the NW corner of the area. They would have four pickup points spread out along the road which was our objective: our pickup point was designated "Foxtrot" for *F*. We were divided up into eight-man squads and carried backpacks with full combat gear, including M-1 carbines. As we started out, it soon became obvious we would not arrive together as an intact unit. One smart ass took off in the wrong direction and would not listen to reason, so I took three guys with me and headed toward our first checkpoint, Alpha, two miles due south of our drop point. Alpha was located on a bluff overlooking a stream and a valley filled with trees where most of the "enemy" were located. The "enemy" were all Vietnam vets dressed in camouflaged jungle fatigues, with their faces all painted black and their M-16s loaded with blanks. They were also armed with simulated claymore mines and hand grenades, which can really scare the hell out of you when detonated in the silence of a dark Texas night! We made it fine to Checkpoint Alpha, and got our tickets punched, and moved on quickly after being informed that the other half of our platoon led by "Mr. Know-it-all" had been ambushed about one and a half miles south of their intended course—the dumb asses! Anyway, we crept along through the tall grass in a slow descent toward the stream bed. I suddenly stepped on something large and alive—up jumped a large buck deer! I don't know who scared who the most, but he really hauled ass! The commotion gave away our position, and one of the "enemy" opened up with an automatic weapon from a group of trees about two hundred yards away. We laughed and hollered, "Poor shot, Ace! You missed us!" and off we ran.

We trudged along for a while and came to the stream, which we crossed quietly. It was about waist deep and was quite cool. I wondered out loud in a whisper how many snakes and alligators it held. We found all our checkpoints without any problem, and other than hearing an occasional burst of automatic weapons fire off in the distance, it was an uneventful trip. We felt that we would have survived the journey even if they had been shooting live ammo, and in that case we could have shot back.

We came out on the road about one hundred yards north of pickup point Foxtrot and were pleasantly surprised to learn that we had traveled the course in just under three and a half hours.

We had departed at 8:00 P.M. and arrived at 11:20 P.M. We lay around until about 1:00 A.M., waiting for the rest of the patrols to come in, and when we finally left at 1:15 A.M., there was a helicopter with a searchlight flying all over the area, looking for a few stragglers who still hadn't made it back. I was proud to be among the earliest teams in, as I could see the value in learning how to cross unfamiliar terrain at night with only a compass to guide you. It might save our lives in the upcoming year.

I later learned that some platoons didn't come back in until after 3:00 A.M. And, as the sergeant had predicted, one team actually ended up back at the drop point. Incredible! Well, we still have some class work to finish up, but we are beginning to look more like combat-ready soldiers than a mob of out-of-shape doctors. Some of us are actually becoming gung ho about it. I figure if I've got to do it, I might as well make the most of it, especially when it's my ass they will be shooting at. I'll learn anything that might help me survive the year intact. Well, time to catch some Zs as wake-up comes early . . .

3 Oct 1968

Fort Sam Houston

Well, we got our haircuts today, and now we really do look like GI Joe! I made my reservations out of Memphis. I will leave on Flight 299 at 8:50 P.M. on October 16. I have to be at Travis AFB, California, at 7:00 A.M. on the seventeenth, and we will probably leave for Vietnam between 10:00 and 11:00 A.M. on October 17. I can't believe this is really happening to me. Now that I know the exact dates and times, it is a hard, cold fact that I really am headed for Vietnam.

17 Oct 1968

Day One—364 to go!

I'll never forget that balmy night in October 1968 when I arrived in South Vietnam. As our World Airways Boeing 707 approached the coast of South Vietnam, the captain turned out all the interior lights as well as the navigation lights. He announced over the loudspeaker that, although they had never lost an airliner over Vietnam, he did not want to risk breaking a good record, so that all lights would remain extinguished until we were safely on the ground at Bien Hoa. It was a clear night, and every few minutes we could see brilliant flashes of light from exploding artillery shells somewhere off in the distance. It was beautiful in an eerie and silent sort of way—but served as a grim reminder of the unhealthy climate of our destination.

After an uneventful approach and landing, during which each of us was certain our airplane would be shot out of the sky, we finally arrived in Vietnam. Only eighteen hours earlier I had boarded that same plane in sunny California, along with one hundred fifty other doctors, each one trying to convince the others that he really wasn't scared. Now, after that grueling eighteen-hour flight, during which the sun didn't set until one and a half hours out from Vietnam, the same plane dumped us in a hostile war zone and was rapidly being refueled and reloaded with seasoned veterans who were about to return to the world. Our seats weren't even cold by the time these characters were boarding their "freedom bird" in an unbelievably ecstatic departure from a country and a war that they had all come to loathe. Off to one side, seven gray metal coffins were waiting to be loaded in the baggage compartment—an even more grim reminder that we had indeed arrived. No one spoke a word. It was as if no one even saw them. The thought kept thundering through my mind, Will I be sent home like that?

We were immediately herded off to a large shed where we

were divided alphabetically into groups. We were amazed to see GIs, South Vietnamese soldiers—soon to be known to us as ARVNs (pronounced Arvins)—walking around casually in the dark without any sign of a weapon! We expected a Viet Cong to jump out from behind every bush—but none had appeared.

After a lights-out bus ride across twelve miles of the roughest road in Southeast Asia, we arrived at Long Binh military base where we were to spend our very first night in Vietnam. Our temporary quarters turned out to be a joke. They consisted of flimsy wooden shacks with corrugated tin roofs, the walls only going up about four feet high, with screens covering the windows and the doors. And the mosquitoes were unreal—each one seemed to be after a total body transfusion! There were two rows of triple-deck bunks. I lucked out and got one of the middle bunks. We had hardly gotten bedded down when a warning came to expect lots of wind and rain during the night. A typhoon was blowing in off the South China Sea and was expected to hit our area in two or three hours.

I had hardly fallen asleep when we were rocked by the loudest noise I had ever heard! This had to be the dreaded mortar or rocket attacks which we had heard so much about. Here was Charlie's chance to wipe out a whole year's supply of doctors in one swoop! We jumped out of our bunks and ran out into the darkness in search of a bunker, only to find that these fine structures were knee-deep in mud and *rats*! Needless to say, most of us decided to take our chances back in our bunks. Well, the mortar attack went on for two hours, and it wasn't until the following morning that we learned, quite sheepishly, that Long Binh base had not received a single incoming round of mortar fire. It had all been our own artillery firing in support of various infantry units out in the bush!

About 1:00 A.M., the typhoon arrived, and it proved to be all they had promised us and more. It succeeded in blowing half the roof off our shack, and the poor fellows in the upper bunks ended up sleeping down on the dirty—now muddy—floors under the bottom bunks. The fury of the storm finally died down about 3:00 A.M. and we finally dozed off. Only to be awakened at 4:00 A.M. by a bloodcurdling scream. It seemed that one of our new docs was having a very realistic nightmare in which he was being choked to death by—you guessed it—a Viet Cong! Needless to say, the sun rose on a pitiful looking bunch of guys.

As we began to stir, we were struck by the most nauseating

and putrid odor one could imagine. It smelled like something burning, but we couldn't identify it. When our briefing officer came in to make sure we were awake, we asked him what was stinking so bad? ''They're burning shit. They burn it every morning. There are no sewer systems over here, and the guys doing the burning are on shit detail as a punishment for some misdeed. This aroma *fills* the air around all the American military bases, and it has become known affectionately as the 'perfume of Vietnam.' Well, welcome to the 90th Replacement Battalion, gentlemen. After a shave and a shower, you can grab a quick breakfast down at the mess hall. We will expect each of you to be at the adjutant's office at 0900 hours. It is now 0700 hours.''

What a surprise to step outside and find, of all things, wooden sidewalks. We had all seen them in the western movies but had no idea that we would encounter them over here. The heat and humidity were already overpowering, even at this hour. We were further surprised to find that our showers would be taken in an open air wooden structure that barely covered the ''essentials.'' Little did I realize that I would later look back on these conditions as luxurious.

After our showers, we initially felt better but were soon hot and muggy. Still dressed in our Stateside kahkis, we headed off to find the mess hall. We were a little surprised to see that the base was located among low rolling hills. About halfway there, we came across a most unusual reminder of just how far away we were from home—a totem pole affair with signs pointing in all different directions, each with the name of a city and the distance in miles to that location. The one which got my attention read ''Pittsburgh—10,270 mi.'' Wow, that's like halfway around the world! Another read ''Hanoi—748 mi.'' Wow, that's like too close! We really are here, and I already can tell that I'm not going to like this place.

24 Oct 1968

Dong Tam

Well, as you can tell from my return address, I have finally been assigned. I am with the 4th Battalion of the 39th Regiment of the 9th Infantry Division, with base headquarters at Dong Tam on a tributary of the Mekong River, about thirty-five miles southwest of Saigon. There are estimated to be *several thousand* VC (Viet Cong) within a ten-mile radius of our division base camp. I am now being oriented by several doctors about local skin diseases that I will encounter out in the field. In a day or two I will be moved to my permanent unit, which is currently out on operations in an area known as the Plain of Reeds. It is a large expanse of wet, deep saw grass, broken up by crisscrossing canals and streams with an occasional stand of palm trees known locally as nipa palm. It is in these tree lines that Charlie frequently lies in ambush for the unsuspecting grunt (GI). The veterans here say that the Plain of Reeds is very similar in climate and terrain to the Everglades in Florida, but here there aren't any alligators to worry about—just leeches, snakes, millions of malaria infested mosquitoes, and of course, the Cong! As I understand it, I will have a permanent room at Dong Tam base camp in a wooden building where I can leave most of my possessions. But I will spend ninety percent of my time out in the boonies with my battalion. Out there, I will *hopefully* be sleeping in a bunker. Apparently, our battalion moves around quite a lot by choppers, and I don't know if they are presently bunkered in or not. If not, I will sure get to work on having a bunkered aid station to sleep in if at all possible. We are bound to have some litters (stretchers) and mosquito netting, so I will do just fine.

We do a lot of traveling out on the roads in jeeps with M-60 (.30-caliber) machine guns mounted on the hoods, wearing our steel pots (helmets), flak jackets (bulletproof vests) and armed to the teeth. I will be expected to make three or four trips per

Military Organization Chart

| Division | 15,000 to 20,000 soldiers |

```
┌───┬───┐
I   II  III          Brigade—approx. 3500 soldiers
┌───┼───┐
2/39 3/39 4/39       Battalion—approx. 1000 to 1250 men
┌─┬─┬─┬─┐
A B C D HQ           Company—approx. 200 soldiers, ea.
┌─┬─┬─┐
1 2 3 4              Platoon—approx. 40 soldiers, ea.
```

4/39th Infantry Battalion
2nd Brigade
Ninth Infantry Division
Headquarters Company
Organizational Chart

S1 Adiminstrative (Adjutant, etc.)
S2 Intelligence
S3 Operations
S4 Supply
Medical platoon

week to the local villages to treat their ill, in an effort to "win the hearts and minds" of the natives. This is all part of a program called MEDCAP, which stands for MEDical Civil Action Program. However, all the docs I've talked to stress the importance of being well armed as they are occasionally mortared or ambushed. What gratitude! Seriously though, this points out one of the biggest problems for any American over here—just who is the enemy, and how can you tell him from the typical peasant farmer who lives out in the paddies and wears black pajamas and thong sandals just like Charlie? Well, now that I've scared the hell out of you, I'll tell you that in spite of all this, I'm really not scared. I'm sure I will be when Charlie starts shooting at me. I really believe that if I take all the precautions offered to me, my chances of being killed are quite slim compared to the infantrymen I will be caring for.

As the battalion surgeon of the 4/39th Infantry Battalion, I will have a wide variety of duties. I will be in command of a platoon of about forty men who will be spread between a rear aid station at the division headquarters at Dong Tam, a forward aid station out in the field, where I will usually be, and four rifle companies out in the field. The rifle companies usually contain four platoons with two medics per platoon. That leaves eight medics to be divided between the two aid stations. There's always a certain percentage of the grunts, as the foot-soldier is called, who are on "profile" [a physical limitation, noted in the soldier's record, which exempts him from performing certain types of physical activity] or on sick leave. This requires the presence of a small team of medics at the rear aid station to monitor the progress of those on profile. Naturally, there will always be a certain number of guys who will fake illnesses in order to try to avoid going to the field.

I will personally decide who stays in the rear and who goes out to the battlefield. It's like playing chess, only in this case it's with real people's lives. It is an awesome responsibility when you think about it. My thoughts now are to try to strike a good balance between those with some combat experience and the FNGs (fucking new guys) as all of us new men are called. Ideally, I would like to have one of each per platoon. Time will tell. I will be expected to coordinate personal leaves and R & Rs and be ready to replace wounded or killed medics with little or no notice. Everyone says "Don't make friends over here, it just makes it harder when you lose them." I'm sure that will be a problem I will have to deal with in my own way. I plan to get to know my men as soon as possible in order to be able to distribute them effectively. I plan to be available for personal counseling for each of my men as needed. The filing of efficiency reports is one chore I plan to delegate to my MSC (medical service corps) officer, but I will tell him how I want them rated. I will be required to participate in court-martial hearings when I am in Dong Tam and will have to be part of the judiciary panel. I'm not real happy about that but will just have to do what is required of me. Of course, maintenance of discipline will be one of my big responsibilities, but I'm not too worried about that as I intend to lead by example. I'm planning a series of lectures to keep my medics well informed about such subjects as heatstroke, fungal skin infections, immersion foot, and venereal disease.

I will oversee the general sanitation of the base camp areas to include the latrine systems, water supply, and mess hall facilities. Once I'm satisfied with these areas, I will turn these inspections over to my MSC officer.

My medics and I will be responsible for malaria prevention by weekly administration of chloroquine-primaquine tablets. These tablets are usually handed out on Mondays and are not real popular since they cause diarrhea for a day or two in most people, myself included! I will be expected to attend daily early A.M. tactical briefings with the battalion commanding officer (CO), executive officer (XO), and all the company commanders, at which time I will keep them informed of the general health of the command and give recommendations such as how much dry-out time is needed by those with immersion foot and other fungal skin conditions, which are aggravated by prolonged exposure to moisture. In this regard, I am really the best friend some of these guys have over here.

The Mekong Delta is comprised largely of rice paddies, rivers, streams, and swamps, with some tropical jungle interspersed among the more open areas. The grunts walk all day and sometimes into the night, constantly sloshing around in the mud and water, sometimes from their knees up to their armpits. They are routinely infested with leeches up to six inches long.

Southeast Asia is under the influence of the Malaysian-Australian monsoonal system, and therefore, from May through October, the weather is typified by oppressive heat, humidity, and periodic downpours known as the monsoons. It is during this season that typhoons occur. Typhoons are similar to hurricanes in having sustained heavy winds and rain. They cause extensive flooding in the low-lying areas of the Delta.

The period from November through February is considered the dry, cool season, but those who live here say it only gets cool at night, and the days are just not quite as hot as during the summer. March and April are considered the hot, dry season. But most say that, in reality, there are only two seasons in South Vietnam—*hot and dry* or *hot and wet*!

They have a local saying that "When it rains the delta swells up like a sponge." When I flew in here, the rivers were all out of their banks, and the only dry land visible were the few one- or two-lane roads which exist. We can't walk up on the dikes because the VC have mined and booby-trapped them. So, on occasion, when troops get caught out on patrol, they end up sleeping and doing all their basic toilet needs while standing in waist-deep water! Isn't that awful? I guess that's one of the worst things about being over here, the utter lack of luxuries for the foot soldier.

I thank God every day for America, and I vow to kiss her good earth the minute I get off that big freedom bird 358 days hence! We have the finest country in the world, and anybody who doubts it should come to Nam for a spell as a grunt.

I am rooming with a black doctor from Memphis, a Louis Twigg, and he is funny as hell and keeps us all in stitches. He reminds me of Satchmo. We are the only two out of six who came down here to the 9th Division who are going out to the bush.

My battalion is currently north of Cai Lay in the Plain of Reeds. Other villages in the area are Binh Phuoc, My Tho, Vinh Long, Tan An, Tan Tru, and Ben Luc. This might help you in listening to news reports, etc.

Well, the 8-inch and the 155mm howitzers have started firing, and the noise is deafening! I sure hope they will stop soon. This will definitely take some getting used to. The dust-off choppers which bring in the wounded from the field to the MASH here at Dong Tam 3d Surgical Hospital have really been busy, and I can't help wondering if one will be hauling my butt back here some day. It's finally beginning to seem realistic. I really am in Vietnam! It's no longer a report to watch on the evening news over supper. Now I am part of the story. Save my letters, and maybe someday I will write a book. Must close for now.

Our unit, the 9th Infantry Division, has distinguished itself by being the first to be organized, equipped, and trained for deployment to an overseas combat zone since World War II. Nicknamed "The Old Reliables," they have been over here since December, 1966, and have had numerous engagements with Viet Cong main-force units and recently captured the largest weapons cache of the war following the rout of a VC battalion. We have been involved in continuous military operations in the soggy Mekong Delta, in large part with our "brown water navy," known officially as the MRF, or Mobile Riverine Force. They travel in patrol boats with .50-caliber machine guns mounted on the bow and carry flame throwers too. They are able to operate in very shallow water and have often surprised Charlie with their mobility, speed, and firepower. We have air support from both the U.S. Navy's carriers offshore and the U.S. Air Force as well as our own air cavalry, the 3/5th Armored

Cav. They are a colorful bunch with all sorts of nifty sayings and nicknames painted on the noses of their choppers along with the crossed swords of the cavalry. They not only haul us around on operations, but they supply air-assault cover with Cobra gunships, which fire rockets and miniguns. We also have support from the 9th Aviation Battalion which hauls us and our equipment in large twin-bladed choppers called Chinooks, more affectionately known as "shit-hooks" for their ability to drop a cable out of their belly and literally pull a downed airman from the thick jungle or, if conditions allow, to pick up a "bird" (chopper) and fly it back home for repairs. We will be spending lots of hours flying around the Delta in an assortment of choppers as there are so few roads.

Don't let me forget the dust-off choppers, which in essence are air ambulances with huge red crosses on white backgrounds painted on their sides. Some say that Charlie uses the red cross as a target, but I'll soon see for myself.

Our first division base camp was located near the Binh Sohn rubber plantation, the main source of the rubber used in Michelin tires. We are now operating out of Dong Tam base, located about seven miles west of My Tho. Dong Tam, the first permanent infantry base in the Viet Cong–infested Delta, was literally dredged up out of the Mekong River to provide a dry foundation above the surrounding rivers, streams, canals, and rice paddies. From what I've heard, it gets pretty sloppy during the rainy season and is a dust bowl during the dry season. It too has wooden sidewalks. There is little or no vegetation on the base as the heat quickly kills anything not growing in water. There are roads, wooden buildings, the 3d MASH Hospital in an inflated building, a PX, and an open-air movie theater. Scattered open booths are manned during the day by local barbers, some of them VC cadre, I am sure.

The varied terrain presents problems for the American infantryman never before encountered in a hostile combat zone. As the mighty, muddy Mekong River flows down from neighboring Cambodia, it spreads out into countless smaller rivers and streams, virtually engulfing the entire region in water during the rainy season. From the air during the dry season, the delta looks like a checkerboard because of the thousands of acres of individual rice paddies which are then visible. They are crisscrossed by countless canals used for irrigation and transportation.

Toward Cambodia lies one of the most barren areas of the

Delta, the Plain of Reeds, long considered a virtual impenetrable sanctuary for the Viet Cong. This is the area we are operating in now, and I approach it with more than a little concern. The mud and muck are so sticky that there is a rumor that a soldier was being sucked down under the surface and even a helicopter couldn't pull him out! True or false, it sounds like one hell of a place to try to chase an enemy, much less kill him.

About twenty miles south of Saigon, there is a large mangrove swamp known as the Rung Sat, which extends all the way to the coastline. We recently came back off maneuvers in that area. Those who have been to both places say they prefer the Rung Sat to the Plain of Reeds, since at least in the Rung Sat you will find an occasional island of large mangroves where you can climb up out of the water for a rest, that is, if you can convince the snakes to give up their spot in the sunshine!

25 Oct 1968

Dong Tam, RVN

. . . Dong Tam sits right in the heart of the Mekong River Delta, known hereabouts simply as "the Delta." Dong Tam is relatively secure except for fairly regular mortar and rocket attacks. The base camp covers about four hundred acres and has a large helipad as well as a crude runway constructed of PSP (perforated steel planking) laid on top of a muddy river bank.

The flight down from Long Binh was a real hoot! The aircraft was a twin-engine prop plane, a Caribou, used to haul freight or up to twenty troops. It has a large loading ramp, which is used by everyone to enter or exit the rear of the aircraft. When in flight, the ramp comes up part way but leaves an opening large enough to drive a truck through, so you have the feeling you could fall out the back if it got too turbulent. Needless to say, I kept my seat belt on the whole time! Anyway, when we boarded, we figured the pilot was already on board. The cockpit is elevated six or eight feet above the floor of the cargo bay and has a ladder leading up to the cockpit, which is open to the cargo bay. Among our passengers were several Vietnamese civilians, complete with ducks in baskets!

All of a sudden two GIs hopped on board, jiving to a portable radio blasting the Beatles' ''Hey Jude,'' and one of them had on some plastic, colored hippy beads. They both had long hair and handlebar mustaches, and I thought, Oh boy, these will probably be some of my troops! Well, you can imagine my shock when they started up the ladder to the cockpit! My God, I can't believe I'm putting my life in the hands of hippies who are hardly old enough to shave. Well, I would soon learn that these hippy kids had their shit together and were doing a man's job and doing it well.

From the air, it was amazing to see all the rivers and streams flooded out of their banks, and the scattered stilt huts with thatched roofs and a sampan or two tied up to the ladder stairs. What a place to live! I thought.

Our landing was a hairy experience. It looked like we were going to land in the river or hit a row of palm trees. When we touched down, the metal runway made a god-awful racket, and the pilot reversed thrust on his props in order to slow down as quickly as possible. The noise of the engines added to the chaos, as the ducks quacked, and the Vietnamese jabbered back and forth. We slammed on full brakes and slid the last one hundred yards or so right up to the end of the runway which was surrounded by mud and more palm trees. Someone blurted out, ''Controlled crash!'' and everybody else cracked up. We then climbed out to be greeted by the heat, the humidity, and the bugs! Lucky us!

Apparently I will be spending a lot of time out on operations in the field with the troops, treating a variety of skin diseases, leech bites, punji-stake wounds, noncritical shrapnel and gunshot wounds. Because of the tremendous level of heat and humidity, something can turn green from mold in a matter of a few days! I can just imagine how quickly infection spreads under these conditions. The environment is a perfect culture medium for fungi and bacteria. Most of the natives have faces marked from smallpox suffered in childhood. Most of the grunts suffer with a condition called immersion foot. It is a peculiar type of cellulitis, which causes a very painful red, scaly, swollen foot, ankle, and lower leg, usually not extending above the knee. It usually begins to occur after five to seven days of continuous exposure to water loaded with bacteria and fungi. There are several dermatologists over here studying the problem. One was a professor from the University of Miami School of Medicine! They were instrumental in the development of our canvas combat boots, which have thick rubber soles over a steel shank. The boots have drainage holes near the soles on the sides, but the problem is, if they will let the water out, they will also let the water in! As long as the Delta is wet, the problem will persist. Maybe it will be better during the dry season.

Lots of times the grunts have to urinate and defecate in waist-deep water. To avoid rashes men don't wear undershorts, and they are reluctant to drop their pants in leech-infested waters. So they literally get "wet-rot" of the feet and legs. The only way to get it cleared up is to get them out of the water to dry out and treat their condition with a variety of oral and topical antibiotics and antifungals, along with elevation. They are told to wear thongs and cutoff fatigue pants. The informality bothers some of the lifer officers, but that's too bad. You don't see any of them sloshing around in this crap and getting immersion foot. One of my biggest battles will be in getting the troops enough "dry time."

I have been told there is a radio communications system available to us known as the MARS network. What it amounts to is this—our shortwave operators in Dong Tam get in touch with a ham operator in the United States, and he in turn makes a long-distance telephone call to the party we are trying to reach. Then the party reached only has to pay for the long-distance call from the ham operator's location, e.g., in California, Texas, or wherever. One of my buddies talked to his wife in Memphis—free—the other night as they were able to reach a ham operator in Memphis, so I will try reaching you that way. You have to remember that it is not two-way communication, i.e., you have to say what you want to say and then say "over," and then it is my turn. Not too practical or romantic, but beggars can't afford to be choosers. And of course you have to figure the time changes, e.g., when it is 1:00 P.M. Friday in Memphis, it is 3:00 A.M. Saturday over here in paradise!

I'm doing fine, just a little homesick, and I really do miss all the luxuries of our fine homeland, but I haven't been scared . . . yet. I'm sure I will be when Charlie starts shooting at me or mortars my camp, but I will handle that situation when it arrives.

27 Oct 1968

Dong Tam, RVN

I've been moved to my unit, the 4/39 Infantry at Dong Tam, where we have a rear detachment, with wooden barracks (nonair-conditioned), and a permanent aid station (again, nonair-conditioned!). Our battalion has about seventy-five men here. The rest, about eight hundred men, are operating out of a Special Forces camp out in the Plain of Reeds near My Phuoc Tay ("mee fook tay"). This area can only be reached by boat or helicopter as there are no roads. I am supposed to go out by chopper tomorrow morning, apparently by myself. I share a small room here in Dong Tam with a Lt. Richard Alexander, the medical service officer for the medical battalion. I guess you could say his duties are similar to those of a hospital administrator back in the real world. Over here, they become jacks-of-all-trades. I haven't met him yet, but I understand he is a short-timer and will be transferred to the rear soon.

This room is a joke! We have a small shelf-type desk, double-deck bunks, a wall locker, and two chairs. Junky back home, almost luxurious over here! However, what it amounts to is that this will be a place for me to leave my footlocker, as I will be spending most of my time out in the field.

I went to chapel services this morning. Our chaplain is a very nice Lutheran minister from St. Louis. We observed the Lord's Supper, and it was very heartwarming to see blacks and whites of all ranks and backgrounds sitting, singing, praying, and wor-shiping. I don't think I could ever become a religious nut, but I believe I will be much closer to God when I leave here than when I arrived.

I haven't received any mail yet, but I've been on the move so much that a letter could not have reached me. My morale is pretty good now, and I will try to keep it up as much as possible. The men I have met back here with my unit look to be sharp fellows, and they seem to appreciate my presence. When I go out to the field, I will probably stay out there about a month at a time, with a three- or four-day stand-down at Dong Tam on occasion. However, we do have mail call daily, as long as the weather and war permit helicopters to fly. When I return to base camp, I will try to reach you by MARS radiotelephone, even though it's awkward having to say "over" each time and having two strangers listen to our conversation. Well, only 355 days to go.

28 Oct 1968

Dong Tam

Last night I was finally introduced to the war. About ten minutes before 2:00 A.M., I heard some loud explosions, which shook the building, and almost immediately, sirens began screaming in the night. Through the open screen window of my room, I could see red lights flashing on the roof of the building next door. I heard someone holler "Red alert!" which means we are under attack. I jumped out of my upper bunk in a flash and lay on the floor against the outer wall, which is sandbagged on the outside up to about four feet. The explosions continued, and I could tell they were getting closer by the loud crunching sound they made on impact. I also could hear the sound of shrapnel hitting metal nearby. Upstairs, the radios in the communications shack were saying, "This is Dong Tam base. We are presently under mortar attack and have received eighteen rounds as of this moment." I was immediately struck with two thoughts: (1) How calm this dude sounded, almost like he was giving a routine weather report; and (2) Who was this guy, where was he sitting at this minute, and who the hell is he talking to? Anybody in his right mind would be on the floor or in a bunker, trying to save his ass, and what can be done about the attack anyway? I would later learn that he was sitting securely inside a command bunker and was talking to the people at Div Arty, which is short for division artillery. Anyway, this nonsense went on for about another forty-five minutes, and that damn floor got awfully hard! Soon there was an awful lot of our artillery returning fire. All the noise made our fourth of July celebrations sound like a prayer service. The most surprising thing to me was that I had not been nearly as afraid as I had thought I would be.

I learned this morning that one of the new two-story enlisted barracks, about two blocks from my bunk, was practically destroyed. Thank goodness it was empty! They were out in the field on maneuvers. Being out in the boonies saved their asses last night. It was this realization that changed my attitude about going out in the field on combat operations. At least out there, you were on the move, and Charlie wouldn't always know where you were—here at base camp, we are all sitting ducks!

Another strange sensation that came over me was an almost surrealistic feeling—like this must be happening to someone else, Holley; this really can't be happening to you, boy! But it did, and I'm none the worse for it. I only hope that if my hooch ever gets hit and I'm wounded, that it's enough to get me evacuated out of here. I would really rather stay healthy for a year and come home in one piece, but I tell you it's a helpless feeling to know that some gook is sitting out there in the tree line, lobbing miniature bombs in at you, and all you can do is lie there and pray that one doesn't land on top of you. The vets over here say that as long as you can hear them not to sweat it, because you never hear the one that kills you—some comfort, huh?

Well, I briefly met Dick Alexander today, and he seemed kind of cocky, but I guess that's understandable after six months in combat. He's a short, stocky kid, with glasses, from California who, I'm sure, would rather be surfing in Malibu than sweating it out over here.

29 Oct 1968

Long Truong

Here I sit out in the Delta, very crudely camped on a dirt road out in the boonies, with rice paddies on one side and a small river on the other side, with a village—friendly I hope—across the river. The village is quite picturesque, actually, with about a dozen thatched huts raised on stilts, sitting among stands of nipa palm and banana trees. Right next to our aid station tent is a graveyard with mausoleum vaults above the ground because the ground in the cemetery is under three feet of water! My first thought was, Well, if we get zapped here, they won't have far to take us. They can just roll us off the road and float us over to an empty vault. It really is kinda spooky having a graveyard within spitting distance from where you lay your head down to sleep.

We were quite surprised to find the canal out of its banks and right up to the edge of our tent at high tide last night. There are no bunkers or foxholes because it's too wet to dig anywhere, so if we get a mortar attack, I guess we just hit the canal. Last night, about 3:00 A.M., there was a tremendous flash and explosion from one of our own guns, and one of our sergeants, a twenty-nine-day short-timer, thought it was incoming and headed for the canal. Well, he is a big dude, and it sounded like a cow had fallen in, so we all jumped up to see what was happening. You can imagine our reaction when we saw him come climbing up the bank, covered in mud and draped in water lilies! We all fell down on the road, we were laughing so hard! It is amazing how funny something can seem when you are frightened and then learn that all is OK.

I had to cut leeches out of two grunts this A.M., one on the thigh and one in the groin. The head gets buried under the skin, and the only way to get it out is to cut it out with a scalpel, after local anesthesia of course. I doubt I will ever want to camp again after I leave this place. The only consolation is that everybody feels the same. No one wants to be here, but we all do our best.

It is really quite picturesque and peaceful looking at first glance, until the solitude is interrupted by the loud blast of our howitzers firing artillery rounds. The locals are really fascinating in the way they go about their routine, almost oblivious to our presence. They are clothed in the typical peasant uniform, which consists of a set of black pajamas and two-piece rubber thongs or sandals. Most wear a straw hat of some sort, and I still haven't figured out how we are supposed to tell the difference between them and the enemy. It is just possible they are the enemy! In the mornings, the women come down to the bank and do their laundry, take their baths with their pj's on, let their kids go to the bathroom, and then they wash their Honda motorbikes—all in the same filthy water. I might add, they also use the same water for cooking and drinking! No wonder there is so much disease. I'll tell you, I love America like I never did before. You have no idea how fortunate our country is. God truly blessed us, and I will be a better citizen on returning because of having lived amongst this poverty and squalor.

There are several villages in the area, and I have already treated some mighty sick babies and children since my arrival a few days ago. There are lots of things going on around here to even scare the hell out of John Wayne, but so far, I think I am holding up as well as the men around me. I should say "boys" because most of them are only eighteen or nineteen, with even a few seventeen-year-olds who lied about their age to get to the Nam. They look at me—all of twenty-seven—as the "old man," and I guess compared to them, I am! Just continue to pray for me, as I really believe that makes a difference. I have asked Uncle Sam not to notify any of you if I am wounded. I would rather tell you in person—knowing the army, they would probably screw it up and tell you I was dead instead!

Today the natives came out by the droves when word spread that there was an American doctor in the camp. I treated two babies with the worst cradle cap I have ever seen—their faces and scalps were covered with layer on layer of scabs, with pus oozing out in all directions! It was enough to make me sick to my stomach, if it weren't for the fact that my heart was so heavy for the little tykes that compassion overruled my disgust at the sight and odor of their little heads. I worked on one of them for over two hours, debriding and cutting scabs, until finally I got down to healthy skin. I dressed his scalp with Vioform and Chloromycetin ointment.

You wouldn't believe the abject poverty over here. These people are living just like their ancestors have for hundreds and hundreds of years, with no electricity, sewage, or medical supplies. Across the canal, I see babies and children by the dozens, crawling around on the ground, mixing freely with ducks, pigs, and other animals, all of them defecating and urinating in the mud. And in the rice paddy, which drains directly into the canal, are three or four water buffalo, which lie around all day, adding their feces to the stew pot. It's no wonder the kids are covered with the creeping crud. I don't think any of them own a bar of soap or would know what to do with it if they had one, probably try to eat it!

Today we were briefed that there are three VC battalions, approximately three hundred men each, operating within a two to five mile range of our camp. The nearest one is a mortar battalion, which may be the reason we are camped practically in the front yards of these villagers, thinking the VC won't mortar us for fear of hitting the locals. It sure as hell isn't anything like any conventional war I've ever heard about! Lt. Col. Franklin Hart, the battalion commanding officer, seems nice enough, but this camp acts like a National Guard camp, and I feel real vulnerable out here on this road. It just doesn't instill much confidence in our leader.

I've been sitting out here this evening, listening to our battalion frequencies, monitoring conversations between our ambush patrols set up along the canal banks a few hundred yards from here, and so far it is pretty quiet. It's quite dark, as a high overcast is hiding the moon, so we expect some traffic on the river tonight. It is common knowledge that there is a curfew all across the Delta—that means that when it turns dark, you had better be inside your hut, or you are fair game for any GI or ARVN. So much of the VC ammo and food is moved under the cover of darkness—down here in the Delta by water and in the highlands by jungle trail. There are so few paved roads in the entire country that they are easy to cover. One of our main goals is to control the endless, interconnecting waterways, rivers, and canals at night and take that supply route away from Charlie. Of course, tons of supplies are smuggled right under our noses during the day in sampans with false bottoms. So, if we see one moving quietly down a canal at night, we don't stop to ask questions—we just blast them out of the water.

I've just received word that our Charlie Company has just ambushed a sampan loaded with people and ammo, and has five confirmed kills. One of our boys got hit with shrapnel and is coming in for me to take a look at him now. I heard all hell break loose a little way down the canal a few minutes ago, so I guess that was them.

Well, I just got through removing some shrapnel from this grunt's shoulder, and I believe his mental wounds are much deeper than his physical one. He was a member of the platoon which ambushed the sampan a little while ago, and he is new in the field, a so-called FNG (fucking new guy). He has just tearfully described the ambush to me and one of my medics. He is really torn up about it, and I can't say that I blame him. They were hidden in the palm trees and brush along the canal bank when they heard a very faint sound—the soft *put-put* of an outboard motor. The boy said, "My first reaction was, surely the VC aren't dumb enough to run at night—by now nearly midnight—with their motor running! Maybe they are farmers or some villagers who got caught out after dark. Look, they even have a small light on the stern of the boat. 'Sarge, maybe we should just stop them and search their boat.' Sarge says, 'Fuck em, they should know better, wait til I give the signal, and then we all let em have it at once.' Well, on his signal everybody started shooting their M-16s and the sarge landed a broadside with his M-79 grenade launcher. The sampan caught on fire and lit up the area enough to see that there were at least two women and a couple of small kids on board, as well as three or four men in black pajamas. There were two small dogs and a few baskets of ducks on the deck. 'Sarge, for Christ's sake, stop the firing—these people aren't VC!' Well, about that time there was one hell of a roar and thunderous explosion from deep within the sampan, and the whole damn thing was blown into a billion pieces, with wood, straw, ducks, and people flying in all directions. 'Goddamn it, they're fucking VC after all!' I heard some splashing at the edge of the water and peered down into the face of one of the women. She was missing about half of her jaw, and her right arm was dangling half out of the socket. 'What the hell do I do now, Sarge?'

'Shoot the bitch!' he barked, and went scurrying down the canal bank looking for more bodies, cool as a cucumber on a rabbit hunt. Well, Doc, I went ahead and shot her just to put her out of her misery—in fact the blood and crap all over my face is hers. I started vomiting and crying and wished I was dead. Doc, do you think you could have saved her? God, I don't know if I can stand a year of this fucking shit, Doc. All my life I've been taught to respect human life, and especially ladies, but if I had done it my way, we all probably would have been shot. The sarge was right, but I hated his guts at the time. Two of my buddies had almost the same experience, only they got to finish off a couple of two-year-olds and their puppy. Is this war insane, or what, Doc?''

What the hell could I tell this seventeen-year-old kid from South Carolina? That his reaction was a normal one for a civilized decent kid? That the sarge has become an animal, or a killing machine who can't afford the luxury of having feelings when he is out on ambush patrol? When in Rome do as the Romans do? How would I have reacted myself? Will I become as hardened as the sarge after seeing some of my own men blown away or tortured? So many questions, so few answers.

Everyone is quite anxious about a mortar or ground attack tonight, even the old-timers. All intelligence reports point to that conclusion. We dug a shallow bunker in the roadbed and piled sandbags up, forming a wall about two feet high—a lot of good it would do, but at least it gave my medics something to do to keep their minds off this place. But I guess we are better prepared than we were last night. In addition I now have my own M-16 with five hundred rounds of ammo and a .45 automatic pistol with two hundred rounds, so I'll sleep with my steel helmet and flak jacket on, with my pistol at my side and my M-16 in my lap. Unless a rocket lands right on top of my head, I should be able to take care of my sweet ass! Even Ashley, my number one medic, is loaded for bear. A very competent and muscular black career soldier, Ashley looks like he could easily play linebacker for the Florida Gators. He is highly loyal and very protective of my safety. He is invaluable in helping to maintain discipline and knows the routine well. I think my medical company would make a pretty good infantry outfit in a pinch, and they sure make a good bunch of bodyguards. Don't ever believe that bullshit about doctors not being out where the enemy is. I am convinced that tonight I am spending the evening in his front yard. Actually, I believe we are here for two reasons: one, to block these three VC battalions in the event the proposed offensive on Saigon comes off in the next few days before the presidential elections back home; and two, to see if we can draw some fire from Charlie and get him involved in a firefight so that we can engage one of his battalions.

You wouldn't believe my chopper flight out here to meet the 4/39th for the first time. I figured it would be a little bit formal, you know, what with me being a doctor and a captain, etc. Well, looking back on it, it was a real joke. At the time, I was a little bit apprehensive and more than a little bit pissed off to boot! I was told to go down to the chopper pad at 0900 hours and to carry only my weapons and whatever I could stuff into my backpack. There was a LOH (light observation helicopter—pronounced "loach") warming up on the pad. The copilot ran over, purposefully ducking to avoid the slowly whirling blades, and hollers, "Are you the doc?" to which I reply with a nod. He hollers, "Hop aboard, sir," and we were on our way. There is only room for the pilot, the copilot, and two passengers—one behind each pilot. There are no doors and no seat belts, just a tubular metal seat covered with canvas, and lots of fresh air. The pilots wore helmets with headsets and were engaged in a seemingly good time while I was trying to get settled. The other passenger was a little Oriental soldier in a camouflage jungle suit and carrying an old M-1 carbine with a wooden stock, which looked like it had seen better days. I tried in vain to strike up a conversation with him but finally gave up, figuring he couldn't hear me above the sound of the rushing wind and the roar of the engine.

We climbed to several thousand feet and soon were flying in and out of puffy cumulus clouds, some of which were full of rain. The air got real cool, something I had not experienced since arriving in this hellhole, so I began to hope we were in for a long flight. About thirty minutes passed before we began a rapid turning descent. I began to look below for some sort of army camp or an American flag, etc. We were coming down over terrain which was quite flat, quite wet, and appeared to be quite unpopulated, except for some rice paddies and a few water buffalo. I could see a small river meandering through the area, with large stands of palm trees on either bank. Lower and slower we went, and still no sign of the battalion or of any people, for that matter. Well, we finally landed right in the middle of the rice paddy, and the little gook jumps out into about two feet of water. I thought, Poor bastard, I wonder where he is going out there in the middle of nowhere? About that time, the copilot starts motioning for me to jump out, too! "Where the hell are my soldiers?" I shouted, only to receive an encouraging thumbs-up gesture from the copilot as they ascended back up into the cool atmosphere from which we had come. I turned around to look for the little gook, and he was hoofing it out across the paddy toward the tree line. In the opposite direction, barely visible on the horizon, was a low mud fortlike structure with what appeared to be a yellow South Vietnamese flag flying above it. Which way should I go? I quickly decided to take my chances with the little gook, since he must be on our side if they gave him a ride out here. When I caught up to him, he just stood there looking at me like I was an idiot or something. "Where are we supposed to be going?" I asked. He continued standing there looking at me and then started gesturing and speaking in Vietnamese. He didn't speak English. Good Luck! I thought, here I am in the middle of the Mekong Delta with a gook who doesn't know how to speak English or where he is going. About the time I was turning to head for the distant ARVN fort, I caught a glimpse of some activity near a neighboring tree line and realized that there were some artillery pieces set up in that area. The closer we sloshed, the more I became convinced that this was my outfit. We finally came across a dirt road which snaked out through the paddies and headed toward the tree line, so we headed down the road. Before we had gone too far, a jeep came speeding up, with a real cheerful looking kid with a floppy cloth hat and a big thick mustache. "You must be Doc Holley. We've been expecting you. I'm Mitch, your driver. Welcome to the 4/39th, sir!" Mitch, officially Sp4. Larry Mitchell, would become one of my closer friends—always polite, always punctual, and a damned good driver.

30 Oct 1968

Long Truong, RVN

We are still here at Long Truong, camped in the road. Our Alpha Company is out on operations a couple of miles from here. They have made contact with a large enemy force, and our mortars are really hitting them hard! These things are so loud, they shake the ground all around you, but I must be getting used to it because I actually got a pretty good night's sleep in spite of their firing off and on all through the night. We didn't get mortared after all. Maybe because we are right under the noses of some of their families across the canal. Makes you wonder, doesn't it?

I saw over one hundred people today, mostly with various types of ringworm, but many with immersion foot, chancroid, LGV (lymphogranuloma venereum), and Lord only knows what else! It's a pretty, cloudless night, and the moon is shining brightly. There is actually a cool breeze and no mosquitoes. The little hamlet across the canal is lit up with kerosene lanterns in each window. Between the explosions of outgoing artillery, it almost seems peaceful, rather like a Seminole Indian village in the Everglades. Boy, don't I wish I was there instead. I wouldn't even complain about the mosquitoes!

I just received word that one of my men has been shot in the leg, and one of my medics has called in a dust-off. They will fly over us and take him directly to 3d Surgical Hospital at Dong Tam. It's a MASH unit which operates in one of these inflatable buildings that looks like an igloo. Well, I've gone three straight days without a shower, and I don't have the courage to bathe in that canal! So, I just shave and brush my teeth out of my canteen cup. I'm really starting to feel grimy, not to mention the smell! Maybe that's why the mosquitoes aren't bothering us tonight!

31 Oct 1968

Long Truong

I'm sitting at my card-table desk, under a tent with the flap open, and it's a beautiful day, with a cool breeze blowing. All day long, sampans—which are very similar to the dugout canoes used by the Seminoles in the Glades, only bigger—ply back and forth on this river, laden with anything from bananas and canta-loupes to cases of Coke, ducks and chickens in crude home-made, wooden cages, pigs and dogs and people of all ages from infants to old mamma-sans who appear to be eighty or ninety but in all probability are more like forty or fifty. Living their lives in this harsh environment takes its toll on them. Their skin is thick, tough, and wrinkled and actually reminds me of ele-phant hide.

We are still located at Long Truong, a small hamlet about six miles north of the Mekong River. Yesterday, one of my troopers came down with malaria, and I had to call in a chopper to evac-uate him. This is a dust-off mission and was the first of many to come. I actually figured the coordinates from the map myself and called it in over the radiotelephone on channel 45.70. I figure anything I can learn to do myself may come in handy someday—you know, the old CYA theory! My call sign is Band-Aid 6 or Big Band-Aid. My medics are Band-Aid-Charley 1 or Band-Aid-Alpha 1, etc., depending which company and platoon they are assigned to. Anyway, I must have passed map reading because in a few minutes, we heard the *whomp-whomp-whomp* of an approaching Huey helicopter. I was really glad to get this kid out of the field. He had a fever of 104 degrees which was rising in spite of an alcohol sponging. He had the most violent shaking chills I have ever seen, and a couple of times I thought he was seizuring. There just wasn't much more I could do for him in the boonies. We did start an IV and gave him small doses of phenobarbital for the seizures. I couldn't believe our medics didn't have one vial of quinine for intravenous use in the field.

I will sure as hell see that this doesn't happen again. He was having excruciating headaches, to the point I was afraid he might become delirious and try to shoot himself. I don't believe I have ever seen anyone sweat so profusely—it just dripped off him. His electrolytes are probably a mess!

Each day we spend about one and a half hours treating the local residents. It's interesting that most are women and children. Most young men are dead or "gone away." VC? These people have some of the most incredible cases of impetigo, and God only knows what other types of skin rashes, open weeping sores, draining lymph nodes, as well as a wild variety of ringworm type lesions. It's a real dermatologist's mecca and is pretty disgusting for an aspiring ophthalmologist. I examined one of our boys yesterday, who was just one big ringworm from his waist to his feet. Of course, it seems they all have VD—civilians and Americans alike—but more on that later.

You would really crack up if you could see the good doctor's uniform now. Floppy, green swamp hat; no shirt; baggy, green jungle fatigue pants; combat boots; dog tags, and a stethoscope hanging around my neck. And to top it off, my very own personal Colt .45, complete with a shoulder holster! I look like Doc Holliday from the Old West!

I just lit up a Winston and returned to the tent after an hour of moon gazing. I sat on top of our bunker and watched the moon, which is about three-quarters full now. Knowing it's the same moon you looked at last night seems to make me feel a little less far from home, kind of like it's a link between us. It's a clear, moonlit night, complete with jungle sounds, the solitude of which is interrupted every few minutes by outgoing four-deuce mortar rounds. The mortar tubes are located about seventy-five yards from the aid station, and the rounds are going right over our heads. I mean to tell you they can naturally scare the hell out of you! They shake the ground all around and make a fantastic flash of brilliant white light. You don't have any warning even though the crew are supposed to yell "Fire!" But half the time you can't hear them. Even the seasoned veterans over here jump out of their skin sometimes. One big black soldier from Alabama, who does everything in slow motion, was lying in his cot with mosquito net draped all around him when one of those rounds went off unexpectedly. He jumped up with all that net hanging off him! He slowly looked around and started laughing and said, "Oh man, I can't stand that shit!" in a beautiful southern drawl, and everybody cracked up.

Laughter really is a great escape valve when you are under the gun, and I've been real impressed with the morale of my medical company. It is almost like a fraternity; thirty-two men under my command, and most of them are great. Three are blacks from the Deep South. I think I really surprised them the other day. We were digging out our bunker and filling sandbags when I grabbed the shovel out of one of their hands and started digging myself. They really seemed to appreciate the fact that I wasn't too good to get my hands dirty. But I told them I wouldn't ask anything of them that I wouldn't do myself, and I figured that was a good way to show it. Besides, the bunker is being dug right next to my cot, so if mortars start coming in, I'll be the first one in the bunker!

Tonight being Halloween, we are expecting some action, as the VC usually like to help us celebrate our American holidays with a little fireworks of their own! Word just came in that we move out for Dong Tam tomorrow, and I can't wait to get a shower. I haven't had one for four days, and I'm starting to smell pretty rank. Of course, the mosquitoes haven't been bothering me too much lately! I really stink to high heaven!

2 Nov 1968

Dong Tam

Well, here we are back at Dong Tam for a few days of dry-out, clean-up time. Then we are off to My Phuoc Tay for three days, then to Long Truong for a week or so, and finally on to Nha Be. We are really a gypsy outfit. Charlie has his hands full just keeping up with where we are at any given time. Shoot, I have a hard time keeping up with it myself!

I had a very interesting experience tonight. I sat in on a five-man board holding a special court-martial. We tried five men for offenses ranging from being caught asleep while on guard duty to being AWOL for two months. The punishments ranged from three months in prison at hard labor with three months of two-thirds loss of pay, to six months of both. I never had any idea that I would ever be trying soldiers in a court-martial. It's a strange feeling sitting there with someone's future in your hands—with you being both judge and jury. I didn't particularly enjoy it. We started at 1900 hours and finished at 2300 hours.

We never did get mortared at Long Truong, but we did have an interesting experience on the way back to Dong Tam. We were traveling in a typical military convoy, pulling our aid station in a small two-wheel trailer behind the jeep. We were about halfway back in the convoy when our trailer came loose and ran off the side of the road. Well, would you believe that everybody just pulled around us and hauled ass, leaving us high and dry out in the middle of Viet Cong country. Sergeant Defenbaugh, Spec Six Ashley, Spec Four Blakely, and my driver, Spec Four Mitchell, each had M-16 rifles, and I had my everpresent Colt .45, but we certainly would not have been any match for a VC platoon. This occurred about three miles from the area where one of our tanks, which sweeps the roads for mines each A.M., was blown up by a command-detonated mine, killing four men and wounding two men. This happened yesterday morning. In fact, we saw it sitting on the side of the road on the way in—a twisted hunk of metal, streaked with blood.

Well, you can believe I was just a little pissed off, and when we got back to base camp, I had a lively discussion with my executive officer who assured me that in the future he would have a rifle platoon at the rear of the convoy to stay with any stragglers. I didn't even know the way back to Dong Tam, as I had flown out there and had never before traveled the road. Thank God, my driver Mitch knew the road well, so we didn't have any problem—no thanks to the battalion! I had a general idea where it was, but I wouldn't have found the unit without some help.

I am taking every precaution available to me, and old Charlie will have to get up awfully early to get old Doc Holley.

I sleep real light when we are out in the field. I sleep with my boots and glasses on, my pistol, loaded, in its holster and on, and my steel pot, flak jacket, and M-16 all within arm's reach. I'm no hero, and I sure as hell don't plan to do anything foolish, but I do remember the Boy Scouts' motto, "Be prepared"—I am.

You wouldn't believe the incredible amount of venereal disease that I am seeing and treating over here. I diagnosed two cases of primary syphilis today and saw several cases of lymphogranuloma venereum (LGV), chancroid, and granuloma inguinale (GI). I'm really developing a reputation in the battalion as being hard-nosed about VD. In fact, I am planning to pull a series of "short-arm" inspections soon—"Open fly, pecker out!"—since, out of fear or ignorance, many kids with sores on their penises won't come in. No telling how many of them have lues (syphilis) and don't even know it!

I've already had several of the guys come to me with very heavy personal problems. One soldier was supposed to meet his wife in Hawaii, and a week before he was supposed to leave, he received a letter from her, explaining that she would not be able to meet him there because she was five months pregnant—he has been over here for eight months. Well, he had been fighting a strong urge to kill himself, so I got him shipped out to spend some time with a shrink in Long Binh. Hopefully, he will see that she is not worth dying for; however, over here death is such an everpresent companion that many times it seems that it might be a way of escape from this hellhole.

Definitions. Chancroid is a venereal disease caused by a bacteria called the Ducrey bacillus. It presents as a painful shallow ulcer on the penis which progresses to involvement of the lymph nodes in the groin in about half the cases. The lymph nodes may swell up as large as a potato and become so painful that walking becomes very difficult. Many times the node will burst open, producing an open, weeping sore. Treatment is usually quite effective and consists of bed rest, plus Gantrisin or Sulfadiazine, four grams daily for seven to twelve days, or tetracycline two grams daily for seven days followed by one gram daily for fourteen days.

Lymphogranuloma venereum, or LGV as it is commonly called, is a viral venereal disease which causes primarily an enlargement of the lymph nodes in the groin without causing a visible sore on the penis. Severe systemic manifestations such as meningitis, encephalitis, skin lesions, keratitis, or arthritis may occur. Treatment is similar to that for chancroid.

Gonorrhea, or GC, is an infection of the lining of the genital tract caused by a bacteria called the gonococcus, hence the term GC. This condition is commonly called clap or strain, and is the most frequent form of VD seen in Vietnam. Gonorrhea in the male patient usually presents as painful burning on urination, with discharge of pus from the tip of the penis. It usually occurs from three to seven days after sexual intercourse with an infected female. GC in the female usually results in a condition called PID or pelvic inflammatory disease and causes pus to form in the fallopian tubes and the vagina and cervix. It frequently results in scarring which leads to sterility. Treatment involves the injection of three million units of depot penicillin in males and twice that dose for two weeks in the female.

Granuloma inguinale is a bacterial infection of the penis which presents as a painless, sharply demarcated ulcer with a red granular base, which bleeds easily. It has an incubation period that varies from one to twelve weeks. It may lead to an enlargement of the genital organs, known as elephantiasis, due to blockage of the lymph drainage. It is less likely to cause enlargement of the lymph nodes of the groin (buboes) than is LGV or chancroid and usually responds to the same type of antibiotic treatment as these conditions.

Syphilis or lues. Prior to the introduction of the HIV virus and AIDS, syphilis was considered the most deadly and dangerous form of venereal disease. It is caused by a spirochete called Treponema pallidum and can cause tissue destruction and chronic inflammation in almost any organ in the body. A chancre, or painless ulcer of the penis or vulva, develops at the site of inoculation three to six weeks after infection. If left untreated, it will heal spontaneously in about six weeks, only to be followed by a rash indicating the spread of the organisms throughout the body. This stage of the disease is known as secondary syphilis. If not treated at this stage, the rash may disappear spontaneously, and the disease may lay dormant for ten to twenty years before signs of neurosyphilis or cardiovascular syphilis appear. Treatment consists of the intramuscular injection of 2.4 million units of long-acting bicillin initially and one week

later. All of these diseases can be prevented by the use
of condoms.

3 Nov 1968

Dong Tam

Well, it finally had to happen, and today it did. My ambulance
crew and I were fired on by a sniper while we were driving out
to an area where our Bravo Company is located on the outer
perimeter of Dong Tam. He must have been a pretty poor shot
because he missed the whole jeep, thank goodness! This whole
area surrounding Dong Tam is heavily infested with Viet Cong.

Just prior to leaving to return to base camp, we overheard
radio chatter from two of our Bravo Company drivers about a
mile south of us, and they were in the middle of being ambushed. They were on the same road that we would have to travel
to return to Dong Tam. My CO got involved and got us an escort
from a deuce-and-a-half (two-and-a-half-ton truck) with a .50-
caliber machine gun mounted on the hood. Everything was quiet
until we were passing through an area known as "Ambush
Alley," because of the frequency of the event. Here the jungle
comes right up to the road, and you can't see back into it for
more than a few yards. Well, we were moving along at a pretty
good clip when, all of a sudden, five shots rang out from the
nearby jungle. You could actually hear them whiz over the top
of our jeep, and Mitch swerved wildly and sped up. He looked
over at me, grinning, and said, "That wasn't even close, Doc.
Besides, you never hear the one that kills you anyway!" We all
burst out laughing. It's really amazing how humor plays along
with fear. We glanced back at the jungle, not really expecting
to see the gooks who had fired at us. We didn't see anything but
dust, palm trees, and vines.

This is an ugly war, and I am concerned that the bombing
halt called recently is the wrong move. If things continue as

expected, we will probably have another Tet offensive, which will probably find us in Nha Be or Saigon. The thought of either location makes me nervous. I really prefer it out in the more open Delta country. Right now we plan to stay at Dong Tam for three or four more days. I'm really enjoying the luxury of daily baths and clean sheets.

I had to sit on another court-martial tonight for a poor guy who went AWOL because his wife sent him a Dear John letter when he'd been eleven months over here. I really can't say I blame him. There are some real heartbreaking situations over here, and I guess after a while they will become routine, but right now they really get to me sometimes.

I wish you could see how cute some of the little native kids are. Most of them wear some kind of hand-me-down hat, which is usually way too large for their tiny little heads. They usually stand at attention by the side of the road and either wave or salute us as we pass. Of course, some of them either give us the finger or just glare, while others make obscene gestures for sex and yell out something about the prices to ''boom-boom'' their sisters. The contrast is unreal.

There appears to be only two classes of nonmilitary people living over here. Either they are high-class and live in mansions in the larger cities, where their kids attend private schools, or very low-class, living in slum conditions in the cities or barely scraping an existence from the land out in the boonies. Over and over, I keep saying to myself, ''God truly did bless America!'' More people should have to come over here and see how millions of other people live, barely surviving. I guess these kids are what the whole damn war is about, and as confusing as it is for me, can you imagine how it must be to their little minds? Whereas most of the kids seem to like us, most of the South Vietnamese soldiers show no expression at all when we pass. I think half of them are probably VC!

4 Nov 1968

Dong Tam Base

We are at Dong Tam, but plans are to move out soon for Cai Be, a small hamlet located on the bank of a river, about fifteen miles from here. Apparently Cai Be will serve as a staging area from which we will go out on search-and-destroy missions. From what I've heard from some of our grunts, these missions can get real hairy because it is so hard to tell who is the enemy and who are the innocent peasant farmers. It seems that a lot of noncommunist farmers and their families get run over in some of these raids.

It usually ends up with their hooches being burned by flame throwers and their rice hauled off to the ARVNs. When the ARVNs come across large stockpiles of rice or other foodstuff, they automatically assume that it is being held for delivery to the Viet Cong. I guess it never occurs to them that a rice farmer would have large amounts of grain on hand until he could get it hauled into the market. But their attitude seems to be: if in doubt, blast away and ask questions later. In a way, I can understand that philosophy, but, on the other hand, it seems so unfair. I really think it is a no-win situation as far as your conscience is concerned. The only major objective we each have is to stay alive another day, and if innocent farmers get killed along the way, it's better them than us. Sounds hard as nails, but you don't get a second chance if you guess wrong the first time around.

I'm doing fine, really! It has finally sunk home that I'm here, and I don't feel afraid anymore. Believe it or not. I take all the necessary precautions, and I'm prepared for the worst. I go into the field armed with an M-16 automatic rifle, a Colt .45 automatic pistol, wearing a steel pot and a flak jacket, which will stop most shrapnel and covers my chest and back. So don't worry too much about me. I'm being careful, and I believe I can take pretty good care of myself, not to mention my own personal troop of bodyguards, who have a vested interest in my continued good health.

We are on standby to go into Nha Be in the event of a major attack on Saigon. We have a large tank farm there, where millions of gallons of gasoline and diesel fuel are stored. It might get kind of scary being around those storage tanks, with rockets and mortars flying through the air! Maybe we will get lucky and not have to go over there. There are some fairly good intelligence reports that seem to indicate that an attack by the VC is a good possibility on or shortly after election day, but it's really hard to know for sure.

4 Nov 1968

Dong Tam

I don't guess I can ever begin to fully explain the many feelings which crowded my mind those last few days and hours at Travis AFB waiting to ship out for Vietnam. It's an experience someone has to go through himself to fully appreciate it. Sort of like being in Vietnam. It's so dirty and grubby that mere words can't adequately describe it.

We just got word a little while ago that we will move out for Cai Be in the morning. We are supposed to be there for three to five days, and then anybody's guess. I assume it depends on whether Saigon gets hit hard or not.

No one I've spoken to is in favor of the bombing halt. Most feel that this is the chance Charlie has been waiting for in order to prepare for a postelection offensive. We have been on thirty-minute alert ever since I arrived at the division base camp. I know I'll be scared if the shooting really gets heavy in my area, but somehow I'm not afraid yet. Even when that sniper shot at us yesterday—it made me mad, but it really didn't scare me. I'm just going to take all the precautions available to me and leave it in the Lord's hands. He has brought me through quite a few close calls in my relatively short life, and I know His will will be done.

I really like most of the crew I have here now. But I had one old alcoholic lifer sarge who was having vodka martinis for breakfast. He was slurring his speech and smelled to high heaven from the booze seeping from his pores. I had a talk with him, and I think it's too late. He started crying like a little kid, so I'm going to get him transferred to a permanent job in the rear. I'm afraid he will get some of us killed.

Most of the medics seem to like me, and they are all busy scrounging up all kinds of supplies, new otoscope, ophthalmoscopes, and three new stethoscopes. Scrounging is the army term for "appropriating" supplies from other units. They are even talking about procuring me my own personal jeep with "Super Quack" painted on the front! We had a three-quarter-ton truck-ambulance, but it was blown to pieces by a land mine a few weeks ago. Top says, "Don't sweat the small stuff, Doc, we sometimes find spare ambulances laying around with the key in the ignition. Ha! Ha!" What a crew! There is a lot of camaraderie, and I can already sense a feeling of relief on their part that they have a battalion surgeon who cares about their well-being and will back them up.

Well, time for a little shut-eye in comfort while I can get it.

5 Nov 1968

Dong Tam

What have I been doing the past few days? Well, each morning from 0730 to 1130 hours, I hold sick call, and my medics and I see anywhere from forty to one hundred and fifty men: lots of venereal disease, quite a few "flakes" (fakes), and a good number of legitimate cases of immersion foot and various skin diseases, as well as a fair number with emotional problems. We are really starting to crack down on the flakes and getting them back in the field. When I arrived, over half the troops were back in the rear area with some kind of pisspoor excuse. Now we are at close to eighty percent of our field strength, mainly as a result of Ashley and me kicking ass. We probably won't win the popularity contest this month, but I really don't care. I figure if we are here to do a job, then let's get off our butts and do it and do it right!

We've been seeing anywhere from ten to thirty civilians each day outside our base camp. I load up a trailer and jeep with medicines and ammo, and grab a small rifle platoon and a couple of medics, and we drive to the outskirts of a few of the hamlets that can be reached by road, and hold general medical clinic. I guess I almost killed an old lady with a penicillin shot yesterday. She went into shock, but unlike most Caucasians, she turned beet red, even though her blood pressure (BP) was hovering around 60/30, with a feeble, erratic pulse. My medics were almost panicking, and it became obvious that even though they are good at patching up wounded soldiers, they don't know much about medicine. If I hadn't been there, she would have died for sure. I gave her 0.5 milliliter [ml] of adrenaline subcutaneously, with one hundred milligrams [mg] hydrocortisone intravenously, along with fifty mg of Benadryl intramuscularly. Nasal oxygen at twelve liters per minute, and she was as good as new in about an hour. "How did you know what to give her, Doc?" asked my medics. I explained that these medicines had been lifesaving when used in a patient who was indeed in shock, but that the same medicines could kill a patient who really didn't need them, e.g., a vaso-vagal reaction. I told them not to try to act like MDs.

Well, we just underwent another mortar attack. I was sitting here writing when I heard two loud crunching explosions, and about fifty guys started screaming "Incoming!" at the top of their lungs. So, I hauled butt into our bunker, and it soon passed, kind of like a tornado in Arkansas. I'm getting to where I can sleep through outgoing rounds now, but I sure don't want to learn to sleep through the incoming ones! Lots of nights, though, I just lay there and hear every damn sound. A good night's sleep over here is five uninterrupted hours. That probably happens once or twice a week on average.

Tomorrow A.M. we head out for a brief stay at Cai Be, and then by helicopter to a Viet Cong stronghold called the Wagon Wheel. It is so named because from the air you can see the junction of three large navigation canals, which resemble a wheel with six spokes. We will set up camp at the center of the Wheel, thus being able to monitor all the traffic on these principal waterways. The closest road is fifty miles away, so we are going to swim or fly out to that area! The Wheel is located in a large wet expanse of sawgrass and scattered patches of jungle known as the Plain of Reeds. Teng, our Tiger Scout was telling me the other day how his grandfather had told him stories about helping to dig these canals back in the thirties when the nation was under French rule. The French believed they could dig a canal all the way to the Chinese border, but they, like a lot of people, underestimated the dreadful working conditions down here in the Delta, and so the project was never finished. However, they did succeed in building hundreds of miles of navigable canals, and Charlie knows each one like the back of his hand. We really are strangers in their land, and this fact is constantly made clear to us by the wide variety of unfamiliar obstacles we encounter.

8 Nov 1968

Dong Tam

Last night we were under a mortar and automatic weapons attack for nearly forty-five minutes, about forty miles west of here. I was not hurt, but only skinned up my knees and my back, snaking for a bunker. Today I was put up for the CMB (Combat Medical Badge) for my actions in treating casualties wounded during this brief but ferocious attack. This was really my "baptism by fire."

We were camped overnight at an old French fort, located on the bend of a small river with a thick canopy of jungle on the opposite shore. We had arrived there about dusk with only two rifle platoons. We all had a creepy feeling because this camp was pretty much a shambles and had obviously been mortared and shot up before, and several buildings had been burned down by a prior Viet Cong raid on ARVNs who had been overrun in the past. Lots of ghosts of dead soldiers in this place, I remember thinking. Another complete company of men was supposed to meet up with us there, but they were waylaid by the enemy south of here, so we were somewhat undermanned. Believe it or not, I was the ranking officer present, a young lieutenant being in command of the troops. This made me just a little nervous, thinking that if he gets killed it leaves me in charge. I'm pretty green when it comes to combat field experience. Well, we all kept kidding ourselves about being stuck out here with so few men (about forty men, including five medics), but there were also a dozen or so ARVNs, along with a handful of their women and kids. What a motley crew, I remember thinking as I contemplated what we would do if we were attacked by the Viet Cong. My first actions were to get the young lieutenant and make a quick inspection of the perimeter of the camp. There was a low sand/mud wall, or berm as they call it, with one row of concertina wire spread out about ten to fifteen yards from the berm. There were machine-gun positions located at the four corners of the fort, and a fast-moving river ran along the western edge. I knew it was the western edge because I remembered watching the brilliant orange-red glow of the tropical sun as it set behind the thick silhouette of the jungle on the opposite shore. We decided to split up the troops into four groups of eight to ten each, placing two men in each of the machine-gun positions, with the remainder being spread along the berm. Each miniplatoon had an M-16 outfitted with a Starlight Scope, a device like a telescope which amplifies ambient light to allow you to see at night. Apparently it amplifies available light from the moon or stars by a factor of 70,000!

There was one old dilapidated bunker that looked like it could not withstand a direct hit. The floor was dirt, and the timbers that supported the roof were rotten. It was pitch dark in there, and the air was musty as hell. While we were inside inspecting it, one of the local ARVN soldiers brought in a kerosene lantern, which lit it up enough to show that it was as dingy as we had thought it was. Well, in a pinch it will be better to treat the wounded than no place, I thought.

Our aid station was set up in one end of a building which had been burned and had about fifteen feet of roof left. We heated up some C rations and afterwards were sitting around shooting the breeze when all hell broke loose! With a tremendous, loud explosion, an incoming mortar round exploded about forty feet from where we were sitting. Dirt and rocks and shrapnel were flying everywhere, with the sound of metal striking metal all around. Almost simultaneously with the first impact, another round landed less than twenty feet from our position and embedded itself in the soft dirt—a dud! If it had been a live round, we would all have been wiped out. Well, all of a sudden a lot

of things started happening at once, and I can honestly say that I
didn't have time to get very frightened. There was so much to do
that my mind stayed amazingly clear! I looked up. The black sky
had become an interlacing network of red and green tracers crisscrossing the air above the fort. The incessant chatter of automatic
weapons drowned out the jungle sounds as M-16s returned fire.
I quickly learned the characteristic sound of the AK-47s.

"Stay low, my man," I remember telling myself as the sounds
of wounded men screaming "Medic, medic!" sounded over the
din. I slithered like a snake to the old bunker, which was looking
better by the minute. You just can't imagine the noise. And
seeing all those tracers going right above our heads! My last
sight before entering the bunker was that beautiful moon with
tracers flashing past it. I remember thinking, Thank God Sondra
can't see what's happening to me now. All the damn gooks were
yelling and jabbering like monkeys, and we were really letting
them have it with a couple of M-60 machine guns. Meanwhile,
more mortars were pounding our perimeter.

Someone hollered that one hundred and fifty VC were over-
running the place. I don't mind telling you I felt like I could shit
a brick about then!

Inside the bunker were about six young GIs and an ARVN
and his young and somewhat attractive wife. Incredibly, the
ARVN came up to me and said, "*Dai Uy*, *Bac Si* (Captain,
Doctor), you want boom-boom my wife? Only one hundred
piasters." I was astonished! Here we were in the middle of the
boonies, under attack, with wounded men in the bunker, and
this jerk wants me to screw his wife for a hundred bucks, Vietnamese currency—about one dollar, American! "Hey, asshole,
there is a war going on outside, and even if there wasn't, I
wouldn't want to screw your wife, so get the hell out of here so
I can take care of my troops." Needless to say, he hauled butt
out of there, and I moved in to inspect the wounded.

I was even further surprised by the reaction, or rather the lack
of reaction of my troops at the man's attempt to sell his wife's
pleasures to me under these circumstances.

"Shit, Doc, these people are so fucked up that nothing means
anything to them, not like real people back in the World." I
quickly learned that this short-timer was very perceptive. He
had only six days left in country and had slipped in here just to
avoid the firefight. He was all of eighteen years old, but he

looked much older. He lit up a Marlboro and said, "How about a smoke, Doc?" At this particular moment it seemed the proper thing to do, so I said, "Sure, why not?" His hand was steady as a rock, as was mine, and I remember thinking, If this kid can stay so cool after a year over here, surely I can do the same.

He pitched in and helped me patch up the few shrapnel wounds we had and then said, "Hey, Doc, want to have some fun? Let's go outside and see what's happening." This really shocked me—it was as if he could take it or leave it—because the sounds of battle continued to rage on. We quick-crawled out to the machine-gun position on the northwest corner of the fort along the river.

The young lieutenant was inside the bunker, looking out a port with a Starlight Scope, and gave this assessment of the current situation. "Doc, it seems that the mortar fire is coming from the opposite bank, just beyond the curve, and we have been taking lots of AK-47 fire from the jungle right across the river from us. I have called for artillery support from division, but it doesn't sound too promising, something about priority missions in another area—same from the Air Cav, so it looks like we're on our own."

I could see occasional muzzle flashes coming from the dark jungle on the opposite bank of the river, but I could barely make out the outline of the trees along the river. Without warning, voices yelled from out of the jungle, "Fuck you, GI! Tonight you die!" Over and over the same high-pitched oriental voice wailed from across the river.

"Get Sergeant Jones over here pronto!" the lieutenant barked. Jonesey had the reputation as our most accurate shot with the M-79 grenade launcher, and he was about to be given a challenge that even he later admitted would require a good deal of luck.

Jones came puffing up to the berm and was quickly apprised of the situation. "Have everybody cease fire, and I believe I can nail him, Lieutenant, if he will just keep on hollering a little longer." We stopped firing and so did the gooks, but the screamer continued to scream until Sergeant Jones had fixed his position in his mind and let fly with back-to-back shots from the M-79. We heard a brief scream and then silence. A few minutes later three bodies were seen floating downstream.

Through the Starlight Scope, we saw six more gooks pushing two sampans into the river from the opposite shoreline, just beyond the bend. Again Sergeant Jones was called upon to pull off a miracle, only this time he had the luxury of being able to see his targets, even though they were out at the maximum range of his weapon. *Boom! Boom!* Two direct hits, two more bodies floating downstream as Charlie turned tail and ran back into the darkness. I was impressed. I'm glad Jonesey and guys like him are on my side. I don't think I'll spend too much time worrying about my safety over here with these guys for personal body-guards.

Baby, I know this must sound ghastly to you, but believe me, when you know that these lunatic maniacs are just sitting out there waiting for a chance to kill or mutilate you, you learn to hate them real quick. Self-survival is one hell of a strong in-stinct, and I remember thinking, Holley, you sure don't want to die in this rat hole of a place, so you'd better get out there and start shooting those damn gooks! and I did.

Needless to say, I didn't sleep too soundly the rest of that night, and the sun shone just a little brighter the next day. I kept going back in my mind to the previous night's experience. I was amazed at the almost surrealistic slow-motion effect of the whole thing, like it was happening to someone else. I had the strange sensation, again, of watching the enemy through the Starlight Scope, with him thinking he was scurrying around under the cover of darkness while, all along, we were watching his every move.

Sergeant Hornfeck—who goes by the name of "Top," for top sergeant—came by the next day back at Dong Tam to congrat-ulate me on my welcome-to-the-Nam party. "Doc, I just wanted to come by and tell you that your men are really bragging on you; they said the captain was really tough. I told them I wasn't surprised, that I knew you would be."

Top is a wily, tough old bird with steel blue eyes, sandy blond hair, and a great droopy mustache that really imparts a look of wisdom combined with toughness—a bandito look. I don't know how old he is, but he must be pushing forty—which is ancient over here for a foot soldier. I do know he is highly respected by all the guys.

Well, those comments from the first sergeant and my men were worth more than any medal I could have gotten. Now I was a veteran of hostile fire and not just another FNG. I have always suspected that I am not a coward, but you never know how you will react until the shooting begins and they are trying to kill you! The horror of the war affects people in many different ways. One of our best company commanders, Capt. Paul Mer-lin, a real nice clean-cut guy of about thirty, feels so bad about losing a couple of his men that he is seriously considering re-signing from the army. It is such a waste of young lives. I'll have lots to tell by the time I come back home. I hope I'll be able to talk about this and not keep it all inside me.

This A.M., on the way back to Dong Tam, we saw several places where the road had been mined, and one hole was eight feet deep by eight feet wide (in an asphalt road, mind you) and had completely destroyed a truckload of civilians. Our chaplain was about eighty feet behind the truck when it was blown up, and he is still jumpy. He only has twenty-one days to go, and I don't blame him. Everybody is jumpy, especially since the bombing halt went into effect. We passed several groups of small children who "shot birds" at us and hollered "Number Ten!" (opposite of number one, which is the best). Obviously they are children of the local VC. Some of the kids are real sweet, but many of them show their hate openly. It's no wonder so many GIs are confused about why we are over here—we don't exactly get greeted with open arms by the people we are supposed to be liberating.

10 Nov 1968

Dong Tam

I spent a worthwhile afternoon at the orphanage at My Tho today. The place is filled with little kids whose parents have been slaughtered by the VC, and they are so pitiful. They all hang on to you, just begging for some affection. You can easily spot the newcomers, as they have a blank stare in their pretty dark little eyes, and they are quite withdrawn.

They sleep in double-deck wire beds with straw mattresses. At the far end of the big room, which they all share, there is a large sandbagged bunker. It was used just two nights ago when eighteen people were killed in their neighborhood. These little fellows are the closest thing to giving me a justification for being over here that I have experienced since my arrival. Their innocent little faces will haunt me for a long time, I fear. Their future is so very bleak.

We are waiting in the rear at Dong Tam while our companies fly search-and-destroy missions by chopper. I'm enjoying the brief rest and the chance to see an occasional western movie at our outdoor theater—a large sheet stretched between two flag-poles, outdoors, with the stench of the latrine and the constant buzz of mosquitoes. Still, it is a break. I imagine we will move out in a few days. Even though it's more dangerous out in the field, I prefer it to sitting around Dong Tam waiting for a rocket attack. And the time really seems to fly.

Today at the orphanage, the chaplain and the Red Cross volunteers were playing the guitar and singing hymns like "Jesus Loves Me" in Vietnamese and singing Christmas carols. It was very touching. Indeed, it was almost overwhelming; I soon had to get out of the place and back to reality.

Last night, one of my buddies, Captain Merlin, came by to shoot the breeze for a while as he was really shook up. In the past two days, he has lost nine wounded in action [WIAs] and one killed in action [KIA] from booby traps near Dong Tam. He's so upset that he wants to get out of the army and is asking for my advice. The KIA was a real nice-looking young guy. He had found a wired hand grenade, and an officer told him to disarm it and throw it in the river. Well, he didn't mean for him to pull the pin, but the young soldier pulled it anyway. It literally blew his head completely off at the shoulders, including his right arm, right before their very eyes! In your wildest dreams you can't begin to imagine the effect that something like that can have on you or your troops.

Thank God, I was spared the horror of having to witness that scene. It was hard enough having to hear it first hand; the captain had tears streaming down his cheeks as he relayed the story to me. "Doc, I don't believe in what we are doing over here any-more, and I can't stand the thought of losing any more of my young kids so needlessly."

The very same day his lieutenant got his foot blown off, and when they laid him down on the ground to work on him, they discovered that he was on a pressure-release grenade which would have gone off if he got up. Luckily for all concerned, he felt it, and one of his buddies quickly picked it up and tossed it out in the river, where it exploded about forty feet away from them. Even so, they all got some minor shrapnel wounds from it. Well, I talked and listened till 0300 hours, and the captain just left to get some shut-eye. I hope I've helped him. I think I did. Only, I now feel worse for the experience.

12 Nov 1968

Dong Tam

Yesterday, something interesting happened. We have Vietnamese men on our side called Tiger Scouts. They are former Viet Cong soldiers who have seen the light and have agreed to come over to our side and help us against their former comrades. Well, one of them, a fellow named Teng who speaks fairly good English, came up and told me about one of the other Tiger Scouts whose little daughter had what sounded like meningitis, with high fever and a rigid neck. This was about four in the afternoon, and the patient was located at their home in My Tho, about six or seven miles east of Dong Tam. Well, the road is patrolled and fairly secure until 4:30 P.M. After that, you are on your own. Most people think it is suicide to drive anywhere out in the country after dark. If you do get caught out, they recommend traveling with lights out.

It would be a close call, but I decided I couldn't deny the man what he needed. I would have felt terrible if I didn't go and the baby died overnight. So, I grabbed my weapons and my medical bag and told Mitch to haul ass to My Tho. Well, Mitch reminds you of a New York City taxi driver, and we were approaching My Tho as the shadows began to fall. Our party consisted of Mitch, Teng, the non-English-speaking Tiger Scout whose child we were to see, and one slightly apprehensive Florida cracker doctor! On arriving, Teng directed Mitch down to an earthen landing on the bank of the muddy, wide Mekong River. He pointed to a tree-covered island out in the middle of the channel and said, "She lives out there." There was one dilapidated sampan pulled up on the shore, and somewhat reluctantly, I climbed aboard to join the two Tiger Scouts. "Come on, Mitch!" I hollered as they began pushing off into the swiftly moving current. "Doc, I've got to stay and guard the jeep or else it won't be here when we get back," he yelled as we slowly moved away from shore. Damn, I thought, I should have thought about that and brought an extra GI along for my security! Now, here I was crossing a flood-swollen river in a sampan about the size of a Seminole Indian dugout with two known former Viet Cong. I hope I haven't overlooked any more minor details, I thought. "Teng, what is the name of the island, and how far out in the river is it?" I asked.

"Island is little more than two klicks (kilometers) from bank. Most people here call it VC Island," he answered. I decided not to ask why.

Well, you should have seen the people come running up when we arrived, all staring, glaring, and jabbering. I think half of them were VC. Well, they led me into a small, land-locked boat, about twenty feet long, but it was so full of hanging baskets and all kinds of crap that I could hardly move, much less examine a child in the place, so I told Teng we had to have a place with better lighting. Without waiting for one word from Teng, the father picked up his daughter and motioned for me to follow him out through the low door. Well, he might not know how to speak English, but he sure as hell understands it pretty well!

We walked through a dense stand of assorted palm and banana trees toward a larger thatched hut, which Teng identified as the local tavern.

Inside the dimly lit hut were about twenty VC-looking characters, all dressed in black pajamas and smoking pot or opium, I wasn't sure which as I had only smelled marijuana in the past. They were sprawled over and around a large rattan table in the center of the room, and most appeared to be drinking sake (rice wine). Their average age was sixteen to twenty-five. Oh shit, too late to back out now! I thought.

Thick smoke hung in layers around the room, and the humidity was stifling. The only light was provided by a World War II–vintage oil lantern. Teng began shouting at the others to get away from the table. Reluctantly they moved, but none of them were smiling, and I was really starting to feel uneasy.

Teng could sense my apprehension and kept looking back at me and saying "No sweat, Bac Si, no sweat!" I just stood there with one hand on my M-16 and the other on my medical bag, as the locals continued to glare at me. All of a sudden the reality of my current predicament hit me. I was all alone in a local VC cadre tavern and my only possible ticket out of there was to save that baby!! At almost the same instant, I casually observed six AK-47 assault rifles standing in a corner and several VC ammo pouches hanging from a corner post. While they all crowded around, I examined the tiny patient for nuchal rigidity (stiff neck) which would be present if she had spinal meningitis. Her neck muscles were relaxed. Her problem really involved her lungs, which were severely congested. This finding, along with a fever in excess of 104 degrees confirmed a diagnosis of bilateral pneumonia. I knew I could probably save her with a large dose of intramuscular penicillin, but suddenly my mind was seized with the recollection of a nurse in Miami who had recently given a small infant a similar injection only to have the little tyke die before her eyes from an acute anaphylactic reaction!! In fact, she had been unable to continue in her field. I could suddenly see a much worse fate in store for me if the child reacted in a similar fashion.

I initially considered giving her a harmless injection of saline, but my conscience knew she would probably die without the penicillin. I couldn't stand to think about that, so I quickly drew up two five-ml syringes of aqueous penicillin and thrust the first one in her tiny little buttocks. She screamed, everybody jumped, and I prayed that she would not drop dead! She soon quieted down, and for the first time the locals began to smile, then laugh, and finally cheer! I took the opportunity to shoot the other cheek with life-saving medicine and quickly got out.

On the way back across the river, the damn sampan started leaking like a sieve, and Teng looked up at me and said with a grin, "This damn number-ten boat!" and laughed. I cracked up, too, mostly from relief. I learned on the way back across the river that I had been correct in all of my assumptions. They were all VC, and several of them were his cousins. Teng proudly explained that even the VC have a code of ethics. Even though each one of them hated me for my presence in his country, they did realize that I possessed a skill which might save one of their own, and therefore, they would not harm me on that day. Tomorrow, in combat, that would be a different story. He also told me that the same father had already lost two infants to tropical diseases after they were treated by their local "medicine man," so they were all hoping I could pull off a miracle. So was I! Somehow I felt a little safer as our jeep sped back through the tropical countryside in a race with the setting sun. As the orange sky turned a brilliant red, I was suddenly reminded how easily it could have gone the other way. I silently said, "Thank you, Jesus," as we approached the outskirts of Dong Tam base.

13 Nov 1968

Dong Tam

I was just reading the Pacific edition of the *Stars and Stripes*, and it showed Memphis with a low temperature of thirty-one degrees Fahrenheit for the morning of 11 November. Wow, is that ever hard to imagine as I sit over here sweltering in this place!

Well, we are finally moving out in the morning. We will be traveling by Chinook, a large two-bladed helicopter. They are loud, and, man, do they kick up the dust! A guy with contact lenses would be in a world of hurt over here around those things. These giants are capable of picking up a two-and-half-ton truck or carrying up to sixty troops.

I'm really ready to get back out in the field. The only good thing about being here is the five o'clock mail call, which gets me your letters one day sooner than when I'm out on operations. We are supposed to stay out there for anywhere from two weeks to two months, depending on what kinds of contact we can make and also on what happens around Saigon. Of course, these plans can change very quickly, but we are taking ten thousand sand-bags with us, so I believe we will be out there for a while. Our supply sarge just hollered at someone to be sure they don't forget the 7,500 feet of barbed wire. This is really shaping up into quite a challenge for the S-4 department, which coordinates all the ordering and shipping of supplies. Somebody is getting rich off this war, no question about that. My troops are really dreading the physical labor which lies ahead.

I wonder what the life expectancy is over here for a civilian, wartime casualties aside. Between the heat and the disease, I'm sure a forty-year-old peasant is really considered old here. Well, I'd better close for now and pack, clean my weapons, and finish getting ready to go. We board our Chinooks at 0900 hours, and I must be up by 0600 hours.

16 Nov 1968

My Phuoc Tay

Here I sit in my aid station, under a tent with the sides rolled up to let the breeze blow through. Actually, today is a pretty day with a nice, almost cool breeze blowing off the Plain. The sky is a deep royal blue, with little white puff clouds blowing in from the north. I guess this is Vietnam's version of a cold front! I just stuffed myself at the chow hall—open-air type—and it really wasn't bad. Decent food on occasion does a lot for our morale, so today we had steak and potatoes, just like back in the World.

We are finally settling in at My Phuoc Tay. I don't know why they call it that. I think "Ghost Town" would be more appropriate. Hey, maybe My Phuoc Tay is Vietnamese for ghost town!

We are set up in a cluster of old burned-out buildings of French Colonial architecture, sitting slap-dab in the middle of nowhere. I mean there are no roads, no hooches, no local taverns, and most noticeable of all, no people. This place reminds me of newsreel footage I saw as a child of war-ruined areas in Europe. It still blows my mind that they ever built buildings of this type way out here in the middle of rice paddies, reeds, and jungle. Everything had to be brought in by boat or by airplane and dropped by parachute as there is no place dry enough to have a landing strip, and this was long before the helicopter was in use.

We are set up in an old burned-out building, so at least we have the luxury of a hard cement floor rather than the usual dirt or mud. The roof is still partially intact but not too safe looking, so we opted to use the end without a roof and set up tents for shelter from the rain. I could just see that old tile roof crashing down on my head in the middle of a mortar attack. Some of the medics were planning to set up sleeping bags down at that end until I pointed out the potential danger. I figure there are enough unknown factors at work trying to shorten our lives without us helping them out by being stupid!

I have a treatment area at one end of the tent, with our mosquito nets and litters at the other. Cots are optional at this point, but somehow I feel safer sleeping closer to the ground. I joined in with the men and we dug a bunker late into the night, so we are fairly secure from mortar attack, unless they use 122mm rockets.

Charlie mortared a Special Forces camp near here three nights ago, so Ashley and I went over to check out their facilities. It was quite an experience. It's a "permanent" camp, so they have spent some bucks in fixing it up fairly nice—for over here. They have diesel-operated electric generators which provide light, television, air-conditioning, etc. They have built a real neat lounge complete with bar, bar stools, TV, and a beautiful red, white, and blue flag tacked up on the wall behind the bar with gold stars which spell out HO CHI MINH KISS MY ASS! It really is a morale boost to walk inside a place like this out in the middle of nowhere and find that the old American humor still prevails.

The Special Forces camp should probably be called "The Oasis." They are quite a spirited bunch, these Green Berets. There are twelve of them stationed here, and they are in charge of over six hundred ARVNs, approximately ten percent of whom are feeding information back to the Viet Cong. The CO was telling us how both of his predecessors had been shot in the back of the head while leading their ARVN troops into battle. As I continue to say, identification of the enemy is the hardest and most crucial task we face. His advice, "Don't trust anyone with slant eyes, only trust the round eyes." From what I've heard, sometimes even those with round eyes will assassinate their leaders if they get fed up enough. Talk about a balancing act, if you're not crazy when you get over here, be patient, because you will probably get that way soon.

We wish now we had known they had showers yesterday when we came in by Chinook. We were filthy from the blowing dust, which caked in our ears and anyplace there was an exposed opening. With large bandanas over our noses and mouths, we all look like bandits, otherwise we would choke to death in the dust storm.

We all stripped and went skinny-dipping in a large canal near our mess tent. What we didn't know was that some villagers had just gutted hogs upstream. All of a sudden, I came up with about ten feet of hog intestines draped over my shoulders. I thought everybody would die laughing, until they realized that they too were in the middle of a bunch of hog parts. We all practically walked on water getting out of there!

We then rigged up a neat device called an Australian shower. It consisted of a canvas bag with a showerhead screwed into the bottom of it. You unscrew the head to control the flow of water. It will hold about five or six gallons of water so we made a fire and heated up a lot of water and had a community shower, complete with soap and a cool rinse from an irrigation tanker.

One of my black medics kept saying "Shit, man, I can make us some good chitlins from dem hog guts." We were all unanimous in our decision to toss his black ass back out in the canal if he tried it!

Our engineers came by a little while ago and are now putting the finishing touches on a portable shower which will pump the water out of the canal and through a filter system before our use. Ah, sweet luxuries of life.

Well, I'd better close for now as I have to go radio for a patrol boat to take some of us downriver. We need to hold sick call for some of our troops who have been holed up downstream for about two weeks. Some of them sound pretty sick. We have had some pretty heavy contact during the past few days, killing twenty-one VC and losing one of ours to a head injury, and suffering ten WIA. Well, I see the patrol boat on the horizon, and knowing the way these crazy kids drive them, he will be here before I am ready. We saw one the other day pulling a makeshift surfboard! Kids will be kids, whether they're in a war zone or not.

17 Nov 1968

My Phuoc Tay

We are still at My Phuoc Tay. All yesterday and most of this morning, we have been observing a very interesting operation. Our ground forces came across a huge underground complex where a VC regiment was holed up. We believe a large number of them are still holed up in these tunnels and bunkers. We called in our friends from the air force, and there has been almost continuous air strikes with jet fighter-bombers dropping five-hundred-pound bombs and napalm. This is all taking place about four miles from our location and is really a spectacle to watch. The noise is deafening! It is beautiful in an eerie sort of way. Napalm is a highly inflammable substance that is carried in canisters, and when it hits the earth, its gelatinous contents ignite instantly and cover everything in sight with an intensely flaming substance. It roars like a fire in the fireplace when it gets a fresh supply of oxygen, and the smell of napalm is so unique that once you have smelled it you will never forget it. Thank God, they don't use it against us! These fly-boys come cruising in at about four-thousand feet and begin a steep full-throttle dive with afterburners screaming. The roar is awesome. They really haul ass, and lots of them will make flyovers and do barrel rolls, split Ss, and other acrobatic maneuvers for our entertainment. I think it's their way of saying "thanks" to us for being there. Not that they don't take risks, but most nights will find them asleep in an air-conditioned room with clean sheets, real pillows, TV, etc. There's no question that the infantry soldier has the grimiest, dirtiest, most thankless job in Vietnam today, and the "junior birdmen" have one of the plushest, especially the navy fly-boys. Oh well, I learned long ago that life is not always fair, so we just have to grin and bear it. But, I am damn glad they are on our side, I'll tell you that in a hurry!

The boy I mentioned being killed in action yesterday had just returned from a compassionate Stateside leave, which I had arranged. His wife was running around on him and threatening to leave him. Two days after returning to the Nam, he received a letter from her saying that she still "couldn't promise anything . . ." Well, the very next day he walked slam into a VC booby trap that blew his head off. His men said he had been very depressed and apparently was not watching where he was walking, and he led ten other men into the same trap. He took the brunt of it himself, the rest of them getting shrapnel wounds only. Thus his bitch of a wife messed up several people and by now has probably received her $10,000 check from his Servicemen's Group Life Insurance policy—pretty damn ironic, huh?

In a couple of days, we will be moving out for a tiny hamlet on a canal (aren't they all?) called Thu Thua (pronounced too-

too-uh). This is near the famous Ben Luc bridge which General Westmoreland boasted could never be blown up and which Charlie promptly did, one week later. This is also near the spot where our medics were killed in the minefield incident I mentioned earlier. We are supposed to build a VC-proof base in an old abandoned fort, which the VC overran three months ago, killing over one hundred men in a nighttime raid. Sounds like fun, eh?

Charley Company just brought in a VC POW. They all look the same after a while. One prisoner, after some "friendly persuasion," helped us locate two VC battalions, totaling almost one thousand men. There are 600 located about four miles north of us, where the air strikes have been going in, and about 350 located about three miles south of us. We flew troops in to the southern location, but Charlie quickly ran and hid, and we haven't been able to engage him in a good fight yet. I have learned that Charlie may be poor, but he is not stupid. He usually chooses the time and place for his battles when the cards are right for his best chance of success. It is almost impossible to get him involved in a fight when it is not at his own time and place. I guess he has learned over succeeding generations how to pick and choose the optimum situation. They have been at war forever, first with the Chinese and for the past one hundred years with the French. We are truly the new kids on the block in this theater.

18 Nov 1968

My Phuoc Tay

As I sit here writing this letter, I am being glared at by a Viet Cong prisoner we captured early this morning. You can't begin to imagine the hatred in his eyes. Not fear, but pure old-fashioned hate. It's a strange and rather unsettling feeling to sit here knowing full well that he would kill me in a minute if he had the chance. He is sitting in the grass about ten feet away from my aid station. He is wearing the traditional black pajama outfit and is bareheaded and barefooted as well. His hands are tied behind him, and he just squats there in the shade with this very defiant look on his face. A few minutes ago, I went out with an interpreter and tried to explain to him that he didn't have to worry about being tortured or anything like that, and tried to give him some water to drink, but he refused any help. Right now, he is being guarded, for his own protection as well as ours. If he doesn't have a change of heart soon, he will be in for a very rough interrogation session with our intelligence people. They are holding him near the aid station now as they feel like we represent the compassionate side of the outfit.

We killed ten VC this morning and captured two others, both loaded down with ammo. Two days ago we killed thirty-one and captured ten. In a strange way, it is exciting to be over here. I've learned to handle my M-16 with good accuracy, as well as my Colt .45 pistol. I can't say that I have killed anyone yet, as the only firefight I have been in was at night, but I'm prepared and feel confident in my capabilities. I'm fifty percent doctor and anywhere from fifty percent to one hundred percent soldier, depending on the circumstances. In the field, I live in a small twenty-by-thirty tent, one end of which serves as sleeping quarters for me and five medics. We sleep on litters and air mattresses, under mosquito netting, which seems to help a lot. I sleep in my fatigue pants, with my glasses on, with my Colt .45 pistol, safety on, right under the edge of my air mattress. We usually build bunkers with steel culverts and sandbags flown in by Chinooks. We are always worried about mortar attacks like the kind that kept Khe Sanh under siege for weeks on end. Our only protection is the bunker. Since our bases are smaller and less permanent than those at Khe Sanh, we probably won't get into a similar situation.

We anticipate moving to Tan An in a few days. It is a larger town near the Vam Co Tay River, which is the location of the Ben Luc bridge. This bridge, if knocked out, would virtually cut off all points south from Saigon, and the type of military assistance road convoys can supply. So the security of that bridge is of paramount importance. Word is that we will be involved in rooting out the VC unit which has been harassing the bridge security unit.

18 Nov 1968

My Phuoc Tay

Today it was so quiet, we actually got bored, so Top Hornfeck came by and said, "Doc, it's about time you learned to shoot the M-79 grenade launcher. Come out in the paddies, and I'll teach you how." We went out a ways from camp, where he had one of his grunts set up targets at one hundred, two hundred, three hundred, and four hundred yards. Keep in mind that a football field is one hundred yards, and you can imagine the kind of distance this shotgun-looking weapon can fire a grenade. They are really a neat toy, and they sound like a miniature cannon when they go off. They have a potential killing radius of ninety feet. I gained confidence rapidly as round after round landed at the base of my intended target. The round is lobbed in a high arc, and you can actually watch it head for the target. It's like having your own small howitzer. Several of our boys don't even have M-16s, preferring to carry the M-79 instead. We were also introduced to a small bazookalike weapon called a LAW (light antitank weapon). They are a disposable, one-shot weapon, but if you are accurate it will literally blow the hell out of a tank, truck, house, or whatever. Rule number one is *never* stand behind anyone who is fixing to fire a LAW. On discharge, a trail of fire and powder is blown out the back, and more than one unsuspecting grunt has been severely injured in such accidents. I got to shoot one at an old bunker across the canal from us, and it was amazing what so light a weapon could do in terms of destructive force. I had to laugh when the sarge asked this one mean-looking rifleman to let me have his LAW. He said, "Not this one, sir, it's all prettied up for Charlie." He had several pictures and sayings painted on it, but one which really cracked me up said simply, Don't Fuck with the LAW. We also got some target practice with our M-16s and my Colt .45. An automatic weapon has a tendency to rise on you when you are firing a sustained burst. It requires a great deal of discipline to

control that tendency. It sounded like World War II had broke
out, with all the firing going on.

19 Nov 1968

My Phuoc Tay

You wouldn't believe the horrible venereal disease I see over
here. Since I told my men I wouldn't have anything to do with
any women over here, that I intended to be a straight arrow,
they seem to really respect me for it. In fact, since I stood up
and spoke my piece about it, there have been several of the
married guys, who had messed around previously, who are now
walking the chalk line. I think they just needed someone to look
up to and set an example. These poor dumb kids just don't have
any idea of some of the serious diseases they can get into with
some of the women they are sleeping with. But "Father Byron"
is slowly but surely educating their pointed little heads with
weekly lectures on VD.

We made headlines the other day with our kill of thirty-one
VC. Last night, two of our companies were mortared with 82mm
mortars, about five miles from here. Intelligence reports from
our POWs indicate we are supposed to get hit tonight. We are
dug in pretty well and will add a few more sandbags this afternoon.

One of our Cobra gunships was shot down by small-arms fire
last night. The pilot was able to get it airborne, and flew it into
our location about midnight. He had only a few scratches, but
his bird was shot up pretty badly. Yesterday we had sixteen
choppers—ten Hueys and six Cobras. These choppers are awesome! I'm really glad Charlie doesn't have them, too!

20 Nov 1968

My Phuoc Tay

We are supposed to return to Delta Tango (code for Dong Tam) tomorrow by Chinook. We just drive our jeep, with trailer attached, right up into the belly of the chopper, and along with my medics and another soldier or two, we swoop away to terrorize the Cong in another AO (area of operations). After a two-day stand-down, dry-out, and resupply, we will head out to Tan An, where we have been promised we can build a relatively "permanent" command post with an aid station. I'll believe it when I see it!

Dong Tam was hit pretty hard last night with 122mm Russian rockets. It completely leveled one two-story barracks, killing one poor devil in his sleep and seriously wounding five others. I honestly feel safer out in the field than sitting like a duck in a pond at Dong Tam.

Moving all the time is really mentally and physically demanding, but I really believe it is in our best interest—harder to hit a moving target, you know!

For a nice change, it was quiet last night. I played hearts with three other guys until about 2300 hours, and then hit the old mosquito net and air mattress. No more cots in the field, with all the moving, it's just too damn much junk to haul around. I do sleep on a canvas stretcher (litter) when I can find one that's not too bloodstained. It was a clear night, and I could see the Little Dipper as clearly as if it was a mile or two away, but no moon. Just the kind of night that Charlie likes to lurk around in the shadows.

Another one of our choppers got shot down yesterday, but fortunately no one was killed or wounded seriously. It was carrying our brigade commander, Col. John P. Geraci. He is one cool dude. He had just lifted off from our command post when, about five minutes later, they took hits from a .50 caliber and went down in a real swampy area near here. It seems that "Mal

71

Hombre'' (Colonel Geraci's call sign) overheard a request for a dust-off for some WIAs from our sister unit, the 2/60th Infantry, and was shot down after ordering his own chopper in for the medevac dust-off. The 3/17th Air Cav gunships kept applying heat to the Cong long enough to allow Geraci and his troops to maneuver through a muddy canal and finally get extracted from a nearby rice paddy. He is a real John Wayne type, and I'm proud to be serving under his command. He is a real kick-ass, take-charge type of guy, not a candy-ass like some of our West Pointers. I don't know for sure, but I would guess that he came up through the NCO ranks. Also, we had to dust-off another case of malaria with a temperature in excess of 105 degrees. I've been in the field for a month now, and it's become almost routine. It seems like I've been here forever.

Thanksgiving will be here soon, and we are supposed to have turkey, not that it really matters. All I want is to get the hell out of here, and all the damn turkey in the world won't speed that up. Right now the prospects for a peaceful solution don't look very promising, do they?

Alpha Company's medic just brought in a Vietnamese woman whose face is one big glob of goo and blood, but she is quite conscious and is just jabbering away in gook lingo. Apparently, she got the business end of an incoming mortar round, and now we have to try to put her face back together. Miraculously, she appears only to have one hell of a laceration going down to the skull, and I believe we can fix her up in our little traveling aid station. I'm not sure where we stand legally in cases like this, but we usually try to do the humane thing. I am sure we have unwittingly patched up many a VC, *but what the hell, there's lots of humanity to go around, right!*?

22 Nov 1968

Dong Tam

We returned to Dong Tam yesterday and found things pretty screwed up administratively in our rear station. So, I've been pretty busy chopping heads today. Tonight I removed some shrapnel from a kid's head. It was embedded in the periosteum of his skull. It has been in there for over two weeks and had really started bothering him. The first doc told him they got it all out, but I thought I could still feel some. Of course, we don't have the luxury of X rays, so I decided to explore his skull here in our fancy bunker-surgical suite. When I scheduled him, the gunner boys assured me they wouldn't be firing their eight-inchers till around midnight. So Ashley and I got this kid all prepped, injected his scalp with xylocaine, and sliced his scalp open down to the skull, when without warning, the eight-inch guns started firing, with six of them going off every thirty to sixty seconds! Well, it's not hard to imagine the initial reaction of the patient, who by the very fact that he already has shrapnel in his head has a pretty good reason to be shell-shocked and a little on the jumpy side. He jumped two feet in the air, dragging the drapes and instruments with him. A quick-thinking Ashley caught the sterile instruments in midair, and another medic grabbed the patient, with his now flowing drapes, and I sat back and roared with laughter as the poor patient muttered, "Shit, Doc, I wish they wouldn't do me like that." Well, we soon picked up the cadence of their salvos and went about routinely removing three fairly hefty chunks of steel from this GI's obviously thick skull. Once you get the rhythm down, it's a piece of cake operating in an earthquaking environment. Seriously, what you do is rest the heels of your hands on the patient's head, or whatever, and if he moves, then you and your hands move with him. I learned that little trick in the middle of the night out on the Plain of Reeds, while trying, successfully, to remove a jagged piece of shrapnel which was embedded right between a corporal's jugular vein and his right common cartoid artery, and this during a prolonged mortar attack. By comparison, tonight was a cakewalk. This fellow was telling us how he had almost forgotten his steel pot and had run back to get it. Even with the steel helmet on, the shrapnel from this damn booby trap pierced the helmet and his scalp, and came within a quarter of an inch of perforating his skull and brain. In all probability, he would have died. We have been passing his helmet around for everybody to see what a lifesaver one can be. Most grunts hate them because of the weight, preferring to wear the floppy, soft cloth hats instead. I must admit to feeling the same way, but after what I saw tonight, I believe I will wear my helmet a lot more!

This afternoon, a young stud went storming into his company commander's office in Dong Tam with a live grenade in his closed fist, threatening to kill both himself and the captain. A clerk at the other end of the room told me how he hit the floor just as the captain cooly grabbed the grenade out of this jerk's hand and calmly walked over to the door and threw it out in an open area between two barracks. The difference between living and dying over here is decided over and over by split-second decisions and events, most of which we have no control over. Fate truly is the hunter, and I'm sure that many of us will never know just how close we have come to buying the farm in this wonderful place. The captain had me see to it that the nut got shipped out to the funny farm. I'm sure he was high on drugs, which is one of the real dangers we encounter over here in the rear areas. We are starting a check-your-weapons-in-at-the-saloon policy, which should cut down on the occasional high or drunken soldier who decides to get in a shoot-out with whomever he's pissed off at. Isn't it incredible, the things we have to put up with over here on the other side of the world?

As I wind this down, they have started up their firing again. The shells are passing right over our aid station, and the sounds produced make thunder sound like a whisper! The whole bunker and my head are shaking like hell!

23 Nov 1968

Dong Tam Base

I received the Christmas cookies today and also the cookies from Mary Elizabeth. The cookies were delicious, but I will wait till Christmas to open the packages. It's really nice to be thought of by all you folks. It's almost Thanksgiving, and it seems like one long, hot summer over here. I'm keeping busy, but I do have boring days when it seems I will be here forever. But nearly every one ends with a beautiful sunset, and I always thank God for taking me through another day.

I have a difficult task trying to command thirty-two men of different races and social backgrounds. I had one black soldier refuse to go to the field. I told him "I'll court-martial you in a minute if you don't get your ass on that damn helicopter!" Well, his thick head must have understood that message because he hopped his butt on the chopper without any further delay.

We are planning a move to Tan An soon, a city south of Saigon but north of here in Long An Province. While there, we are to build a base camp from which we will supposedly be setting up ambush patrols along a major supply route from Cambodia. Of course, any army plans are subject to change, immediately if not sooner!

I was glad to hear that Papa Holley had his cataract surgery and hope it will be successful. I really miss that old guy. The "Grand Ole Opry" is playing on AFVN radio and it makes me so homesick!

24 Nov 1968

Tan An

We choppered in to Tan An today, just another riverside hamlet, with a few more hooches than the usual, and probably more VC! We are setting up in an abandoned French fort, and from the looks of it, I can understand why they left!

We now share our space with about a hundred artillerymen (gunners) and their battery of eight-inch guns. These are the loudest mothers I have ever heard, and they reputedly have a range in excess of twenty-five miles. Considering the noise and concussion they make, I'd believe they could hit a target on the moon!

Our main tactical operations center (TOC) is located at Thu Thua, about six miles north of here. I am the highest ranking officer at our current location, so technically, I am in command of this little fort. You can't begin to imagine the types of problems people keep bringing in here for me to solve. I'm getting a reputation as a hard-nosed bastard because of the way I stick up for my men and don't take crap from anybody. Why should I? Lieutenant Groves from the artillery battery just came over to talk about the security—or rather I should say the lack of security—at this location. Night before last there was a hell of a big firefight in the rice paddies a few hundred yards south of here, and a few weeks before that, the VC tried to overrun the place. When the smoke cleared they found thirty-seven dead VC hanging on the concertina wire strung around the perimeter. Nice place, huh? The lieutenant and I saw eye-to-eye on the security aspect of our little "Fort Holley." He will supply the main security force, with backup from my sparse crew.

Today we built a fairly nice, by RVN standards—trashy anywhere else—aid station. It is in an old bombed-out building, but it has an intact roof and a cement floor, so we are in hog heaven. We even got our old cots back, so we will all be sleeping in high cotton tonight! There are two very old earthen bunkers at each end of the building, which we will tear down and rebuild. I want walk-in, stand-up bunkers so I can treat patients and do surgery in relative comfort. I am tired of operating bent over in the mud, with some dude holding a flashlight on my patient's wounds. They keep promising us we will be here long enough to make it worth our while putting in all these improvements. I figure, even if we move in a week or two, it will at least keep us busy. Who knows when we might just bop over here and rest for a day or two. I think it will be OK here, if it wasn't for those damn eight-inchers going off all the time without any warning. You just can't imagine the concussion and sound effects produced every time one of those guns goes off. The whole building shakes, and dirt falls down from the rafters all over everything. A neat person would really go batshit over here in this hellhole!

I've been having a hard time sleeping lately—lots of nightmares and tossing and turning in my sleep. Now with this damn "cannon factory" under our noses, we are really in deep shit. Oh well, what can one expect from a war anyway? Especially one fought in the Nam. I am really bushed tonight. I have hammered and sawed with the best of them today, and I can really feel it now. Some of my boys are starting up a poker game, but I believe I will pass on it tonight and get some early shut-eye. I promised the lieutenant I would be up about 0330 hours, checking on security, and that will be here before you know it.

25 Nov 1968

Tan An

Isn't it disgusting the way Saigon refuses to sit at the peace table with the North Vietnamese representatives? Uncle Sam should tell them all to shove it up their butts. They continue to play politics while good young American blood flows on the ground here in Nam. I hope and pray that something breaks open in the peace talks soon. It seems to get worse over here with every day that passes. Two nights ago, the VC raided My Tho, burning,

looting, raping, and murdering. We were up here at Tan An, or
we probably would have gotten involved someway.

I went out to the 9th Medical Battalion clearing station today
at Tan An and ran into Ken Dooly, the doc I sat next to on that
long, boring flight over here. He has a real nice setup here,
complete with two dentists. I made an appointment to have a
cleaning and to have that chipped tooth filled on December 5.
I'll probably be way the hell out in the boonies then, but if not,
maybe I can keep the appointment.

I just got through sewing up a gook's neck, slashed with a
straightedge razor I would guess! Just like the days at good old
Jackson Memorial in Miami with the Saturday night "Knife and
Gun Club"—and the beat goes on!

Supposed to go out with a rifle platoon for an overnight ambush patrol tonight. Don't really have to, but kind of want to
see for myself what it's like, so more on this tomorrow.

26 Nov 1968

Near Thu Thua

The night ambush patrol is behind me, and I'm glad I went, but
wouldn't want to make a habit of doing it. The odds begin to
stack up against you if you do that sort of thing too often. Well,
we moved in about dusk to a position along the bank of a small,
winding river and settled down as the darkness quickly settled
over the water. We sat in the shadows and, later, lay in ambush
in the cool dampness as the night sounds continued, undisturbed. An occasional nighthawk's cry echoed from the distant
tree line, which was now just barely visible in the gathering fog.
An occasional fish splashed nearby as the constant drone of the
mosquitoes began to die down. From the far bend of the river,
a slight hint of movement, seen briefly, then shrouded in the fog
. . . now coming again into view—a convoy of sampans, moving directly toward us, obviously unaware of our presence. There
were three VC in each sampan, five sampans in all. "Wow, this
may be a bonanza, Doc! Keep your heads down, and don't any-

body move or fire until I give the order," whispered Corporal Rollins. Slowly, the convoy makes its way toward us, and we could begin to make out a few figures, all dressed in black pajamas. The dipping sound of their oars was barely audible as they silently paddled down the slowly moving stream. One last-minute check to be sure we wouldn't be caught in a cross fire and then, "Let her rip!" The eerie silence was shattered by the harsh sound of continuous automatic-weapons fire, the red tracers reflecting off the surface of the river. Instant chaos for the gooks. Lots of screaming. Two jump overboard and disappear beneath the surface. Two others shoot their AK-47s in our direction but are high as their tracers trail ineffectually over our heads.

The lead sampan was now on fire, and the others were milling around in aimless circles. The earlier darkness was now broken up by fires on the river, casting a strange glow, with dancing shadows on the surrounding riverbank. *Bam! Bam! Bam!* "I got the swimmers, Sarge," one grunt hollers from down the bank. Just then I began to realize that I, too, was firing. It all happened so fast that I felt detached from the battle. It seemed so impersonal, firing at boats with black pj's on board. Not real people like us, you know, slopes, gooks, the enemy, for crying out loud. Killing machines don't have time to consider the consequences of their actions. As the fiery wreckage, the debris, and the corpses began to float downstream past our positions, our thoughts turned to the inevitable question, Why them and not us tonight? Who were they, and where were they going? Another night ambush patrol goes in the battalion log, and the body count continues to grow. For tonight, I can vouch for the reported count—fifteen enemy KIAs, no friendly casualties. No, no physical casualties, but I can assure you that operations like this leave their scars, only you can't see them on the outside.

They are down deep inside each of us. I'm glad I don't have to do this every day. It has made me appreciate my job all the more.

29 Nov 1968

Tan An Base

We got mortared again last night. That's twice since moving to Tan An. No casualties either time, but it still tends to frazzle your nerves. One of our rifle companies killed ten VC last night, that's twenty-six for three nights, not bad, huh? I just finished operating on another kid with a big piece of shrapnel from a booby trap. This time it was sticking out of his chest wall. It came very close to being a sucking chest wound, as I could see pleura between the ribs by the time I got it out. Had he been wearing his flak jacket, he wouldn't have gotten hit. But they are so heavy and bulky that very few people wear them. I quit wearing mine after my first convoy. However, I do wear my cloth floppy hat as much as possible.

Darling, I'm kind of concerned about my hearing. We are located about sixty feet away from a battery of 155mm howitzers, and they blast away all night long. It actually rocks the litter and shakes things off shelves as well as knocking the hell out of my sleep. My ears sort of have a steady ringing now, and when I listen through my stethoscope, it has a metallic echo to it. I found some ear plugs, which my medics and I used last night. We couldn't hear the sirens, screams of "incoming," or anything else. We thought the concussions were from our outgoing 155 fire. We would have been in deep shit if we had been overrun by a ground attack—so no more ear plugs! This man's army sure isn't worrying about my hearing, or any other part of my body. At least an ophthalmologist doesn't have to have excellent hearing—just steady hands, and so far mine are staying steady as a rock, even after some pretty hairy experiences.

This morning I was driving my jeep over to the hospital at Thu Thua, a small hamlet near here. They had asked me to inspect their hospital and make any suggestions for needed improvement. They would like for me to make rounds twice a week while we are camped in this area. Can't you just see me, the big "heavy" from the States—making grand rounds with all the little slopes following along behind! Me with my .45 strapped to my waist and my stethoscope hanging around my neck! Quite a contrast from Baptist Memorial, huh?

Early yesterday some local natives brought me a little three-month-old baby girl who had a bad cold six weeks ago and now is paralyzed from her waist down. She is such a sweet little thing. Her little legs just hang there like a rag doll. I'm quite sure she had poliomyelitis. The poor natives over here are so pitiful—proud but pitiful. We have so much to be thankful for in the United States. Just enjoy the luxuries you have. Believe me, I'll never take them for granted again.

11 Dec 1968

Dong Tam Security

For the past two weeks, I have been too sick to write and have been in the sack back at Dong Tam for several days. I'm doing better but not up to par yet. I'm trying to work fewer nights now, but that is difficult.

Today, one of my good friends, Maj. Jeff Templeton, got hit in the head with the tail rotor blade of a helicopter. When I first heard about it, I figured he was dead as several guys have got their heads chopped off this way. Jeff and I are pretty good friends. He is a real sharp West Point graduate, and he seems to respect me quite a bit, too. Well, I felt terrible to hear this news over the tactical radio, so I hopped in our jeep and hauled ass to 3d Surgical Hospital where he had been dusted-off to. He was lucky as hell! The rotor split his scalp right down to the skull without even nicking the bone. He was pretty shook up, and he said it felt like it took the entire back of his head off! I was tickled to see him sitting up on the examining table, with a big grin on his face, by the time I arrived at the hospital. His skull X rays were negative, so all I had to do was suture up his scalp laceration. We also had another KIA and several more wounded by claymore mines today. We are suffering lots of booby-trap casualties since we started providing security for Dong Tam.

13 Dec 1968

Dong Tam

Today is my twenty-eighth birthday. *Big deal.* I can't feel very excited about it, just another year older and maybe a little wiser. I got a birthday cake from my mom, angel food with chocolate icing. It was real good. One of my medics turns twenty-one today and is flying home this afternoon. We shared my birthday cake the other night before he left Dong Tam. Another of my medics had been AWOL for two weeks. He came in, dragging ass, yesterday, and naturally, I chewed his ass royally! So, now I have all kinds of administrative bull crap to go through to save him from a court-martial. He is a good kid, and I really would hate to lose him. He got to Hong Kong and just kind of went crazy, screwing and drinking twenty-four hours a day, and said he lost touch with reality. The horrible memories of what awaited him back here were more than his young mind could handle. I can dig it, really. They expect a lot out of us over here.

I did get my new MSC officer, a Lt. Bill Casey. He is a real nice young fellow, very well mannered and anxious to take as much of the administrative load off my shoulders as possible. He is so polite, he seems shy, almost withdrawn, and I am a little concerned about how he will react to this living hell over here. I plan to keep him in the rear area as much as possible. He can keep an eye on things at the rear aid station so that it will be one less thing for me to worry about. Of course, that's not without danger either, considering the frequent mortar attacks on Dong Tam base. Bill is a very good administrator, and he will be able to take a load of paperwork off Sp6. Ashley and me.

I have lost so many personnel lately that I am down to about 65 percent of my authorized personnel. Lots of them have DEROS'd (rotated or returned back home), but quite a few have been wounded or killed. I had to go see the division surgeon and raise hell before he finally gave me four medics on "loan" until some replacements come in. This whole deal sucks over here, the army, the war, and the country! I have four companies of two hundred men each, and each one is supposed to have four line medics. All four units are down to two medics each, so I have been rotating my time with each unit to fill one of the slots myself. That can get kind of old quick, and it isn't really too smart either. It's not what Uncle Sam would refer to as "efficient use of personnel," especially if I go down out in the field and get shipped out—then who will run the outfit? I probably shouldn't even write when I am in such a foul mood, but it helps to be able to ventilate to someone besides a grunt!

13 Dec 1968

Dong Tam

This will be short as it is the second letter I've written to you today. I'm feeling better. For one thing, I'm half tight—not drunk but just very relaxed. My medics bought me the neatest cigarette lighter with the Combat Medical Badge on one side and DOC HOLLEY—4/39TH INF engraved on the other side and gave it to me today. It really touched me that this hard-nosed bunch of kids would be that thoughtful. For the most part, they are a great group, and they are all the family I have over here. We do tend to stick together, despite our differences. So, I had a few brews with the crew tonight, and I'm out of the doldrums for a while. I am going to try to get up at 0600 hours Sunday to try to get you on the MARS system. The other night I sat down there from 9:30 P.M. until 4:00 A.M., waiting for my turn. Just as they finished the call for the guy ahead of me, they lost contact with their Pacific relay station, and after twenty minutes of failed attempts, the radioman turned to me and said, "Sorry, pal, try again tomorrow night." Needless to say, I was very disappointed. It was about 5:00 A.M. by the time I got back to the aid station, and then I couldn't go to sleep, so I just sat up and

read until the mess hall opened at 6:00 A.M. I will write you a
long letter and bring you up to date on all that's happening. I'm
just too damn tired and a little too shit-faced tonight.

15 Dec 1968

Dong Tam 0130 hours

Darling, this will have to be short as I have been working like a
dog, and I'm bushed—bone tired! I have two young Vietnamese
kids—aged thirteen and fifteen—who have malaria, and I am
having to treat them here in my aid station. They were hired by
our line companies to serve as Tiger Scouts i.e., to go out in the
field on operations and help point out booby traps, etc. They
both were born near here, so they know all the trails and hiding
places. I am sure they have saved countless lives, and I really
feel obligated to help them in their hour of need. Well, tonight
they came down with fevers of 105.8 degrees and 106 degrees
respectively, and the clearing company I routinely refer medical
problems to refused to take them in, so here we are! We have
IVs going and have sponged them in alcohol baths for about
four-and-a-half hours.

Ashley just came by and told me their fevers are starting to
break, so maybe I can get some shut-eye soon. They were having
such severe chills, they almost fell off the litter. Bless their hearts,
they are such brave little boys! I will just keep them in the aid
station until they are well enough to go home, wherever that is.
They may be orphans, who knows? They could even be Viet
Cong, but I really doubt it. I just checked them and their temps
were 98.4 degrees and 98.6 degrees respectively. I think the
crisis is over, so I'm going to go hop in the sack since I am
planning to get up in about four hours and try again to call you
on the MARS line. I really need to make these calls while we
are in the rear area because when we finish Dong Tam security
we will be back to flying all over hell's half acre, and I won't
have access to the phones. I am enclosing a VC propaganda
leaflet we found in a hooch on one of our Medcaps in a local

hamlet. Can you believe the spelling and grammar? You'd think they would have found someone to do a little better job with the English:

AMERICAN GI's

From the 1st to nov 5th 1.968. The united states commitec for demand of ending the US aggressive war in Vietnam hold "the week for united states armymen" which support to your opposing the war movement en demand for repatriation. Don't let american youths go on to south Vietnam and dic uselessly and senselessly. The Vietnam people and youths and students and pupil as well as the world people warmly wellcome and give whole hearted support and response to the creation of the united states committee.

GI's

. . . . .Oppose the US aggressive war Vietnam.

. . . . .Demand the US government to stop immediately the US aggressive war in Vietnam and it must negotiate directly south Vietnam national front of liberation.

. . . . .Demand the US Government brings home all US troops.

. . . . .Let the Vietnamese settle themselves their our affairs.

. . . . .Demand your repatriation refuse to go to the battefiel oppose your going to slaughler the Vietnamese people who are struggling for their independence, freedom and peace.

That's the only way for you to defend the honer and pestige of america and save the happiness of your families and yousse lves.

17–18 Dec 1968

Dong Tam Base

Please forgive me for not writing lately, baby. I have been so damned busy that I have not even gotten much sleep. We are having an epidemic of influenza, possibly Hong Kong flu, I'm just being run practically crazy with patients! Do you remember my patients with malaria. I am enclosing pictures of them. They are Tiger Scouts as I explained in the last letter, and they are good boys. They are in their early teens, which almost makes them middle-aged over here. One of them developed nausea and vomiting yesterday, so I gave him 5.0 mg of Compazine. Today he had a pretty severe reaction to it. He went into pseudoparkinson and oculogyric crisis, and I had to give him intravenous Benadryl to bring him out of it.

I got called away on an emergency last night and didn't get to finish this letter. At 0500, I went down to the MARS radio station and waited until 0930 to get through to your phone number. When I finally did get through, it just rang and rang, so I sent you a MARSgram telegram instead.

Monday, I drove up to the 3d Field Hospital in Saigon to see the commanding officer. It is the largest hospital in Vietnam, and they have an ophthalmologist there, a Dr. Elia. He was very nice. I met with Colonel Thomas and told him I wanted to get some OJT (on the job training) in the field of ophthalmology. He said, "No problem! If your division will release you, we would love to have you in our hospital, assisting our eye man." He said they only have three eye surgeons in country, and the other two are at 24th Evac at Long Binh. He said I would get training that would be equivalent to a first-year resident. He was real pleased to meet someone who was interested in eye surgery as he said they really could use the help. He told me to tell my division surgeon that I had talked to him and he has agreed to take me on his staff, although I would probably be sent to Long Binh because of the larger volume of eye work done there. He promised to introduce me to Colonel Austin, who has the authority to move any doctor in Vietnam anywhere he pleases, so I'll have to make an appointment to see him and then, hopefully, the wheels will start turning. It seems too good to be true, but at least I'm trying. This could happen before March, but I told him I was in no hurry to leave the battalion unless they needed me sooner. He told me to go ahead and fill out my transfer papers now. I'm so excited, I never thought it would be so easy. My dad always said you never know what you can get or do unless you ask. I'll keep you posted on these developments.

While there, I was in a real air-conditioned room! My first since arriving in country—and, I got to sit on a real flushing commode! Wow! What a luxury! By the way, I was coming around a corner and literally ran into an old friend from the States, Dr. Max Mass. I had known him in Gainesville, where he was a friend of Wendell Hall, and met him again at medical school in Miami, where he was one of my residents in internal medicine. What a pleasant surprise to run into someone over here that you knew back on the other side of the world. Our paths keep crossing in the damndest ways. He leaves here in six months to start private practice in Fort Lauderdale, so hopefully we will see him sometime in the future.

While there, I checked on one of my patients from the 4/39th, SFC Leon Field, who was shot through the spleen, kidney, and pancreas on 5 Dec 68. He was real happy to see me, but he didn't look very good. He died December 13, ironically, on my birthday, after four days on renal dialysis at 3d Field Hospital. Oh, how it hurts.

Lt. Larry Tahler recalled Sergeant First Class Field and the night he was critically wounded—"SFC Leon Field was a good NCO. He had a ruddy complexion, was fair-haired, and had the round belly that people sometimes acquire in their late 30s. I remember him as being good to his troops; however, he didn't take any shit, but dealt fairly with all below him. He was a platoon sergeant in Charlie Company, and our company commander was Capt. Bruce Hartshorn, a very capable infantry soldier. I was platoon leader of 3d Platoon. Charlie Company was on an extended recon-in-force operation in the Delta. According to intelligence reports, there was heavy enemy activity in our immediate area, with the VC in company-size or larger elements. We set up a full company-size night-ambush position in a thicket of woods several klicks (kilometers) in diameter. The company was set up in a loosely defined wagon-circle perimeter. As night fell, everything got very quiet. I don't believe anyone got much sleep because of the imminent possibility of contact with a superior enemy force. The thought of being overrun by a large enemy force was a constant concern anytime we slept out in the boonies and away from the relative security of a base camp.

Sometime after 0100 hours, everyone was startled by the rapid, telltale sound of AK-47 fire coming from the opposite side of the company perimeter. Word quickly spread that Sergeant Field had been shot in the stomach. It seems that he was smoking a cigarette under his poncho liner and had inadvertently given some patiently waiting VC sniper a perfect nighttime target. Captain Hartshorn called me on the company net and asked me to get several men and carry Sergeant Field about four klicks out through the thick jungle to a clearing where he could be dusted-off by a medevac helicopter. Since we all knew it was his only chance of survival, I quickly got four other "volunteers," and we began the difficult and frightening trek out of the jungle. The four grunts carried him in a poncho, and I took point. To realize what was happening here, you must imagine that it is approximately 1:30 A.M. in the middle of a deep, dark patch of jungle, filled with VC just waiting for a light, or some movement so they could target the GIs. Here we were, five troopers stomping through this deadly quiet jungle, carrying a two-hundred-pound man who is groaning constantly. The four enlisted men had their hands full carrying Sergeant Field, and I was the only one who had a weapon ready. We were making so much noise that I just knew we were going to be attacked. How we got through those four klicks to the LZ site without being ripped to pieces, I'll never know. I only know I thanked God about a hundred times after that chopper picked up Sergeant First Class Field and lifted off into the darkness. The trip back to the ambush site was even worse because we all realized how mortal we were. As we approached our ambush position, we knew we had made it back to the relative safety of our fellow soldiers. Our bodies were soaking wet with sweat and aching with fear, but at least we knew we had contributed to saving our comrade's life. Later, we heard that Sergeant First Class Field had died in the hospital in Saigon, and our hearts were greatly saddened."

By the way, Sondra, I have tried to call you about five times but can never find you at home or else the line is busy, but I won't give up, I promise.

I was awarded my Combat Medical Badge (CMB) yesterday and am sending it to you for our scrapbook. I am really proud of it. I must run now as I have about five-and-a-half hours of driving time to cover all my men in the field, and it's now 10:30 A.M. Oh, by the way, Mitch just told me that last night one of my little Tiger Scouts who had malaria became delirious and started saying "VC die!" over and over. An interpreter was brought in and soon discovered that both he and his friend were

VC and had intentionally been leading our boys into booby traps. Looking back on it now, I can see how easily we were duped. And good old Hippocrates, here, risked disciplinary action by treating them overnight in the aid station against orders. Well, live and learn!

18 Dec 1968

Dong Tam

As usual, I had a real busy day, but tonight I had a real treat. They showed Clint Eastwood in *The Good, the Bad, and the Ugly* at our battalion staging area on an outdoor movie screen, and I really enjoyed it. Tell old Jack Allison I finally got to see it—complete with real fireworks! Everybody was really laughing a lot and seemed to be enjoying it when all of a sudden mortars started landing on the helipad about two blocks from here. Red flares went up, and the sirens started blaring, and we hauled ass to our bunkers. A few minutes later the red alert was lifted, and we returned to finish our movie. Well, there was this Civil War scene, and there were incoming cannon rounds in the film, which sounded exactly like real incoming mortar rounds. Someone screamed at the top of his lungs, *"Incoming!"* Everybody scrambled, running into and all over each other. It was hilarious, and we all just lay in the dirt, howling with laughter! We got a bigger laugh out of that than from the entire movie.

Today, Mitch and I drove out to the company areas surrounding Dong Tam's perimeter. All of a sudden, I heard beaucoup automatic-weapons fire, with sporadic M-79 and machine-gun fire, coming from an area about a mile or so ahead of me. I linked up with our Bravo Company commander and played war games with him for a while. He was in radio contact with our Charlie Company commander, and it was really exciting to watch them move their platoons around on a big map, and eventually box Charlie in and close in for the kill. We only got one kill, but we captured three VC and a bunch of weapons. After awhile, I felt it was safe enough for Mitch and me to take our jeep Super Quack through an area where there were still a few small fires burning from the artillery barrage. We tended to a few sick and injured GIs, and then we bopped on back to our base camp. On the way back, I was reflecting about how strange this war was—sitting there last night watching a war movie and getting mortared ourselves. All that was missing was John Wayne and Kirk Douglas!

19 Dec 1968

Dong Tam

I got your sweet Christmas card today with the package of goodies, and also a bunch of goodies from my mom and dad. Mom sent a great homemade fruit cake, and believe me, it didn't last long around here.

Baby, I know you are finding it hard to enjoy the holidays. I heard a Christmas carol over AFVN Radio a while ago, and it seemed so incongruous—I was sitting here in this steamy, hot, dusty aid station, trying to picture you there in Memphis where the temperature was eighteen degrees. I remember the day we walked through the ice down at Riverside Park in the spring blizzard, and it's like that was in another world. I opened my presents tonight so I could use the binoculars for the Bob Hope show. They are just beautiful, darling. I'm just crazy about them, and I can't wait to use them for football games back in the good old USA! Meanwhile, I'm sure I will get lots of use out of them over here. Our army-issue binocs are junk.

I believe I will enjoy the world around me so much more when I return to the real world. You don't miss your water till the well runs dry—so true! I lie down some nights and think about you being so far away, and I get a tight ache in my chest, and I feel like I could cry. I toss and turn the whole night. I do get some consolation from praying when I get that way. I know God is keeping you safe for me. Thank God, I don't have to worry about VC burning and looting your home. We Americans have so much to be thankful for. Take a close look around you. You have no idea how many luxuries you are blessed with.

I had a bad day today. I had to dust-off six seriously wounded boys with a variety of booby-trap injuries. One, a real nice kid from Alabama, had a fragment of steel pierce his skull, and a large piece of gray matter was protruding. God, how do you fix that out in the boonies, or even in the OR? I had just arrived on my daily circuit-rider rounds when it happened. Another one died on the chopper from massive pneumothorax and pulmonary hemorrhage. I think his aorta must have been perforated. One poor kid had a fractured tibia and was shot right through the genitals. Baby, most people have no idea of the hell these young kids are going through over here while those SOBs in Paris argue about the shape of the damn conference table.

Darling, I still feel like I am the same Byron, but I can't help getting bitter towards the Viet Cong when I see so many of America's young men being blown up, killed, and maimed. I would get immense pleasure from killing a VC. It's something you have to live with to fully understand. Seeing the last breath of life leave a young GI, I just stand there, feeling so damned empty, and helpless . . . and sad.

Tonight, I had a big black GI who apparently was going through a withdrawal reaction from heroin. He went berserk, and his nose and eyes were running like a faucet. I started wrestling with him. A switchblade knife fell out of his pocket, and he made a lunge for it. He was strong as a bull, but I kicked it out of his reach and hollered for help. Two big studs came running in, and together, we finally got him sandwiched between two litters (stretchers) and tied them together so he couldn't move. I didn't give him any Thorazine or sedative because I wanted the division psychiatrist to see him in full swing. The last one, we sedated before shipping him, and they made some snide remark about having to wake him up to talk to him and why did we send him in the first place. Well, they won't wonder why we are sending this crazy fucker to their nuthouse! Of course, he might try to rip their faces off if they ask him his name, rank, and serial number.

I tell you, darling, this is like a small general hospital I'm running here. I never seem to have any time just to sit and meditate. I have been interrupted ten times since starting this letter. As dangerous as it is driving out around the perimeters of Dong Tam, I prefer that to this rear aid station. Being out on maneuvers is even better. This security operation is a farce. We hardly ever have any real contact with the enemy, and our boys are just cannon fodder for their booby traps. I don't like the predictability of it, so I try to vary my route and times of departure and arrival to the different outposts.

26 Dec 1968

Dong Tam Base

Well, I had another close call two days ago. I was in my jeep Super Quack, driving down a small dirt road, about seven miles west of Dong Tam, when the VC blew up the road with a command-detonated mine about fifty feet ahead of us. I heard this terrific explosion and felt the concussion simultaneously as, directly in front of the windshield, the road shot fifty feet in the air. Mitch slammed on the brakes, and we jumped out of the jeep and started spraying the tree line down with M-16 fire. There were open rice paddies on our left side, so we concentrated our fire on a stand of banana and nipa palm trees on our right side. We really shot the shit out of the tree line, and if Charlie was planning to hang around to finish us off, he must have made a quick change of plans because we didn't receive any return fire. Mitch was pretty sure he saw a gook in black pajamas running out through the tree line, but it all happened so fast, we couldn't be sure. They like to lie out in the jungle, waiting for an American vehicle to pass over the spot in the road where they have buried explosives just below the surface. They run wire through the grass and connect it to a command-detonation switch, and when they think we are in the right spot, they push the button and *boom!* goes the road and anything or anybody who happens to be on it. They usually plant the explosives at night. They undermine the edge of the road and tunnel in a few feet to the center. Then they cover it all up with dirt. What probably happened to us is that they got confused and forgot the exact spot where the charge was buried, or they overestimated our speed and led us too much. The explosion left a hole, twelve feet deep and eight feet wide, in the road. Needless to say, it would have been the end for us if it had been on the mark. I know God must love me and has a specific purpose for keeping me around because I just keep on having so many close calls and still haven't got a scratch. I got plenty scared from this event though, but strangely enough, not until the next morning when I woke up. At the time, I was more thankful than scared.

26 Dec 1968

Dong Tam Base, RVN

Tomorrow, we go to see the Bob Hope show. I have seen his Vietnam show so many times before and never dreamed that I would be one of those faces in the crowd. I will take lots of pictures and plan to break in my new binoculars. Darling, they are really great. I was using them today, and they are the nicest I've ever used. Thank you again, so much.

Today I made sick call at the different company areas outside the base camp perimeter. Only today's trip was preceded by a mine sweeper! So, no mines today. We were mortared pretty heavily a couple of nights ago, and we are supposed to get it again tonight. Which means we will probably sleep all night long. Our military intelligence leaves a lot to be desired. In fact, its very name is a bit of a self-contradiction!

Our battalion is responsible for providing security for the Bob Hope show, and our CO is more than a little nervous about it. Can you imagine the stink if Bob Hope were killed at our division base camp? I don't even want to think about it. There are many reports of a planned mortar and ground attack to be staged during the show. We are keeping about half our men out on the perimeter, and we have extra air support for the time he will be here. I just feel for the guys who won't get to see him. I've already run into a little difficulty in assigning line medics for that period. I have pulled a few fellows back in as they are more deserving than some of the newer kids.

27 Dec 1968

Dong Tam

I just got back from the Bob Hope show here in Dong Tam. It was really neat seeing him in person after seeing so many of his overseas Christmas shows. This will be shown on 16 January on NBC, so be sure and watch it. I am seated on his right about twenty to thirty rows back. We really enjoyed the binoculars, and I mean *we*! All my friends around me got a real good look at Ann-Margret and Miss World! They were a sight for sore eyes over here, believe me! He also had Les Brown and his Band of Renown, Rosie Greer, and the voluptuous Gold Diggers who were on the summer Dean Martin show. There was an air strike going on at an island downstream, and Bob Hope kept saying, "What the hell is going on? Can't ya'll drop your bombs when I'm not dropping a punch line?" I took a roll of film, and I hope they came out. It was really steamy hot, and we were all sitting out there sweating up a storm.

Well, mail just came, and I didn't get any. I know you can't write everyday, but it gets very lonely and depressing over here. All around me, I see people leaving and going home, and it really bugs me. But then, I also see new recruits coming over, so I know my day will come. It just seems like it's so slow coming, doesn't it?

I guess I already told you that we are still on Dong Tam security. We are supposed to go back out into the field on January 15. There is a possibility we might be assigned to the Mobile Riverine Force, known affectionately as the River Rats. The worst thing about going on the boats would be not getting mail everyday like we do when we have air support. Believe me, mail call is the highlight of our day. Well, I'd better close as I just had a couple of wounded boys come in. It looks like mine is the only office in Dong Tam that never closes.

28 Dec 1968

Dong Tam Base

I drove up to Saigon today to do some shopping at the PX at Tan Son Nhut Air Base. We had a safe trip back except we got run off the road twice by Vietnamese buses. The only paved road out in the country is a narrow two-lane road, the equivalent of the worst country road in Arkansas.

The Vietnamese all drive like maniacs over here. The only way to describe the traffic in Saigon, with its ten million Hondas, buses, small blue and yellow taxi cabs, motorized rickshaws, jeeps, trucks, and bicycles going 360 different directions at the same time, is mass confusion, like someone had opened up a nest of ants. Your horn is more important than your brakes, and it is survival of the fittest. They have several traffic circles where several roads enter a large circle with a statue in the center. It is like our demolition derbies on a Saturday night!

I'm concerned that another major offensive is about to begin. Last night, we received about thirty mortar rounds about two blocks from my hooch, and today we had two KIAs and twenty wounded, two of whom had both their legs blown off. I knew all of them, and it really hurt me. Twelve of them were riding in a chow wagon, going out to Fire Base Mustang near where the mine was blown in front of my jeep. In fact, they had slowed down to drive around the crater when they were ambushed by a platoon of VC. They were hit with an RPG (rocket propelled grenade), which completely blew out the tires, took off the right rear fender. The windshield was riddled with bullet holes. Blood was splattered all over the seats and the dashboard. It was awful. There were over fifty bullet holes in the body of the deuce-and-a-half (two-and-a-half ton) truck. I've been going down that same road every other day for over a month, and I would have been out there today if I hadn't gone to Saigon to call you. In fact, the attack occurred about 3:30 P.M., just about the exact time we were talking on the phone. That's more than luck. That's divine guidance that made me decide to go up to Saigon today.

Everyone feels that something is in the air. There is a marked increase in Viet Cong activity, and in the past three weeks, we have had more than sixty combined casualties. Meanwhile, those silly jackasses in Paris pussyfoot around while over here good, red American blood continues to flow. Baby, it's hard not to become calloused when you see and experience what I have seen and felt. One of the fellows killed today was a friend and was in here kidding around with me just two days ago. Now he is history. Another one, who got his right foot blown off, had been instructed by me just yesterday not to go out to the field because of a severe skin problem. But he felt his buddies needed him, and tore up his sick slip.

Last night, the guy I told you about having the heroin withdrawal went berserk again and shot his M-79 grenade launcher inside his barracks. The grenade has to travel a certain distance before it is activated, and it fell in the corner—an unexploded but hot round. Well, I got called over there, and Ashley and I got a couple of guys in his barracks to help us hold him down and put him in a straitjacket. He kept screaming at me saying "Doc, you motherfucker, I'll get out and kill your white ass, just you wait and see!" I just laughed at him, but I had to practically fight the division psychiatrist to get him to admit him. What a candy-ass of a doctor. Everybody in the army passes the buck, and sometimes people die because of it. I told the patient I was going to have them bury his black ass under the mental hospital and that he would still be there when I returned to the World. That really scared him, and he finally shut up.

1 Jan 1969

Dong Tam

Happy New Year! Finally, it's the year of my return to the World. It never really was Christmas over here. It was so damn hot, and I never did anything different, but we did have a turkey dinner at the chow hall. Christmas is more a state of mind than a date on a calendar. It couldn't be Christmas because of my being over here and you being all the way across the world. It's as if I missed a Christmas—1968. But we will make up for it next year.

Yesterday was some day. I got called up to the TOC in the afternoon. There sat Capt. John Seeker, a very good friend of mine who is now commander of Bravo Company. He was soaking wet and looked quite pale. It hadn't been raining, so I was puzzled as to his condition. I soon learned that he and his men had been in sampans in a canal about one and a half miles north of Dong Tam when they were ambushed by automatic-weapons fire from the shore. Seeker's RTO, Spec Four Sinclair, another friend of mine, was shot in the face and died instantly, turning the sampan over as he fell sideways. John said he fired one twenty-round clip of bullets before he fell into the canal. All at once, he felt a sharp stabbing pain in his belly and realized he had been shot in the abdomen. Another fellow in the sampan was also killed instantly. John and three others swam to shore, climbed out, and walked to Dong Tam. Well, I put him in my ambulance and rushed him over to 3d Surgical, where we soon learned that an AK-47 round had penetrated his abdominal wall, but after being deflected by a belt of ammo he wore around his waist, the bullet traveled around the preperitoneal space and never entered his abdominal cavity! Is that miraculous, or what? He is a terrific guy, and I was so relieved. He and I used to sit on courts-martial together, and he was always a real fair person. He has been over here for one and a half years and was due to go home in three weeks anyway. He is a lifer and one of the top career men I've seen.

Well, as if that wasn't enough, last night the troops around here got drunk and started firing their weapons, and some were even firing machine guns around the battalion area. I had to help the other officers get all this shit stopped, and about 0100 I finally lay down. I was almost asleep when I heard violent coughing right outside my window, so I hopped up, pulled on my fatigue pants, and ran outside to find the whole area engulfed in a cloud of tear gas. I got a good whiff of it, but ran back into my room to put on my gas mask. Some drunken practical joker had thrown a tear-gas grenade into our BOQ, and the gas lingered, so I finally went to the aid station and spent the rest of the night trying to sleep on a litter. What a hell of a way to usher in the New Year!

Today I made my circuit ride out to the company areas, and Charlie blew another mine on Death Road I've told you so much about. It made a hell of an explosion! We had just driven by it about two minutes earlier. Fortunately, no one was hurt this time. I'll be glad to get off Dong Tam security and back out on field operations around the Delta. All this driving around on these mined and booby-trapped roads is for the birds, not to mention the ton of casualties I've had from booby traps out in the local fields. This area surrounding Dong Tam is referred to as AO Kudzu. It's a stupid name, and this is a stupid game. Anytime you begin using the same road over and over again, Charlie is going to sniff out that pattern and ambush you, or worse.

5 Jan 1969

Dong Tam Base

Today was Sunday, and I saw eighty-three patients in the aid station. I work seven days a week. There are no weekends. I work from about sunup to near midnight most days, and some days more. Everyday is the same. Last month we logged in 1,265 patient sick-call visits, 106 WIAs and 15 KIAs. And I believe I saw practically every one of them myself! At least it seems that way. Actually, my medics do a great job, and I could work a lot less if I wanted to, but I feel so strongly that these GIs deserve the best medical treatment available that if I'm available, I see them.

I just stepped outside and there is a full moon out tonight, and it is so beautiful. I hope you saw it last night and thought of me. It's the same moon seen from opposite sides of the globe. I've often thought about how it's the same moon that Jesus gazed at and wept under. Maybe that's one reason our eyes are drawn to it when we see it. Like the song says, all great men over the ages have sweated beneath the same sun and gazed up in wonder at the same moon. When you are stuck over here on the other side of the world, you spend a lot of time at night out in the field, looking up into the heavens. It is so dark out in the boonies and the air is so clear that you can see the stars like you never imagined. The Southern Cross is dramatic, and the Milky Way looks like a highway in the sky. We see scores of shooting stars every time we have a clear night. It's almost a religious experience, it's so beautiful.

Yesterday I hitched a ride down to Can Tho on a supply chopper, about ninety miles from here, to pay a special visit to Captain Seeker and fifteen other boys of mine at 29th Evacuation Hospital. Big John was as delighted to see me as I was to see him and the rest of the guys. It was great to see them on the road to recovery and evacuation out of Nam. The flight down was a delightful trip. With no doors on the chopper, you are really flying through the cool air, and I always hate for it to end. I don't worry about getting shot down. I just have faith, darling, faith that God will bring me home and faith you will be there waiting for me when I step off that big bird in Memphis. Without faith, a man could go crazy over here, and many do!

10 Jan 1969

Dong Tam Base

Today it was proven to me again that I'm just not meant to die over here. As you know, I've been going out to the various company areas in the field surrounding Dong Tam, every other day with the chow convoy. Well, today I started to go, but for some unknown reason, I decided to wait until tomorrow. Well, they got ambushed and had a mine blown on them at exactly the same spot where we had our close call with the prematurely blown mine last month. The explosion turned over a two-and-a-half-ton chow truck and killed one man and wounded three others. The VC began moving in on them to finish them off, and one guy, the driver of the truck, grabbed his M-16 and drove them off. He is a real neat kid from the mountains near Franklin, North Carolina. The others were too injured to fight, except for two soul brothers in the cab of the water-tanker truck who left their weapons in the vehicle and took off running across the paddies like cowards. I believe I would have shot them if I had been there myself. We've got some real brave black soldiers, like Sergeant Ashley, but we've got our share of sorry ones too. If it hadn't been for that one white kid who kept his cool, they all would have been killed. He was shot in the foot, but luckily, it just grazed him. The water tanker took a direct hit with an RPG (rocket propelled grenade), which set it on fire. The deuce-and-a-half was twisted and crumpled like cardboard. It's a miracle that only one was killed. I knew the boy who got killed, but not too well. A good friend of mine, Lieutenant Miller, was riding shotgun and was blown out of the chow truck, sustaining a compression fracture of his second lumbar vertebra. That, my friend, should be a million-dollar wound, not permanently disabling, but serious enough to get him the hell out of this place for good.

I heard all this going on over my two-way radio, and I was at 3d Surgical when the dust-off chopper landed. The poor kid who got killed got the front part of his neck blown away, and his neck appeared to be broken from the angle it was twisted. Just horrible. What a waste!

I thank God I didn't go today because I usually drive about twenty feet behind that same truck. I don't believe it would have made any difference to the kid who got killed if I had been there because it looked like both his internal cartoids and trachea were blown away, and he probably died instantly and never knew what hit him. Still, I always wonder. We are going out there tomorrow, but we are going to have a platoon sweep both sides of the road for VC and mines before we go. Only two more trips, and I'll never have to ride down that damn road again. I knew someone would get killed on that road the very first time I rode out on it. I nicknamed it Death Road then, but our superiors thought we were overreacting. Of course they didn't have to drive it themselves as they always flew out. Oh well, the beat goes on, and it's one less day till DEROS.

12 Jan 1969

Dong Tam

Well, I believe Charlie is beginning to warm up for the Tet offensive we've been told to expect. Last night, we received a heavy mortar attack at Dong Tam, and most of our outposts were under some sort of ground attack. They blew out three bridges on Highway 4, one each at Tan An, Ben Luc, and Long Dinh. We are preparing to move out to the Wagon Wheel on the seventeenth. Lord only knows how long we will be out there.

Today I went out to a big ship, actually a dredge, anchored out in the Mekong River off Dong Tam. One of our rifle platoons provides security for the operation, so I could justify going out there to hold sick call on these fellows plus a few crew members who are civilians. They actually were very grateful to see me, but not nearly as glad as I was to visit their floating palace. They have air-conditioning, hot and cold running water in the showers, and the greatest chow hall this side of Walnut Ridge, Arkansas! I had my first hot shower since leaving the States, and it felt so good, I stayed in it for about fifteen minutes. Then we went to the dining hall, where we sat down at a real dinner table with real silverware and real china cups, saucers, and plates and ate a meal fit for a king. The crew members sat around watching in amazement as we ranted on and on about these luxuries that they take for granted. You could tell that they really enjoyed sharing it with us. After dinner, one of the chiefs said, "Doc, the only thing missing is a nice after-dinner nap in a cool, dark room. Come with me, and let's see if we can find you an empty room for a nap." Well, words cannot describe how much I enjoyed my two-hour nap on clean white sheets, with the air temperature about 68 degrees, and a clean white sheet and light blanket over me. It really rejuvenated me. Ashley and Redfearn were with me, and we just kept on marveling to each other about how great the day had been. We boarded the launch to take us back to hot, dusty Dong Tam. We just couldn't get over the contrast.

Yesterday, I went out to the area where the ambush happened. We were really loaded for bear. We had a rifle platoon with ten M-79s, six LAWs (light antitank weapons), and twenty M-16 rifles. Of course, Charlie never appears when you are prepared for him. Tomorrow is my last trip out on Ambush Alley, or Death Road, whichever you prefer. I just heard that the army engineers put in a pontoon bridge to replace the blown-out Long Dinh bridge. I hope so, because that's the only way I can get over there, and hopefully, it will remain intact long enough for us to do our sick call and get back to Dong Tam.

I received a nice letter from Dan McCue, and he always describes the cold weather, ice, and snow in such a graphic way that I can close my eyes and almost be there. He always sends me his latest *Flying* magazine and writes at least twice a month. I really do appreciate him.

I got a great tape from my mom and dad the other day, and it had both of them on it, as well as Papa Holley, Mary Elizabeth, Aunt Mae and Uncle Jimmie, Aunt Thelma, Barbara, Robert, Rhonda, and Robin. It was really neat. I especially enjoyed hearing Papa Holley talking about going squirrel hunting, etc. Aunt Mae was hilarious because she didn't want to talk to "no dumb machine," and then she just laughed. Listening to that tape brought tears to my eyes, and I'm not sure how often I will want to go through that. Letters are easier on you.

14 Jan 1969

Dong Tam

I'm hot, and I've got the GI trots. I have to take a chloroquine-primaquine pill once weekly for malaria prevention, and it is notorious for causing diarrhea, so I've got to run, be back in a minute!

Well, here I am again, three pounds lighter. The weather is awfully hot and muggy today. I'm in the aid station. I sent Lieu-

Doc Holley standing in front of Battalion Aid Station
at Dong Tam on his birthday, 13 December 1968.

Doc Holley with two malaria patients *(on right)* and their friend.
18 December 1968.

SFC Wayne Defenbaugh shoots some penicillin into the rear of a grunt who slept with the wrong civilian.

Leaving Ben Tranh airfield on Eagle Flight, 21 January 1969. *(Left to right)* Sgt. Toby Hager, Doc Holley, unidentified door gunner.

Colonel Hackworth's command-and-control chopper. January 1969.

(Left to right) Wintzer, Doc Holley, Redfearn, Andy, and Ashley. Four klicks from Cambodia in the Plain of Reeds. 10 February 1969.

Chinese raider? No, just Ash! Spec-6 Robert Ashley at Dong Tam.

Doc Holley, near Cambodia. February 1969.

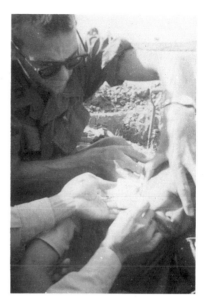

Doc Holley working on the badly abscessed ear of a Vietnamese child.

Award ceremony at Fire Support Base Danger, March 1969. *(Left to right)* unidentified, Sp4 Benny Fontenot, Doc Holley, Sgt. Slater, unidentified.

Colonel Hackworth presents Doc with Army Commendation Medal for heroism. Near Fire Support Base Danger. March 1969.

(Left to right) Lt. William Casey, Sp6 Robert Ashley, Sp4 Mitchell, Doc Holley, Sp6 Darr. Dong Tam, February 1969.

(Left to right) SFC Wayne Defenbaugh, Doc Holley, Sp6 Robert Ashley, Sp4 Grundy, PFC Frazier, SSG Rives on the way to Cai Bei. November 1968.

Sp4 Vernon Iddings and crew on canal bank near where Lt. Robby had his fingers shot off by Cobra gunship because of a colonel's error. 10 March 1969.

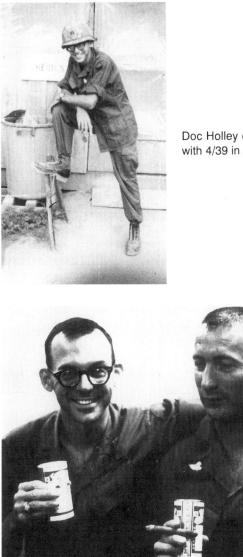

Doc Holley on his last day with 4/39 in April 1969.

Doc Holley enjoying a cool one with Colenel David Hackworth at the MACV General Dispensary, Tan Son Nuht Air Base. 06 July 1969.

tenant Casey and two deserving medics out to the dredge for a little relaxation. I'm beginning to believe I should have gone too, as patients keep dwindling in. It's been an hour since I first started this letter, and I've given two injections of Compazine, three plague shots, three cholera shots, and two tetanus shots, not to mention all the other complaints. I have a busy little aid station here at Dong Tam.

You are probably trying to figure out the enclosed slip of paper. It is a propaganda leaflet we dropped from an airplane after Charlie blew up the Long Dinh bridge near Dong Tam. I don't read Vietnamese worth a damn, but the gist of it is: The noble government of the South Vietnamese struggles to build bridges to strengthen the economy of its government. Meanwhile the despicable Viet Cong blow up these structures to destroy the economy and take food out of your mouth. I thought you might enjoy seeing it. I don't know if they help any. I do know these airplanes sure look like huge litter bugs, dropping all these little papers all over the countryside! I retrieved this one yesterday out on Ambush Alley.

Well, our fickle brigade has changed its mind again, and now we are supposed to go to the Ben Tranh airfield, a little airstrip about ten miles north of My Tho. That won't be as bad as the Wagon Wheel. At least there I'll be able to drive my jeep to Dong Tam once in a while for supplies, and I should receive my mail on the same day as if I were still at Dong Tam. Keep your letters coming. When I don't get one, I hear my men saying, "Well, Doc's got a case of the ass today. He didn't get a letter from Sondra!" That's their expression for being pissed off. But when I do get one or two from you, my huge grin gives good evidence of how happy I am, and when I'm happy, so are my men. People back in the World have no idea what a morale boost mail call is to those of us over here. If I couldn't get letters from you, I think I'd go crazy, really! I read your letters, and for a few minutes, it's almost as if I'm home with you.

Well, the patients keep wandering in, so I'll hang it up for tonight. Oh, one more thing! I took my last trip down Death Road yesterday—without incident. I was relieved to finish that mission. It's a pretty helpless feeling to know that any minute you may have an explosive charge blown up under you. I don't mind being shot at with rifles as much because I can shoot back, but a mine scares the hell out of me because there's no way to fight it. And it usually doesn't kill you. It knocks you out cold, and then Charlie comes in and finishes you off.

17 Jan 1969

Ben Tranh Airfield

We are set up at the Ben Tranh airstrip, about fifteen kilometers south of Tan An. This is a real nice area, with a short airstrip surrounded by ponds. The battalion which preceded us did a great job of building bunkers and even left their tents up for us, so we just moved right in without much work. What a nice change! I don't imagine we will be here too long, though, probably one or two weeks at the most. After that, we are supposed to Chinook out to the Wagon Wheel.

I got six new medics yesterday and three more today. I am beside myself with joy! Seriously, we were starting to hurt for replacements, and with us starting back out in the field, I was getting concerned, as I know I will lose some to injury or worse.

23 Jan 1969

Dong Tam Base

A few days ago, I was sitting around outside the aid station, shooting the breeze with one of our company commanders, Phil Martin, a really capable West Point graduate, talking about how boring my job has become. He said, ''Come out on a search-and-destroy mission with me, and you will appreciate your boring job a little better.'' Well, a couple of days ago I accepted his challenge and went out with his men on a series of ''Eagle Flights'' out of Ben Tranh airstrip. I had mixed emotions about going because it's like flying into the eye of the storm instead of around it, but my adventurous streak won out, and I went on a reconnaissance-in-force mission to the Plain of Reeds with Alpha Company. We had ten slicks (Hueys), which carry a crew of four and six grunts each, and two Cobra gunships, which prep the LZ (landing zone) for us. This Air Cav is really a spirited bunch. They have crossed swords painted across the front of their choppers, and a few of them wore yellow bandanas. One even had a bugle hanging by his seat. The troops looked at me like I must be crazy to go voluntarily into the bush. One of them said, "Doc, don't be stupid, you don't need this shit!" but I said, "No big deal!" and hopped aboard my chopper. I was carrying nothing but my M-16 with a VC ammo pouch, which held eight clips of ammo. I was really surprised by the faces of these kids as we lifted off and headed off for our first drop zone. They all looked so much older than their actual seventeen and eighteen years, and each one seemed to be lost in his own state of deep thought. No smiles. No joking or horsing around. This was a serious business, and the hard looks on their faces bore mute testimony to that fact.

I was enjoying the cool breeze blowing through the chopper and the lush green tropical landscape as it slid by beneath us. Sgt. Toby Hager was to be my companion and watchdog, and he explained that the Cobras were ahead of us, flying low over the area of our first LZ, trying to draw fire. Hager, a platoon sergeant from Mountain Home, Arkansas, is tough as nails and built like a fireplug with the face of a bulldog. They could use his face on a recruiting poster for the Green Berets. He looks like Mr. Infantry. As we began to descend in a big circle, I got a good look at one of my medics, Jose Rodriguez, sitting in the chopper next to ours. He gave me a big grin and a thumbs-up, and I felt better. Sergeant Hager leaned way out of the opening, where the doors had been removed, and looked ahead to the LZ, then turned around and hollered against the sound of the engine and rushing wind, "Red smoke! Hot LZ!" I felt a slight chill run down my spine. It wasn't that I hadn't been exposed to hostile fire because I had, and it hadn't bothered me like I thought it would. But, this was different. This time I knew in advance that Charlie was down there in the tree line, shooting, and we were fixing to jump out of a perfectly good helicopter and land in an open rice paddy. Then we would watch the slicks fly off and back to the relative safety of the base camp, while we tried to avoid becoming statistics.

As we started a rapid descent, I looked out the front window of our bird and saw red smoke rising from the LZ. I remember thinking, Lucky me, my first LZ would have to be a hot one, then I countered with, Well, stupid, nobody made you come out here so go for it.

When we were about forty feet above the paddies, our door gunners opened fire with their M-60 machine guns, and I could see bullets ripping the rice paddy and working their way out into the tree line on either side of the paddy. There were several large explosions out in the open area where we were attempting to land, and I really didn't know where they were coming from. I later learned that it was Charlie firing M-79 grenades from the tree line. The roar of the choppers, combined with all the weapons, created a din unlike any I had ever experienced, and all of a sudden, I was filled with an intense excitement that is hard to explain. This excitement superseded any fear I had been feeling earlier. The Huey hovered, ever so briefly, about three feet above the rice paddy, and we all jumped out into the knee-deep water and sloshed over to the nearest dike for whatever cover it could provide. Sergeant Hager had us hold up there while the Cobra gunships made another pass, in which they strafed the tree lines with rockets and miniguns. It was incredible to lay there so close to where all that firepower was landing and not get hit. I remember thinking, . . . if I was Charlie, I sure as hell wouldn't be sitting in that tree line now. We started a sweep across the paddy. Sergeant Hager had me well surrounded by friendlies as we slowly made our way across the open expanse of water. As we got closer to the trees, we could see white signs with black letters *Tu Dia!* posted on trees and wooden posts all along the tree line. Translated to English this means, ''death place.''

The woods were loaded with booby traps, most of which our Tiger Scouts located and detonated. Whatever VC had been there had obviously hauled ass, so we soon loaded back up for another trip to another LZ.

We had one other hot LZ, which I will never forget. We came in over a tree line and saw about a dozen gooks in black pajamas out in the middle of the rice paddy. As we were so low, they hadn't heard us coming, and we really caught them by surprise. They were each carrying AK-47 assault rifles, and I was surprised they didn't start shooting immediately but instead started running in different directions. Sergeant Hager directed our pilot to follow one who had taken off by himself, trying to reach a small thatched hut at the edge of the trees. He turned back to me and said, "Doc, you'll never get a better chance to shoot one of these bastards, so when we get down in the paddy, I want you to kneel down, take aim and shoot the bastard."

My adrenaline was really pumping as we jumped out into the knee-deep water. Either the gook was a hell of a fast runner, or else I had misjudged his distance from the air as he was quickly shrinking in my sights, so I squeezed off a full clip until he finally dropped. At first I thought he might have been taking cover, but he got up again and hobbled into the hooch. He must have been two hundred yards away when I dropped him. It was a lucky shot! We found a big blood pool where he fell and another in the hooch, then lost the trail at the edge of a tree-lined stream, where he obviously had got away in a sampan. I can still hear Sergeant Hager screaming, "Shoot the fucker, Doc, shoot the fucker!" and then "All right, Doc, you got him. He's on the ground!" I relived it over and over in my mind the rest of the day. Sort of had to put the old Hippocratic oath on the shelf for that one.

About this time, our battalion commander, who was flying overhead in his LOH (light observation helicopter), hollered down to us that there was a much larger force in the tree line behind us, and for us to forget about my prize and hump it over that way ASAP. We soon were in a position to see movement in among the trees and began to trade fire with this sizable force. Quite a few rounds were exchanged. All of a sudden green smoke popped in the tree line, and someone hollered, "Cease fire!" It seems that our large enemy force was in reality a reinforced platoon of ARVNs in camouflaged uniforms. They had been moving in to ambush the Viet Cong we had spotted from the air, when we came along and stole their thunder. They had been so well concealed that we didn't see them from the air. With their uniforms soaking wet, they looked black, and they really did appear to be wearing black pajamas. One of their men was hit with an M-79 grenade fragment, so I bandaged him up. It was not too serious, but if they hadn't popped that smoke grenade, it could have been disastrous for both units. We had one more LZ, and it provided as much excitement as the last one. Corporal Rollins and I were checking out some VC bunkers when we started receiving machine-gun fire from a bunker about fifty yards away. We were shielded from the fire by a stand of trees, so after it became obvious that no one else could get to the bunker, the two of us sort of broken-field ran through the trees to get there. Corporal Rollins let me have the pleasure of nailing the gook with an M-79 grenade. It blew half of his chest away and made tinfoil of his machine gun. He must have been asleep and got left behind, because when we searched the bunkers, we didn't find anybody else, just a lot of propaganda material, a few maps, some ammo, and a Viet Cong flag, which was pinned to a large support post in the main room. Rollins gave me the flag, and I'll send it home soon.

As we were heading back to the LZ, we heard the distinctive staccato of AK-47 fire coming from the area of another thatched hut at the far end of the tree line. The PRC-25 radio crackled with conversations between the CO and the Air Cav. "Colonel, we'll level that fucking shack, you guys just keep your heads down!" Two Cobra gunships came swooping down with their miniguns blazing. The air echoed with the crushing explosions of four rockets as they found their mark, and the hooch began to erupt from secondary explosions. "Lots of secondaries exploding in that place, Doc. Rice doesn't blow up like that," said Rollins, with a matter-of-fact look on his young face. "This is VC country all right."

After the explosions died down, we started to head back to the LZ when this message came over the radio, "Rollins, get the Doc over here ASAP. Believe he will want to see what we found in the hooch." Upon entering the still smoldering hooch, we found four VC sprawled on the floor, each still clutching his AK-47. "Look, Doc, this one is still alive and she's pregnant!" exclaimed a young grunt. Indeed, she was still alive, though barely. She was riddled with bullets, several of which had obviously penetrated her belly. She had been rather attractive, but laying here in this pool of blood . . . "Doc, can we save the baby?" comes the incredulous question. "This woman was in here trying to kill us, and now you want me to try to do a cesarean section on her, out in the jungle, on the floor of a grass hut! You gotta be kidding, pal! Shoot the bitch and put her out of her misery!" I calmly told the confused young soldier. All of a sudden my mind flashed back to the riverbank at Luong Truong and the FNG who lost his lunch on his first night ambush. I had become like the sarge, and I could feel the hatred of the young soldier who, in a moment of compassion, had forgotten who this woman was—the enemy. Same thing with her baby, who would fire a weapon, wire a booby trap, or toss a grenade in your jeep as soon as it became old enough to do it. Well, maybe he will understand in a few months, if he is lucky enough to live that long. No, I don't feel real proud of myself for my actions today. On the surface they appear hard and ugly, but if I've learned anything by being over here, it's that nice guys usually end up in a body bag headed for home, and whatever it takes to avoid that fate, I'll do it and worry about it later.

25 Jan 1969

Dong Tam Base

Today is probably the saddest day I've had since arriving in this hellhole. I had just flown in on a supply chopper when the pilot hollered that I might want to run over to 3d Surgical Hospital as he just heard a dust-off chopper calling to the hospital, inbound from Tan An with nine seriously wounded boys from the 4/39th Infantry. Well, I hoofed it over there and got to their helipad just as they were unloading the wounded. The first casualty I saw was my good friend, Corporal Rollins, and it was obvious he was hurt real bad. He appeared to be bleeding from multiple wounds and was unconscious. The others were also torn up pretty bad, but I went in with Rollins because I thought so much of him. We took him into triage and started cutting his uniform off. I was shocked. His muscular young body was literally riddled with holes about the size of the end of my index finger, over thirty different entrance wounds. He had gotten a claymore mine full blast, head on, and blood was oozing from most of the holes. He had several sucking chest wounds, any one of which could have killed him. In fact, I was amazed that he was still alive and breathing on his own. He had several leg and arm wounds, and one of his fingers was blown completely off. The worst was a neck wound, which had gone through the left carotid artery and left internal jugular vein, and blood was just pumping out of his neck with each heart beat. I applied a lot of external pressure and finally got it slowed down long enough to get blood going in both arms and both legs. I was just finishing up a two-minute tracheostomy when the surgeon came in and asked me to give him a hand. All their surgeons were tied up with all my other troops. He asked me to start putting his carotid artery back together, and he would start on his chest. By now, Rollins had received six units of whole blood, and his blood pressure was 60/0. They put him on the operating table while we were scrubbing. Someone hollered, "Goddamn it, get in here, he's arrested!" We ran in and sliced open his chest, and I started giving him internal cardiac massage. Miraculously, he began to resume a normal heart beat! We continued to pour the blood into him until his blood pressure came back up, then we laid a sterile towel over his chest incision and went to work on his neck wound, trying to reestablish good flow to his brain. We excised the damaged portions of his carotid and jugular and got a beautiful repair on them. We released the clamps, and blood filled the vessels, and they held beautifully. About this time, a waterfall of blood poured out of his chest incision. We pulled his left lung out, and he had eight holes in the left lung, all of which were now leaking like sieves. We paused, and looked at each other, looked up at the monitor, which showed his heart still clicking along, and went back to work. I looked over at the window in the OR door and was surprised to see eight of our good buddies looking over each other's shoulders, crowded around the small porthole of a window. I just shook my head and looked down as I felt the tears begin to well up in my eyes. They dripped down into my friend's chest cavity as I struggled to maintain my composure. I didn't look back up at the window, but I could still feel their presence. The lung wounds hadn't leaked earlier because his blood pressure was so low, but now that his pressure was up, they were leaking like faucets. We finally got all the holes in both lungs patched up and were starting to open his abdomen when he arrested again. We pumped and pumped, and all he would do was fibrillate, so we shocked him with the electric defibrillator. He went straight-line on the monitor and would not return a beat. His gallant fight was over. Our efforts had consumed over three and a half hours and thirty-eight units of whole blood. I've never seen a body with more will to live. By the time I looked up to the window, our pals were gone. I guess they were more realistic than I was. I just can't believe that Rollins is dead. Not Corporal Rollins, our very own John Wayne! Not the brave and fearless young stud who always volunteered to take point on patrols! Not the

Rollins I had seen on sick call at 0630 this A.M. and told to stay in because his feet were raw and bleeding from recurrent immersion foot! Not the Rollins I had told to stay in because he was real short—less than a week to go—and had already used up several of his nine lives in previous skirmishes, in which he had received shrapnel and punji stake wounds! Yes, Rollins had been every man's warrior. He had seemed so invincible. He was a handsome kid, bright blue eyes, blond hair, and a well-kept mustache. He always had that air of confidence about him and had always spoken to me with "yes, sir" or "no, sir." One of America's finest, dead at nineteen. He would have been a star on anybody's football team. Now he's just a fond memory in minds of a bunch of grunts who should be used to this shit by now, but somehow have really been touched today. My heart aches for his mom and dad who are probably at this very moment preparing for his homecoming. Oh God, how senseless this all is! When will it ever end?

27 Jan 1969

Dong Tam Base

Please forgive my slack in writing. I've almost been worked to death. I saw seventy-nine patients yesterday, then all night long they were firing mortars and cannons out of Dong Tam. It's hell trying to sleep amidst all that racket! I will know how to appreciate peace and quiet when I return to the World. Well, baby, to quote you, "There's really not much happening here," to write about. I get so damn tired of the routine of things. There are no days, e.g. Monday, Saturday, or Sunday, just daylight hours with a number attached, e.g. the twenty-seventh. There are no weekends, because every day is the same as the last one. People back in the World don't realize just how lucky they are. I'll be one hell of a better citizen for having spent a year over here.

28 Jan 1969

Dong Tam

We had another bad day, with a Tiger Scout killed and ten wounded—several critically. I went down to 3d Surgical to lend a hand. One poor kid was shot through the top of his skull and had a considerable amount of brain tissue sticking out of the wound. He had another bullet which had entered his left flank, pierced both kidneys and his spinal cord, and exited his right flank. He kept hollering "Am I alive? Get me a dust-off!" No amount of explanation on my part could convince him that he had already been dusted-off and was in the hospital. He was so pitiful. His blood pressure was 40/0, so we got blood going in about six sites, and soon we had his pressure up to 90/50.

Meanwhile the hospital came under mortar attack, which knocked out our power, so we decided to transfer him and some of his buddies to 24th Evac at Long Binh, north of Saigon. Well, they needed a doctor to go with him and watch over the other patients, so I volunteered. It was a flight I'll always remember. We had five others aboard, each on a litter, and each with three or four IV bottles or blood bags going. The litters are strapped onto the seats and onto racks above the seats so there really wasn't any place for me to sit. I spent a lot of my time with the brain injury patient's head cradled in my lap. It just broke my heart listening to him regress back to his childhood and talking to "Mommy" and whining and crying like a two-year-old. He really had totally lost contact with reality, which was a blessing, I guess, considering his poor condition. Even if he is "lucky" enough to recover, his future is pretty bleak.

One of the boys got real scared and confused and started flailing his arms around, and I had a hell of a time preventing him from pulling out everybody's IVs! I did manage to keep all their IV tubing straight and running at the proper rate of flow and even managed to change a couple of bottles which were about to run out. That one poor kid was really fighting to live, and he was still alive when we landed at the helipad at the 24th Evacuation Hospital.

I went in and brought their doctors up to date on what we had done on all the patients and went back out to hop a ride back to Dong Tam. Around 9:00 P.M., I caught a ride with another dust-off who had brought a few more patients out. I really enjoyed the ride back. It was just me and the pilots—no patients—so I could watch the sights of war at night from the air. Saigon is really quite beautiful to fly over at night. When we got farther out in the boonies, we saw several firefights going on south of Saigon. It was pretty in an eerie sort of way, with all the red and green tracers flying back and forth and the parachute flares drifting slowly over the jungle. We had a safe and uneventful trip back to Dong Tam. It took over an hour to get there. Long Binh was where I first entered the country, ten years ago!

I just got back to the aid station and discovered that Ashley and Spec Four Wintzer, one of my medics, had packed up all our supplies for our Chinook ride out to the Plain of Reeds tomorrow A.M. They are really good help, and they knew I would be worn out and upset about all those casualties. I wasn't real close to any of them, but knew all of them from seeing them at sick call at one time or another.

We have to wrap a lot of our supplies in plastic bags as the Chinooks really stir up a huge dust storm that covers everything within about one hundred yards with a thick brown layer of dust. This has to be the dustiest country in the world when it's not trying to be the muddiest! I'd better close and start getting my own things together. I still need to clean my M-16 and .45. I'll write to you next from the Wagon Wheel.

29 Jan 1969

Dong Tam

I'm sitting around this A.M. doing what the army excels in, having you hurry up and wait! We were all packed and loaded for a Chinook ride out to the Wagon Wheel for a brief layover and then on to Muc Hoa, a small hamlet near the Cambodian border. Our intelligence reports indicate that the 9th NVA Division is moving through this area, so we might see some action if we can find them. However, these intelligence reports are not always accurate—understatement of the year! I'm sitting here scratching my leech bites. I got leeches all over my belly on our last operation, when we spent a lot of time going through streams and canals. They bite a little chunk of skin out and attach themselves. They don't hurt until you pull them out. Right now they just itch like hell! In the past seventy-two hours we have really taken a beating, sustaining forty casualties, with two killed. It's depressing as hell!

I know so many of them. To see them all blown up, it's so pitiful. My handwriting is shot—I'm so tired—been up since 0530 treating casualties and dusting them off. Now it's almost 10:00 P.M., and I think we are almost caught up so I can get some rest. *Rest*, that's a real joke over here. You can never really rest because you can't ever get cool or dry or comfortable. You just crash and go into a state of half-sleep and hope nothing disturbs you for a few hours.

I read a good book about life during the Civil War in Mississippi. Only the faces have changed. They suffered the same kind of hardships we do here, only we have better food and transportation. But we have little else in the way of creature comforts. It's title is *By Valour and Arms* by James Streeter. Try to read it if you can, and it will give you some idea of what life is like for the infantry soldier.

1 Feb 1969

The Wagon Wheel—Plain of Reeds

Baby, this will be short. I just wanted to let you know I am OK. We are finally out at the Wagon Wheel, and it is really a mess! We have a new battalion commander, a Lt. Col. David Hackworth, and he is really a fanatic! No more portable showers in the field, no more portable latrines, no more hot chow flown out. We are really grubbing it. In fact, he considered sending our aid station tent back, but decided to leave it after I reminded him I might need some place in the shade to treat heat exposure cases. He is a real hard ass, lucky us! He is probably about thirty-eight years old but really looks like he can handle himself. He is not very tall but has "Popeye" forearms attached to a thick, muscular chest. His arms are covered with tattoos and scars from previous battles. He sports a real short crew cut, which reveals a large scar on his scalp, picked up in Korea. His pale blue eyes can pierce through a timid person, but I saw a big grin flash across his face today, so I suspect he's not all bad. I hear he has already earned six or seven Purple Hearts, and someone said he is the highest decorated, living soldier in the U.S. military today. I am looking forward to seeing this living legend in action.

I have not gotten any mail since we left Dong Tam, and don't know if I will. There will no longer be daily choppers for mail and water as Colonel Hackworth doesn't want Charlie to know where we are. Shit, there's always a helicopter in the air over South Vietnam, so I don't see how that will make us any less conspicuous. Oh well, it's his battalion, not mine. Anyway, now you will understand when my mail slows down. I'm still writing, they're just not picked up as often. The morale is quite low, and lots of our troops have the letters FTA written on their canvas helmet covers—fuck the army! One kid I saw today had this message scrawled across the side of his helmet: Yea tho I walk thru the Valley of the Shadow of Death, I will fear no Evil, cause I am the Meanest SOB in the Valley!

4 Feb 1969

My Diem, South Vietnam

I'm doing fine, just grubby, tired, and lonesome. We have been on one hell of an operation, and I haven't bathed or shaved for seven long, hot days. Wow, do I stink! But it's been very successful. We killed forty-six Viet Cong and didn't have any of our own killed. As I told you, we have a new battalion commander, a Lt. Col. David Hackworth, a real gung ho, Airborne type, who believes in taking everybody out humping in the paddies with him. So we all carry only what we can hump on our backs with us. The aid station has been reduced to one chest of IV bottles and one chest of miscellaneous drugs. We are really roughing it. No cots or tents. Every man sleeps on the ground. I tell you, we all look grubby as hell!

The other day, just before the new colonel arrived, we flew into the Wagon Wheel, so named for it's spokelike pattern of crisscrossing canals as seen from the air. I had just jumped off the slick (Huey) when someone hollered, "Be careful, the whole place is booby-trapped!!" Thirty seconds later, I heard a very loud explosion and saw three of our guys flying through the air, about three hundred yards away! We ran quickly but carefully through the middle of a minefield and got these guys patched up and back to the chopper. Ashley and I flew with them on the Huey as they were bleeding pretty badly.

After getting these troops to 3d Surgical Hospital in Dong Tam, we flew back out to the Wagon Wheel again. By this time, it had gotten dark, and the only way we could see where to land was to look for a soldier who had a strobe light in his helmet. I was thinking, I sure as hell hope he doesn't land this thing on a damned booby trap 'cause we will all be blown to bits if he does! Well, I'll tell you one thing, these chopper pilots are really top-notch. Ours hovered about six inches off the saw grass while we jumped out. This type of flying in a minefield on a foggy, moonless night! Wow, I thought, I'm glad these guys are on our side!

Well, we learned that ten others had been wounded and dusted off while we had been gone. We crept along very slowly in the dark until we finally found my other medics. We had just gotten bedded down on our poncho liners when three tremendous explosions went off, this time just a few yards away! Almost simultaneously, we heard bloodcurdling screams, and again had to run through the minefield—this time in the dark—to find two of our best infantrymen lying in the saw grass, screaming in agony. One look at them, and I could see why they were screaming. Each of them had lost both of their feet! Their buddies found what was left of their boots, with what was left of their feet still in them. But it wasn't enough to salvage anything. Our first job was to get tourniquets on their arteries to save them from bleeding to death. They were pumping blood all over the place. A couple of their buddies lost their cookies, just looking at the gory scene. We got the bleeders stopped, and got IVs started with Ringer's lactate, and got on the horn to the TOC, who got the chopper to turn around and come back for these two. The fog had gotten so dense that you couldn't see more than fifty yards in any direction, and I thought, Good luck! In about twenty minutes, we heard our Huey circling overhead trying to find us. This time it was my turn to hold a strobe light in my helmet. Unbelievably, this cool cat of a pilot inched his way down through the fog until I could just see his skids just above my head. I jumped out of the way, and he made another picture-perfect hover while my medics loaded up the wounded.

We finally got to sleep around midnight and slept pretty well, considering our surroundings. The next morning at about daybreak, I awoke to Ashley's deep steady voice. "Doc, wake up but don't move." I couldn't imagine why or what he was talking about but I knew from the tone of his voice that he was serious. It seems that in the dark, I had chosen a very precarious spot to lay out my poncho liner. My wrist was resting across a trip wire connected to a hand grenade attached to a bamboo pole about three feet away! Someone got our demolition expert over to deactivate the grenade while I made sure not to move. What a hell of a way to wake up from a hard night's sleep out in the boonies!

That A.M., we had the damndest change of command ceremony you could imagine, complete with the commanding general of the 9th Division and all his staff plus the brigade commander and all his staff. They almost needed an air-traffic controller to direct the air traffic. They even had a sound system, complete with loudspeakers. I thought two things immediately: First, this must be some important dude who is fixing to take over our unit; second, they must really want Charlie to know that he is here because they are broadcasting it all over the countryside with those stupid loudspeakers. Charlie sure missed one hell of an opportunity to wipe out the entire upper echelon of our military leaders in the Delta this A.M.

It was really quite a contrast, our grubby unshaven troops and these officers in freshly starched and ironed uniforms, with their waxed, spotless helicopters.

I noticed several things right off about our new leader. For one thing, Colonel Hackworth showed the utmost respect to his superiors, standing at attention with his arms at his sides even when engaged in casual conversation with the others who were standing very casually with their hands on their hips or with their arms folded. I also noticed that he answered every question with a "yes, sir" or "no, sir."

"This guy doesn't cut much slack," Ashley remarked to me.

"I think we may just have a real soldier for our new leader, Ash," I said.

As soon as the choppers lifted off and cleared the surrounding palm trees, the new Sergeant Major Bob Press came over with the news that we were to gather up all our shit and put it in one pile where a chopper could pick it up. We were to keep only what we could carry on our backs. Before we could finish groaning about this order, he continued with, "And we are moving this entire camp three hundred yards south ASAP!" Well, you can imagine how this struck our tired group of grunts who had just dug in the previous night.

After some chow, we settled down to getting things moved and dug a few foxholes. This was really difficult because the terrain consisted of saw grass growing from a moist, spongy base. We were really sitting ducks out there. Other than the unbearable heat and humidity, we had a rather quiet day and completed the move as dusk settled in.

After darkness fell, Charlie began his nighttime games again, and we received about forty rounds of incoming mortars. The mortars didn't result in any casualties, but shook the entire area like a major earthquake, probably because of the spongy nature of the terrain. It was unreal! The VC followed up with 75mm recoilless-rifle fire from two locations across the canal, and then bombarded us with countless rounds of 60mm mortar fire. Miraculously, none of the rounds were hitting home. Then it dawned on us that Hack had outfoxed them with his last-minute three-hundred-yard move at dusk. Charlie was out there pounding away at our previous position! Well, the old man quickly went into action and called out a team of Cobra gunships, and did they ever put on a show for us! It was a pitch-black, starlit night, and we had actually seen the flashes from Charlie's mortar tubes across the water from our position. As we watched the area with anticipation, two Cobra gunships swooped down out of the night sky and unloaded their rocket pods into the riverbank. Then they swung back around and started hosing down the entire area with their miniguns. On a dark night minigun fire looks like a hose spraying a crimson stream of water, and are quite spectacular to watch. It really gave us a thrill, and I'm sure they got Charlie's attention as it remained quiet for the rest of the night. Colonel Hackworth called in some artillery just to make sure.

Yesterday, while we were on some local maneuvers, a VC sniper started taking potshots at us. One of our Chinook pilots flew out over the area and spotted the sniper in a bunker across the canal. He called back to our artillery officer who lined up our 155mm howitzers with the VC bunkers in plain view across the canal. We figured they were empty. Anyway, they lowered their guns and fired point-blank at them! You should have seen the secondary explosions! It looked like the fourth of July!! They blew them all to hell! They must have been loaded with ammo, some of which had the HARD CORE's name on it, I'm sure.

We are presently located at My Diem, about forty miles west of Saigon, and are dug in on a riverbank. Baby, I don't think I will ever want to camp again. We are really roughing it. C rations galore, and dirty brown river water to drink and bathe in. When we do go camping, we will rent a nice camper and go first class, shower and all!

I've met a real nice fellow from Mountain Home, Arkansas, who knows Jack Allison. He used to drag race against Jack in his old Polar Freeze truck. His name is Toby Hager. We went on that recent Eagle Flight together. He is a real *tough* guy. Tell old Jack I wish he was over here with me. I think he would enjoy kicking Charlie's ass as much as I do! I'm going to try to do better with my letter writing. It's just that it's kind of hard to write when you are up to your butt in rice-paddy water!

We just had an air strike about a mile north of us. The USAF had fighter-bombers dropping five-hundred-pound bombs, and they really leveled the place. When they finished, they flew real low right over our position, doing barrel rolls and dipping their wings in tribute to the grunts or ground pounders as we are affectionately called. They are really good, and I am glad they are on our side. We are supposed to be here a few more days, then on to the Cambodian border near Muc Hoa.

I just had a nice visit with Lt. Bob Knapp, "the Knapper" as we call him around here. He is the CO for Bravo Company, and he is really one sharp dude. He's the one who was so excited when he heard that Colonel Hackworth was coming to command our battalion. "Hell, Doc, I studied his Vietnam Primer on guerilla warfare at West Point! It was required reading," he had exclaimed. "This man is a living legend, and we are lucky enough to have him for our CO!" Knapper is a natural comedian and is a lot of fun to be around.

6 Feb 1969

Dong Tam

Today, I flew over the Delta with Colonel Hackworth in his LOH (light observation helicopter). I really enjoy the flying and do it every chance I can get. The air is so much cooler when you are moving through it at one hundred miles per hour. There is so little pleasure over here that I have to do something for fun. Flying out over this beautiful, lush green country is worth any risk I might be taking. I don't really think it's that dangerous. Very few choppers get shot down over here on routine flights at high altitude, and when they do, the crew usually survives as they can normally autorotate to a controlled crash landing. Also, they are in constant radio contact with other choppers, and you are rarely more than a few miles away from help.

I think I'll get my private pilot's license when I return to the World. Flying is such a great way to get away from it all, and nobody can call you on the phone when you are up in the air.

I'm getting to know the colonel, and today he said, "Just call me Hack, Doc." I flew in here yesterday for supplies and will fly back out later today. We are leaving for the Cambodian border tomorrow, and will be based at a small airfield near a little village called Muc Hoa. I don't know how long we will be there, but I picked up supplies for a month, just in case we really get involved in some heavy contact and can't get out for a while. Keep your chin up, and I will, too.

I'm having to stay pretty grubby for weeks at a time now, but I can handle it OK. I used to do it all the time on hunting trips back in Florida with Don Jennings, so this is just a big, long, different kind of hunting trip over here. The real difference is that over here the prey is also hunting you! I'm a little blue this A.M., but I know it will pass. It always does.

7 Feb 1969

Near My Diem in the Plain of Reeds

I'm sitting here on a canal bank out in the middle of the Plain of Reeds, sweltering in the sun. Tomorrow we go to the Cambodian border, which is located about ninety miles west of Saigon. We will probably have night infiltration insertions into Cambodia. Of course, this is completely unofficial and off the record as Cambodia is strictly off limits to all U.S. military personnel. However, it is not off limits to Charlie, who often retreats into the jungles of his western neighbor, knowing full well that we won't come after him. Well, we might just surprise him.

We flew very near the border yesterday and saw several columns of smoke rising out of the jungle on the Cambodian side of the border in areas shown on the map as uninhabited jungle. So it's a big chess game, and they just move their pawns out onto their own private board. Since officially we won't be over there at all, any reports of our actions will probably read "dateline: Muc Hoa." We are supposed to be there until Tet, and after that move back closer to Saigon. I don't know who the hell does all this advance planning because as often as not, the plans change before they can be carried out. Mainly, because Charlie never does what we expect him to do. Almost never, anyway. The Lord only knows for sure, I guess. Please excuse the grubby stationery, but everything I have is grubby right now, sloshing through the Delta muck as we've been doing lately. We are sitting here listening to a little portable radio, with Johnny Cash singing the "Orange Blossom Special"—just a bunch of guys enjoying the music. Of course we can't play it very loud, but any music is better than no music. It is a pretty starlit night, with a cool breeze and no mosquitoes. We have been talking about how we've all turned into crude animals—I know I can tell it from some of my language. Well, Baby, I now cuss like a sailor. It's a survival factor. It seems like the more you cuss, the less chance you have of going batty or nuts over here. I'm still the same old Byron, but I've aged a little, I'm sure. I'll just have to work on cleaning up my act when I see you again.

10 Feb 1969

Phuoc Xien, near Cambodia

Here I sit out on a big expanse of reeds and saw grass, a few miles from the Cambodian border, waiting on a chopper to take us closer to the border. One of our slick pilots accidently landed inside Cambodia today but realized his mistake soon enough to fly out before getting involved in a firefight.

I can't remember when I wrote my last letter as we have been on the go and never settling down long enough to take time to write. We are sleeping on the ground, and if it weren't for our poncho liners, we would be soaked every night as a heavy dew falls before daylight, even during the dry season. When you are humping as much as we are, you are so dog-tired that you don't have much trouble catnapping, although a good night's sleep is virtually nonexistent over here. Ashley found a nylon parachute that we have rigged up as a canopy, and it helps to keep us a little drier. Our baths consist of occasional swims in a nearby canal and our meals of C rations and LRRPS (lurps) for "Long Range Reconnaissance Patrol, Subsistence," which are small freeze-dried packets of different meals, which when reconstituted with water, make a fairly tasty dinner. We just heat up some water with a small, burning chunk of C-4 plastic explosive, which burns like Sterno, and then pour it right into the plastic bag and eat right out of the container. They have beef stew, chicken stew, and spaghetti, which are our three favorites. Some of the others are awful! We have no chairs, stools, or wash bowls, so our steel helmets serve as a lavatory, kitchen sink to wash yourself and your utensils, and a pot to heat up water. They also serve as a makeshift seat when you get tired of sitting on the ground. Lordy, Lordy, will I ever appreciate the luxurious goodies we have back home in the World. Well, I must run now as our chopper is coming in, and I have to get one of the pilots to take this letter back to Dong Tam and mail it.

13 Feb 1969

Somewhere in a jungle southeast of Cambodia

I know my writing has slacked off the past couple of weeks but, as I explained before, we are traveling light and move every other day by chopper to a different location. Most of our stops have been to places where no one else has ever been, so we really haven't done much in the way of digging in as we don't stay long enough to justify the effort. In addition, we are traveling so light that we can't bring sandbags, shovels, etc.

We have been quite lucky that we have been able to find areas high enough to remain relatively dry but low enough that we always have had a river, stream, or canal close by for washing, swim-baths, and drinking water. Nothing like muddy water to get you clean! It's really kind of neat being away from base camps and truly out in the boonies. At night, the sounds of the birds and insects are fascinating when the drone of the mosquitoes quiets down long enough to hear them. It's funny how some nights you can sit out under the stars without a shirt on and actually feel cool and not notice a single mosquito, and then the next night in the same spot be driven to your mosquito nets by sundown. They seem to thrive on insect repellent, especially the U.S. Army brand! Off seems to work fairly well. It's hell to wake up at 0300 hours and need to pee so bad you can explode and then have the mosquito netting so covered with mosquitoes that you can hardly see out through it. Well, I usually lay there until I can't stand it then jump up, pull the net down, run to the first available bush, pee, then run back and dive under the net. This maneuver can be accomplished in about sixty seconds if you're quick.

It's been two weeks since I had a shower and change of clothes.

I have quit smelling my own BO or that of the others. During the day we sweat so much that when it dries, we have concentric rings of salt caked around our jungle fatigues. Nobody wears underwear because it causes such a horrible rash by holding in the moisture with the heat. Talk about diaper rash, wait until you see crotch rot in a grunt after two or three weeks in the same fatigues! It's a scream to watch us thrashing around in a muddy canal with our clothes on, trying to wash them, too, while at other times we will all strip down, looking like refugees from a nudist camp, sitting around waiting for our jungle fatigues to dry. We manage to shave every three or four days, so you can imagine how grubby we look. The VC don't grow beards so they never look quite as grubby as we Americans while living out here in the boonies. The sweat, grime, and mud get real old, but in the past eight days, we have killed sixty-five Viet Cong, so it's worth it.

The sentiment toward Hack seems to be improving as time has shown us that he is really one hell of a fine soldier. He is truly interested in the welfare of the men, and most of them seem to sense it. For a while there was a rumor circulating that there was a price on his head, six hundred to one thousand dollars to any GI who would wipe him out. When I told him of the rumors, he grinned and said, "Shit, Doc, I would have thought I would be worth more than that, wouldn't you?" and we both laughed. I said, "I'm serious, sir, you really need to be extra careful." He answered, "I've already been apprised of the situation, Doc, and I'm planning to go out with Bravo Company tomorrow and take point, just to show the bastards that I'm not afraid of their little rumor."

Well, as it turned out, he did exactly that, and while out in the field, actually made contact with the enemy. Hack showed the boys why he is called "Mr. Infantry" by leading the platoon against a small force of VC and killing several of the enemy without so much as a scratch to any of our men. He later laughed while telling me how he was up front where even a blind man could have bushwhacked him if he had wanted to, but felt they were all too interested in his ability to save their asses to worry about shooting him. He is one courageous SOB, of that I am certain.

We had a meeting when we got back to Dong Tam, right after he took command. He was starting to read me the riot act about something, and I respectfully but firmly let him know that I had heard all about how he was Mr. Infantry and had written the book on guerilla warfare in Vietnam, but I didn't think he knew much about doctoring and keeping his troops healthy, and that if he wouldn't fuck around with my medics, I wouldn't fuck around with his grunts, other than to keep them in the best physical and mental health possible. At first he appeared to bristle, and then he sat back and said, "You got a deal, Doc, sit down and let's talk about some of the problems you encountered before I arrived." We talked about the importance of morale and how poor it had been after suffering heavy casualties while providing Dong Tam security. "Lower than whale shit," is how he described his assessment of the morale of the 4/39. I pointed out that I understood his reasons for getting back to the basics as I, too, had been appalled at the National Guard–bivouac style of most of our operations under his predecessor. But, I pointed out the tremendous positive morale effect that daily mail call had and pleaded with him to try to arrange at least every-other-day mail drops while we were on the move. Hack agreed in principle and promised to try. Of course, I had some selfish motives behind my reasoning. He assured me that as the unit began to improve its appearance, performance, and attitude, we would see a return of some luxuries, such as beer, ice cream, and an occasional hot meal choppered out to us as long as they wouldn't compromise the immediate military situation.

He really isn't a bad guy, and I believe he is as good as Knapper said he was. I feel like my chances of surviving this place have increased significantly since his arrival. Right now I am sitting on an ammo box (empty!) and using another one for a desk to write on. It's 11:00 A.M., and the mosquitoes are still bad. Last night, my netting was solid black from the mosquitoes, and they were so thick they actually blocked the airflow, and it felt like I couldn't breathe. We had to seek shelter under our nets about 8:00 P.M., when the sun went down, because of the hordes of mosquitoes. We are presently camped in an area of deep saw grass, with scattered, raised hammocks full of trees, very reminiscent of the Everglades. It is hot as hell, and even the slightest breeze is very much appreciated. Well, Baby, the supply chopper is inbound, so I need to close this so they can take it.

13 Feb 1969

Somewhere about three miles southeast of the Cambodian border

Letter to Mom and Dad:

Please forgive the delay in writing. We have been on the go ever since 28 January—moving all over the delta—moving approximately every other day by helicopter. I have lost track of the places we have been. Most of our operations have been near the Cambodian border—*very near*—and we have killed sixty-five or seventy Viet Cong and captured a number of weapons, crude French medical supplies consisting of sutures, poor quality hemostats, and a variety of sulfa powders packed in brightly colored paper packets, the way we package sugar in America. They have no expiration dates on them, and they look quite old, almost World War II vintage! We also captured some maps and other military documents.

We are really roughing it—no tents, and everybody sleeps on the ground, covered with a poncho liner and a mosquito net when we can rig one. I haven't had a shower since 28 January and my clothes have eight days of mud, grime, and sweat on them. In the past two and one-half weeks we have had hot meals flown out to us for three meals only, and we are all starting to get pretty tired of C rations and LRRPS. We've only had enough water to shave every three or four days, so we are really a grubby, stinky bunch. The mosquitoes are *terrible*, even during the day. We are sloshing around in saw grass, which holds clouds of mosquitoes and other insects. Nobody in his right mind would choose to live in these conditions. It really is no-man's-land!

Dad, you were asking about open heart massage? Well you just open the patient's chest below the left nipple with a scapel. The heart is sitting right there looking at you. You take the heart in your hand, slipping your thumb behind and squeezing from the bottom upwards, and have someone feel for a pulse to verify that you are pumping forcefully enough. Obviously, it's a last-ditch effort, but occasionally we will save a GI that way. Well, I'm sitting out here getting eaten alive by mosquitoes, so I'll close for now.

19 Feb 1969

Plain of Reeds, South Vietnam

Baby, I hope you have forgiven me for not writing more often the past three weeks, but it is impossible for you to know just how exhausted I have been. My troops are just about to fall on their faces. We have moved so much the past few weeks that I have actually lost track of the many different places we have camped. Charlie must really be on the run because we are chasing after him! On the average, we have moved every other day since the first of the month. Each time we move, we have to repack everything, haul it aboard a Chinook helicopter, and fly it to a new location—usually way the hell out in the boonies—unload again, and set up in the scalding sun. *Dig*, *dig*, and *dig* some more until we have enough sandbags filled to have a fairly safe bunker to treat our wounded in, out of danger of enemy mortar fire. It's the hardest I have worked in a hell of a long time. The heat is unbearable, and the only thing we have is C rations and water. I don't think I ever want to see another canned good in my life, much less go camping! So my reason for not writing is sheer exhaustion. Even my eighteen-, nineteen-, and twenty-year-olds are about to flake out, so you can imagine how the "old man" is doing. I usually pitch right in with the manual labor as I figure if they know I'm not too good to get my hands dirty, then they will be there when I need them. I'm holding up all right except that I'm just too damn tired to do anything that isn't absolutely necessary.

We have killed 126 Viet Cong and stopped most of their infiltration from Cambodia into the Delta. General Ewell, commanding general of the 9th Division, bragged the other morning that the 4/39 was his best battalion, and if Saigon is hit, he will send us there to protect it. The battalion has improved consid-

erably since Col. David Hackworth took over. He is truly outstanding, and we are all rapidly becoming lean and mean.

Baby, this heat is unbelievable! Being from Florida, I thought
I could handle a lot of heat, but this heat and humidity are so
overbearing that it feels like we have hundred-pound sacks on
our backs all the time.

Well, they just brought a grunt in here with a temperature of
103 degrees, so I better stop for now and go have a look at him.
Some of the guys have stopped taking their malaria pills in the
hope of contracting that disease instead of a case of acute lead
poisoning—compliments of Charlie. In a way I really can't blame
them. Some even shoot themselves in the foot to get a trip back
to the World!

20 Feb 1969

Dong Tam Base

I got into Dong Tam for a night's rest, then we flew into Fire
Support Base Moore, about fifteen miles west of Dong Tam,
out of which we will conduct airmobile operations from one to
four weeks, depending on Charlie's reactions. There is a road
from here to Dong Tam, so I will be able to drive back and forth
to the PX for extra goodies and an occasional overnight for a
change. They seem to mortar both bases with equal frequency,
so it's six of one and half a dozen of the other.

We have put in so much helicopter time that my boys and I
have all been put in for our first Air Medals, with clusters likely
to follow. Our adjutant was talking about that the other night
and casually mentioned that he and I and Bob Knapp, a West
Pointer and a real sharp guy who commands Bravo Company,
will all be on the same flight to Hawaii next month. Flight P208
leaves Tan Son Nhut Air Base sometime on 18 March and arrives
in Hawaii sometime earlier on the same day as it crosses the
international date line. I still don't know what time it arrives,
but I will notify you of this as soon as I find out. Oh Baby, I'm

so excited I can hardly believe it's for real—only *twenty-five* more days!

Well, precious, the lights just went off. The first night in weeks I've had electric lights, and the damn generator quits. That's my luck! So the sun has set, and I am sitting out in the front of my hooch, frantically scribbling before it gets completely dark. The eight-inch guns are starting to fire quite regularly, so that means someone is engaged with the enemy nearby. I hope it's not my boys as they have no medical help other than the medics. Well, it's gotten so dark I can hardly see the paper, so I will close for now.

21 Feb 1969

FSB Moore

One of my friends, Lt. Mike Sinclair of Charlie Company, had an interesting experience today. His platoon was on a reconnaissance-in-force operation northwest of Cai Lai, and as they were walking through an area of streams, nipa palm, and banana trees, one of his men spotted a VC poking his head out of a spider hole. He pulled his head back before they could fire, so Mike went over and called *"chieu hoi"* (surrender and come out), but the gook did not answer. So he pulled the pin on a hand grenade and tossed it down the hole just as Charlie tossed one of his own out of the hole! Well, the lieutenant hollered "Hit the deck!" The VC grenade detonated harmlessly as the bunker exploded. They searched the collapsed bunker and found two dead gooks.

22 Feb 1969

Fire Base Moore

Well, we are at FSB Moore resting, from our strenuous hop-scotching mission. None of us can believe how luxurious it is to have three hot meals and a hot shower every day! Everything in life is relative, and this base camp would look like a concentration camp to the average citizen in the United States, but compared to how we lived for the past three weeks, it could be called the "Waldorf Moore." It is not a very large camp, probably not over ten acres at best, but since it is the brigade headquarters, there is an awful lot of chopper and convoy traffic in and out of the camp.

I'm responsible for anything the brigade drags in here, so I don't know how long I will be happy here, but at least it's a nice break from the rigors of living like a swamp rat. I don't think Hack is too crazy about it either, but he, too, realizes that there is a limit to how long you can keep your men out in these conditions. The Viet Cong were born and raised in this climate and are accustomed to living under these primitive conditions, but we aren't. I think that after three weeks, we had reached a point of diminishing returns, from a morale as well as physical viewpoint. However, I think we will be ready to get back to it in a very few days. Colonel Hackworth has really turned us around, and most of the guys are anxious to get about the business of killing gooks. With this man in charge, they have finally seen some positive results, with very few of our own men being lost. The general feeling is that at least we are not just sitting around waiting for Charlie to drop a mortar on top of our heads. Instead, we feel like we have Charles on the run for the first time in a long while. Being here for the transition, I can really attest to the difference. It's like being transferred to a completely different outfit, which resembles an elite bunch of Rangers rather than the ragtag, half-drunk outfit I first met in October. The chief difference seems to be leadership founded on experience and confidence. Hack has an infectious way of drawing the best out of his men and making them want to be better, and if possible, achieve their absolute best in the field. I don't hear any more hate remarks or talk of bounties on his head.

Well, I was interrupted by a brigade Huey that stopped off here for me to try and save a dying Viet Cong POW. His leg was practically blown completely off and was hanging by a thread. I could see the open, oozing end of his femoral artery. The clowns who brought him in hadn't even put on a tourniquet, so he just about bled out on the way in. He was in agonal respirations, and even though his pupils were dilated and fixed, we put a tourniquet on his thigh. I performed a hasty ankle cutdown. His vessels were all completely collapsed, and his BP was 0/0 with a very faint and irregular heartbeat. Incredibly, right in the middle of our efforts, in rushed the interim brigade commander, with a couple of his stooges, insisting that we let him take the patient out to their interrogation room. Colonel Hunt, an engineer with little to no combat experience, has already been a thorn in Hack's side by interfering in our tactical operations, and now he is interfering with my job. It's easy to see why they refer to him as "Mickey Mouse" Hunt. "For Christ's sake, the man is dying!" I exclaimed. "Time is critical if we are going to save his life." He said he didn't give a damn about saving his life, he just wanted to get some info out of him that might save some American lives. I told him to get the hell out of my aid station and let me do my job and reminded them of the Geneva Convention. They threatened to court-martial me for insubordination. I said, "Help yourself, gentlemen. Maybe I'll get out of here a little early." They seemed to think for a moment about their shaky position then retreated, red-faced and angry. Colonel Hunt left one stooge there to keep an eye on the prisoner! Meanwhile the POW went into ventricular fibrillation. We tried to defibrillate him electrically, but it was just too late. I told the stooge who stayed to watch, when he insinuated that we had dropped the ball by not saving him for a session in their hot seat, "Look, sir, next time, tie a tourniquet around his leg and maybe he won't bleed to death enroute. We're not Jesus, you know!" He got all red-faced like his leader and bolted out of the aid station, mumbling something about Hackworth's smart-ass mavericks, to which I answered, "Yeah, but at least we're not dumb!" I think he knew better than to press it any further since all the evidence placed the blame for the prisoner's death squarely on their shoulders, and I would have welcomed the opportunity to tell that to General Ewell himself if need be. I really wasn't concerned about another Viet Cong dying, but I sure as hell wasn't going to let these brigade clowns in their spit-shined boots put the blame on me or my men. We had our shit together, and we knew it. And we also had our doubts about some of these candy-ass officers who flew around above the battles, and for all the world looked just like any other REMF to us.

25 Feb 1969

Fire Base Moore

Letter to Mom and Dad:

I was relieved to hear that y'all survived the freak storm. I had heard about it and wondered if y'all had any serious damage.

Mom, I enjoyed the pictures you sent along with your "early A.M." letter. The aquarium looks like it's real nice, and you look like you might have lost a few pounds, huh? Pictures are worth a thousand words. I have about sixty slides I will take to Hawaii, and Sondra will forward them on to you. They are of the Bob Hope show, some taken of Dong Tam from the Huey I rode in down to Can Tho, as well as a couple of me and Sergeant Toby Hager leaving on the Eagle Flight from the Ben Tranh airstrip.

We have been at Fire Support Base Moore, our 1st Brigade headquarters since 20 February. We were mortared on the night of 22–23 February, receiving about forty to fifty rounds of 82mm mortar fire. We had seven significant casualties, and I had to run all over the base camp, picking up the injured and hauling them back to the fixed bunkered aid station here. We spent about three hours patching them up and stabilizing them in preparation for an 0200-hours dust-off. We received mortar fire off and on from about 2100 hours until after midnight. I talked to the chopper pilot and told him that they could wait until things had quieted down. At night, all choppers look the same and are easier targets, so I always try to wait as long as possible at night, and I certainly wasn't going to ask them to fly into our position while we were still receiving incoming mortar rounds.

Just about dusk tonight, a white phosphorous ("willy peter") artillery round landed on top of a thatched hut in a small village about three-quarters of a mile southwest of our base. It set the roof on fire, and the locals believed one of our rounds was accidently fired short. They brought three women, who were really a mess, into my aid station. They had severe WP burns, and their skin was barely hanging on. I couldn't identify any veins to start an IV, so I had to do veinous cutdowns on each of their ankles and then have them dusted-off to Saigon. I doubt very seriously that any of them will survive as it's pretty damn difficult to live with a total-body skin graft, which is what each one of them will need if they are to have a Chinaman's chance of survival—poor choice of words!

White phosphorous is a very potent, caustic, and deadly agent, which will burn straight through any human tissue it comes in contact with. It will also burn through most man-made materials as well. A piece the size of a lemon must have landed on this one poor woman's thigh just above her knee, as it burned completely through the skin, muscle, over half the femur, and out the back side. You could look straight through her leg, and it looked like someone had held her down and cut a hole in her leg with a four-inch cookie cutter or a four-inch drill. The strange thing is that you would expect it to be pumping blood like crazy. But it was as clean and dry a wound as I have ever seen. I guess the burning phosphorous cauterized the blood vessels as it passed through the tissue. Her femur would probably fracture if she put her body weight on it as three-fourths of it was gone. WP is really mean stuff. We were wondering if it could have been one of our stray rounds which fell short. However, not too long after it was fired, we began to receive our first salvo of incoming mortar rounds, and most of our people believe the stray WP round was a marking round that Charlie had used to range in his mortar tubes. Both sides use WP as marking rounds because it produces an intense white smoke cloud that is easily seen from a considerable distance, therefore making it an ideal reference for adjusting artillery fire on a given target. Hack finally said, "It was a Viet Cong white phospherous marking round. No doubt about it. *Case closed!*'' to which we replied, *"HARD-CORE Recondo, sir!"*

Early the next morning, I was awakened to come down to the gate to "straighten out a little problem." As Wintzer and I approached the gate, we were both struck with the horrible odor of burned flesh, only much stronger than we had ever before experienced. The old papa-san who was the village chief was there, along with about a dozen women of all ages who were wailing and carrying on. They were carrying several wooden U.S. ammo boxes, about one foot wide and four feet long and about eighteen inches deep. We peered down inside the boxes and saw a varied assortment of bloody body parts. One ammo box held the remains of an infant, about nine months of age, with half of its chest melted away. I could see part of its tiny little heart and lungs. Another had about 50 percent of what had been the upper torso of an eight-year-old boy, with part of a T-shirt still in place and a little hat on his head. One box had the upper portion of the chest, neck, right arm to the elbow, and lower half of the skull of what had been a middle-aged woman. The rest of her body had vanished. It was a real horror show! Wintz and I looked at each other and for a moment were speechless. No matter who fires the fucking things, few people who fire them ever get to witness firsthand the gruesome devastation which is wrought on the poor victims. I thought every senator, congressman, and the president himself ought to have to witness this scene, ought to have to hear the moans and screams of the family, see the pain on their faces, and smell the horrible odor, which right now I know I will smell forever.

The incredible icing on the cake was the hard-nosed old papa-san who insisted that it was our shell that produced this horror show. He had an itemized list of the casualties, including the cost of replacing three hooches and two water buffalo! I looked incredulously at Wintz, who still appeared to be in shock from the whole scene we had just witnessed. I told the interpreter to explain to them that it was Charlie who had fired the shell and for him to take the bill to his local Viet Cong cadre. I also said I was sorry it happened but that we weren't the guilty party. He started cussing us out in English, and I said, "Papa-san, you'd better *di di* the fuck out of here before you have some more dead bodies to carry around the countryside!" He sneered as he and his troupe turned around and headed back to their village. It amazed me how the women immediately turned off their grieving when it became apparent that we weren't going to subsidize this fuck-up, no matter who caused it. We don't carry our war dead in ammo boxes, but we have our share of tragic deaths to deal with, too—and we don't even live here! This is supposed to be their home, but they are caught in the middle, and for that, I'm sorry.

We went on back to the aid station. Wintz and I both decided to pass on the scrambled eggs and bacon they were serving in the mess tent this A.M.

We were just finishing up the paperwork from the night's happenings and a small A.M. sick call, when the military police called for us to drive down to Highway 4, where the VC had just blown up a bus loaded with civilians. It had been on its way to the market at My Tho. Traffic was backed up for about four miles, but we finally got there with the help of an MP jeep escort. You would not believe the scene which awaited us! The bus, a colorful blue one with yellow and orange stripes, was sitting in the middle of the road, with its front one-third blown to shreds, overhanging a huge crater in the center of the road, which was at least eight feet wide and eight or ten feet deep. In front of the crater was a huge pile of bodies, some of which were moving and moaning. The most incredible aspect of the gruesome scene was the dozen or so gooks who were taking jewelry off bodies, dead or alive. My first impulse was to shoot the bastards, but I looked over at the MP captain who quickly dispersed the stragglers. Well, Wintz and I, along with a couple of the medics attempted to do a triage of the pile of dead and dying Vietnamese. The mound literally was three feet high, so we started on top and the sides, pulling away the bodies that appeared to be dead. Occasionally one would moan when you moved it. One poor fellow seemed to have a fracture every three or four inches along the entire length of both legs. He must have been sitting directly above the charge when it exploded. His feet were dangling at about 180 degrees from their normal anatomic position. While working on him, I felt something move under my right foot and looked to see an arm, attached to a young woman who was obviously dead. I don't know how or why it moved because she had fixed and dilated pupils, no pulse or blood pressure, and was dead, no question. I hadn't even seen her there in my concentration of trying to save the man I was working on.

While we were working on these pitiful people, the dust-off

arrived and landed in the road next to us. It blew dust all over everything and everybody as we loaded ten casualties and sent it on its way. We were all covered with blood, and the dust turned it into a red-brown mud. I turned to count heads of my men and saw one of my medics over in the ditch, vomiting his poor head off. And he wasn't an FNG, he was a veteran of many combat operations. It was just that the mine and its horror were the straw that broke this particular camel's back. He quickly recovered and apologetically hopped back in the jeep for our return trip to FSB Moore. "Shit, man, don't apologize for that," I said. "It was a normal reaction. I'm surprised you didn't have lots of company in the ditch."

On our two-and-a-half-hour, four-mile return trip, we rehashed our experience. Wintz said one lady was nearly decapitated and over twenty bodies were just dismembered parts. We finally estimated the total number of casualties at about sixty. So much for cramming people in, on, and on top of these buses. Well, the injured were also crammed in for their final helicopter ride. One of my boys said kind of sheepishly, "I hope none of them fall out," and we all broke into laughter. Not that we didn't care, because we did, but the wounded were all in such bad condition, it would probably be a blessing if they all fell out. We seriously wondered if any would survive.

I've had quite a few Viet Cong and NVA soldiers brought in for me to patch up so they can interrogate them before sending them to the *Chieu Hoi* center at Dong Tam. Today I removed an M-16 bullet from an NVA's leg. It really made one hell of a hole. We have a small blood bank here, so we can transfuse them if need be before dust-off. This place is pretty busy, and I haven't had a full night's sleep since arriving here. I'm ready to go back out to the field.

3 Mar 1969

Giao Duc (Jow Duck)

Well, darling, let me tell you where I am and what I am doing. We have moved, by vehicle this time, to Giao Duc, near the town of Vinh Long. We are actually located in the rice paddies right off the main road, Highway 4, and I guess they call the cluster of thatched huts in the tree line Giao Duc, as I don't see anything else near here which resembles a village or hamlet. We are forty miles due west of Dong Tam and are setting up one mile north of the Mekong River. Our mission is to build a first-rate fire support base—which Hack has already named Danger—to provide an area for staging raids into and around Cambodia and the Ho Chi Minh trail. Our artillery will be in the range of this area, and apparently we are the first American unit to attempt to dig in for any degree of permanence in the region. This is definitely VC country. We will have a battery of six 105mm howitzers, and with the wide-open area surrounding us, we have a clear fire-zone for several hundred yards. Charlie would be crazy to try to overrun the place with a ground attack. I am sure that it will be closed down with the return of the monsoons. It is bone-dry now but will be a muddy mess then. Anyway you cut it, I will be out of here by then.

We moved here on 28 February and have been busting our butts ever since. For the very first time since being out in the boonies, we have a bunkered aid station large enough for eight to sleep in, with hardwood floors and protection from mortars. We all worked real hard on it, and Benny Fontenot and Charlie Wintzer brought me a sign to go over the door. It is drawn on the cardboard from a C-ration box and says, GIAO DUC GENERAL and has DOC HOLY, with a halo above my name and the insignias from Ben Casey for death, life, infinity, male, and female, and the arrowhead symbol for the HARDCORE Recondo's. It is real neat and just shows you some of the spirit this bunch of guys have.

While the engineers were bulldozing the area to build up a berm, they uncovered a dead gook with an AK-47 still in his hands. Hack took it and fired off a burst, with a laugh, and said he doubted that an M-16 would fire after being buried for a day, much less a year! The M-16 is notorious for its propensity to jam up when it gets dirt or mud in it.

Charlie mortared the shit out of us the first night, but we were dug in well enough that we didn't sustain any casualties. The fire base is shaping up really well. We have a mud-sod berm on all four sides, with observation posts on each corner, equipped with antipersonnel radar, which detects ground movement at night, so Charlie shouldn't be able to sneak up on us. Firing ports are located on each wall at several locations, and we have strung concertina wire in rows, extending out to over four hundred yards out from the wall. There are strategically placed claymore mines and trip flares, so the sapper team that plans to slip in here may get more than they bargained for. Hack definitely has his shit together! I think I will definitely sleep better now.

There are a hell of a lot of VC around here. Yesterday they ambushed a truckload of ARVN soldiers, about five hundred yards down the road from our position. Colonel Hackworth hopped in his LOH and flew down there to check out the situation. The VC were firing M-79 grenade launchers, AK-47s and machine guns, and it sounded like the Battle of the Bulge. From Danger, we could see Hack's LOH and began to see puffs of smoke going off all around the chopper. A LOH is unarmed, so I knew it had to be coming from the ground.

"Hardcore Six, this is the Big Bandaid. Don't look now, but the little yellow people are shooting at you, boss!"

"You mean to say you are monitoring Alpha Whiskey (automatic weapons) fire being directed at *my* little airplane?"

"Roger that," I replied. Well, he's a nut and comes back with, "Thanks, babe, I think I'd better do an operation Hotel Alpha (haul ass)," and with that this LOH shot straight up about a thousand feet. He called back and said, "Thanks, stud. Appreciate your covering me." To which I replied, "No sweat, sir. Those LOHs cost the taxpayer a lot of money, and we can't afford to lose one!" To which he roared with laughter.

He's quite a guy, and I really get along well with him. He relies on me much more than the previous CO did, and he will frequently call me over to the TOC and take out his maps and go over a particular military operation with me and ask me what I think. He is really interested in medicine, and I share a lot of interesting info with him too. I believe he would perform surgery if I would direct his hands and tell him what to do. There is little he won't try. He has invited me along on several reconnaissance flights, and I really enjoy getting away from the routine in the aid station. Knapp says he is a genuine Korean War hero, having won a battlefield commission from master sergeant to first lieutenant. He has already been awarded five Silver Stars for heroism, and at the rate he is going he will win some more soon. He is about thirty-eight years old and has a home in Germantown, near Memphis. His wife was a senior in nursing school when they married and is now working on her BS in nursing in San Francisco.

Well, I will be going on R & R with two real neat guys. One is Lt. Bob Knapp, a really funny guy who graduated from West Point and who is Bravo Company's commander, and a Lt. Dave Risley who is the battalion adjutant. They are both good friends, and I am looking forward to traveling with them.

Well, precious, I am sitting out in the sun, baking like a potato, so I think I'll close for now and go find some shade.

5 Mar 1969

Giao Duc

I'm sleepy! I just got up and I don't feel like doing a damn thing. So, I will just sit down here and scratch out a few lines to you. Only twelve and a wake-up, and we will be together in Hawaii. It's amazing how time drags when you are waiting for something special. We are still working like dogs on the fire support base. In fact, all the guns are firing right now, and they are about to drive me batty! The concussion almost knocks me off the ammo box I am sitting on as I attempt to write this note. I get so damned tired of hearing those guns go off. Oh Baby, I guess I am just in a foul mood this morning. I shouldn't write when I am. Last night I didn't sleep very well at all. I rolled around

and had nightmares off and on all night long. I guess I really do
need this R & R.

7 Mar 1969

Giao Duc

This will be short as the mail truck is about to pull out. Only
ten and a wake-up, and we will be together again. I can't believe
it is finally happening. I will come in to Hawaii on Pan Am
flight P208 which leaves Tan Son Nhut Airbase near Saigon at
5:30 P.M. on 18 March and arrives in Honolulu at 3:30 P.M. on
18 March. So, thanks to crossing the international date line, I
will arrive there two hours before I actually leave. Is that crazy
or what? Well, a dust-off is coming in with a couple of casualties, so I'll close for now. See you soon.

10 Mar 1969

Giao Duc

Darling, I finished off most of the food tonight. That was such
a nice package. Naturally, I shared it with my men, and they all
send their love and thanks for the goodies. I am sitting in my
bunker at FSB Danger now, and it is hot as hell. I have had a
pretty rough day. Several booby-trap casualties were flown in
here to our little aid station bunker, as we are quite a ways from
Dong Tam, and they were really blown up. We got the bleeding
stopped and got IVs going on all of them about the time the dust-
off choppers arrived to pick them up. Baby, this stupid war is
such a waste! Two of the guys today were real sharp guys and
real good friends of mine. I will never get used to it.

One of my friends just came in with an unreal story. He had been guarding some Viet Cong POWs who were being flown by chopper to division HQ. Well, one of them got untied and tried to push him out of the helicopter. Well, he pushed the VC out the door at twelve hundred feet altitude. They found his remains the next day. I had assisted in the interrogation of the SOB the day he was brought in.

It's amazing how much hate man can build up against his enemy. I'll sure be glad to get back home where I can experience *love* instead of hate. I'm so tired of hate and killing and death. God knows I am tired of this mess! We got mortared two nights ago, but thank God, no one was injured.

We have a fairly good bunker here, so we are fairly safe. Colonel Hackworth said it was all right with him if I transferred to a hospital when my time came, so I will probably be going to "safe country" in April or May. I think I'm ready for it. Being out in the boonies so damn much really wears on your nerves.

11 Mar 1969

Giao Duc

Well, Baby, I got busy with patients last night and didn't get to finish this. It's now 9:00 A.M., and there is a cool breeze blowing through the bunker, and I feel better because in one week we will be together! I still can't believe it. I will go in to Dong Tam on the thirteenth and get my uniforms ready. It will feel funny to have my khakis on. I've had nothing on but jungle fatigues and combat boots for over five months, and it will really feel strange to wear my loafers. I can't wait to find out! Well, a chopper just called in-bound casualties, so I will write later tonight. I continue to see so many gory sights and wounds and dead GIs. I will be so glad to return to a land of *peace*. The word never really meant that much to me before I came over here.

12 Mar 1969

Spec Four Charlie Wintzer just came in with an incredible story. You won't believe the screwup which happened yesterday. One of our fellow units, the 2/39 got into some real heavy contact over near My Phuoc Tay and called for some help. The battlefield was located on a canal near the village of Thanh Phu and was surrounded by open rice paddies. The canal was bordered by foliage surrounding the village where the enemy was holed up. HE rounds had started some of the dry fields burning, and the smoke had reduced visibility to nil. It was almost dark by the time Hack had gotten all our men into position along the north bank of the canal. Hack was flying over the area in his LOH, getting things organized, when all of a sudden he hears Col. Ira "Mickey Mouse" Hunt call in a Cobra gunship to hose down the area with rockets. Hack objected but was ignored, and after two passes by the Cobras, he had his pilot position his LOH directly above his troops, in a hover, with all the navigation lights blazing, just as the Cobra was turning around for his third pass.

Meanwhile, on the ground, one of our fine lieutenants, John Roberson, was on the radio trying to call off the errant fire. Robby and four others were wounded from flying shrapnel.* Wintz told me how he had put Robby's finger back on in a gallant effort to save it and had bandaged it all up, and how he had tried in vain to give the brave young lieutenant an injection of morphine to control the pain. Lieutenant Roberson refused the morphine, saying that he was in command of his platoon, and he felt that no one else was as capable, so he would tough it out

*Lieutenant Roberson never completely recovered from this terrifying experience, and suffered recurring bouts of severe depression, which finally led to his suicide in 1985.

142

until the shit subsided. Wintz also recalled how Robby had looked out at the nearby stream, made a mock gesture of casting a fishing lure, and said, "Hey, no big deal. I can still hold a fly line between these remaining fingers. It could have been worse." What a great soldier, one of the Citadel's finest!

These are the screwups that the American public rarely hears about. They happen often enough over here that we have a term for them—"cluster-fuck"! And the beat goes on . . .

15 Mar 1969

Dong Tam Base

I guess you are packing your bags to come see me. So, you probably won't get this letter until you return, but I've been thinking about you and had to write anyway. I am back at Dong Tam and have gotten my bags packed and my uniform ready. I can't really believe that in three days we will be together! I'm so excited I can hardly stand it. Baby, I'm still a little concerned about how I will seem to you. I know I've changed some. So much has happened to me and around me since I last saw you. One of my very good friends is in critical condition now, and another had his fingers shot off. I've had so many casualties brought in to my little aid station at Giao Duc. I know most of them well, and I can tell it's getting through to me. It's breaking my heart. A little bit of you dies each time you see one of your friends mangled, killed, or mutilated. I can feel myself tied up in knots, so I hope I don't disappoint you. I am still the same old Byron who loves you very much. By the way, I put in my transfer today for the 24th Evacuation Hospital. Cross your fingers.

17 Mar 1969

Prior to R & R Saigon

Wow, do I ever have a hangover this A.M.! Last night, Lt. Bob Knapp, Lt. Dave Risley, and I arrived here in Saigon for a one-night layover before departing for Hawaii. We had a hard time getting away, and I had to wait at Danger till the last minute as Knapper was late coming back in from the field. In fact, he still had his grimy fatigues and boots on when we found a jeep to take us up here. He was delayed because he had to spend extra time with his replacement, Lt. William Torpie, a real neat kid but one with limited command experience in combat situations. Bob was reluctant to leave at all, but he has to get away as he has been under a lot of strain lately, as we all have. Naturally, we headed for a hotel to dump off our stuff and had a nice dinner before heading for the nearest bar. We were at a nice one on Tu Do Street, having a few rounds and swapping war stories, when this older American civilian came over to our stools and said, "I see from your patches that you boys are from the 9th Division. You don't by any chance know Col. David Hackworth do you?" We about flipped and explained that he was our battalion commander. "Well, boys, he is the reason I am over here in Vietnam. I am an army historian, and I am on the way to Fire Base Danger to interview him. He is really quite a famous soldier, and you fellows are really lucky to serve under him!" he replied.

"Yes, sir, we know that from our firsthand experience, and we figure none of us would be alive today if it weren't for Hack," we answered. He seemed to enjoy the company of infantry soldiers and was obviously very knowledgeable about infantry tactics. After a while I asked him if he was in the military.

"No, not any more, but I was in the army for many years. Now I just write about it. In fact, Lieutenant Knapp, I too used to be a company commander, and even wrote a small book about it."

Knapp's eyes met mine, and together we exclaimed, "Holy Shit! You must be Charles B. McDonald! We just finished reading your book!"

"One and the same," he replied.

I had often lain out in the desolate reaches of the Plain of Reeds, reading about his experiences fighting Germans and had really come to admire his courage and abilities. In fact, his book was almost considered required reading for infantry officers. Now we were meeting him in a bar in downtown Saigon. "What a small world we live in," we all exclaimed. Well, after sharing a few more beers and lies, we took off for another bar. After a couple more bars and many more drinks we started trying to find our way back to our hotel. We were all feeling pretty high from the combination of the booze, being on our way to Hawaii, and our incredible experience of meeting Mr. McDonald, and I am sure we were pretty rowdy as we made our way down the dirty sidewalks of Saigon. We were bopping along, minding our business, when all of a sudden a Vietnamese civilian, dressed in dark slacks and blouse, ran over to Knapp and started jabbering something about changing our money to piasters and how much money we could make. He was obviously streetwise and had successfully made this deal before. But he had never met the Knapper before, and Bob started yelling, "He's a dirty VC, let's kill the fucker!" He pulled out a knife—the kind we affectionately called the pigsticker—and started to stab the dude right out in the middle of Tu Do Street. I quickly jumped between them, and as I reached for his knife with my left hand, the blade slapped between my index and middle fingers and sliced them both open. The blood started gushing out of both of them, and the gook took off, running into the darkness. I knew good and well that if Knapp had killed a civilian in the streets of Saigon, he would be treated as any other common criminal; I had heard too many horror stories about the prison system in Saigon to want any part of that. I didn't give a damn about the gook, but I didn't want to give the local National Police any excuse to lock us up. Meanwhile, we wrapped up my fingers and Risley said, "What your fingers need is another drink!" so off we went to the next available bar. The bartender noticed me pouring my bourbon on my wounds and came over and, in broken French-English, offered to let me use some of his antibiotic powders from Paris. He handed me a small yellow packet with red writing, which appeared to be French. I don't know any French, but the word sulfadiazine appeared in letters I could read, so I took off my makeshift dressing, rinsed the wounds with straight Kentucky bourbon, poured the French antibiotic powder into the wounds, which by then were only slightly oozing. I made a bandage from a cloth the bartender gave me.

We finally found our way back to our hotel about 4:00 A.M., and after four-and-one-half hours sleep, I woke up to a throbbing, sore left hand. I got up and caught a cab out to 3d Field Hospital and was sewn up by a corpsman who insulted me by offering to put me in for a Purple Heart for my "wounds sustained in combat zone!" I told him I knew hundreds of brave young men who had earned their Purple Hearts, some posthumously, and he ought to go out in the field and see for himself what goes on over here in the real combat zone.

After a late lunch, it was time to head out to Tan Son Nhut for our freedom bird to Hawaii. What a way to start R & R, I thought.

On the flight over, Knapp kept getting colder and colder and kept piling on more blankets. I reached over and felt his forehead, and he was burning up with fever. All we had to give him was aspirin, and he took two every four hours during the twelve-hour trip. By the time we got to Hawaii, he had to go straight to Tripler Army Hospital. I visited him there later, and they still had not made a definite diagnosis. I sure thought it was malaria.

28 Mar 1969

Fire Support Base Danger Near Giao Duc

Well, darling, I've gotten back from our glorious week in Hawaii, and it's like starting all over again. You wouldn't believe all the crap that happened while I was away. I'm glad I was gone spending time with you, but another part of me feels guilty for not being there when my men needed me. Actually, Captain Schwartz, the air force doc who filled in for me, did a great job from what everyone says.

Bob Knapp's company, Bravo Company, engaged a VC bat-

talion, the 261 Alpha Battalion. He had left his XO, Lt. William J.
Torpie, in charge. Torpie, as he was known to all of us, was
a real neat, clean-cut, all-American type kid, who always had a
big grin on his face and could always find something positive to
say about even the most negative situation. Knapp had been
concerned that Torpie was a little too inexperienced to command a company as he had even limited experience as a platoon
leader. But no seasoned captain-type company commanders
were available, and Knapper had already put off one R & R for
similar reasons. Since he and Dave Risley and I had long ago
planned to take our R & Rs together, he had come to me with
the dilemma. Bob, like myself, had seen his share of combat
with its casualties over the past few months, and we were both
in bad need of a change of scenery, if only for a few days. I told
Knapp that if he tried to cancel his R & R that I would ground
him for medical reasons. He had to agree that his rubber band
was stretched pretty tight and agreed to go. Well, as you know,
it's just as well he did go because he ended up in the hospital
with some wierd tropical febrile illness. He is still at Tripler
General, and word has it that he won't be back to the field. Well,
anyway, after two days of fighting, the HARDCORE had killed
177 Viet Cong, while sustaining only 6 KIAs and 20 WIAs,
with 12 killed in another battalion that was helping us. One of
those killed was Torpie. It seems his men were pinned down in
an open paddy, and for some reason, he stood up and got riddled
by machine-gun fire. I've often seen men break under the intense
pressure of fire, and panic in an effort to just get away from the
present situation. I guess we will never know for sure why he
stood up. I do know that the Knapper is going to be sick when
he hears about it. I was, and I immediately asked myself, What
if you hadn't made Knapp go on R & R? Would Torpie still be
alive? The Knapper never would have stood up in the heat of
battle. Torpie was such a sweet, good kid, and I will never forget
his grin. I was also told that Hack was coming down for the
third time to pick up wounded men when his bird took heavy
AK-47 fire from the wood line, and he and three others were
shot in their legs. They told me he had loaded up his chopper to
the point where there wasn't any room for him inside, so he
stood on the skids as the chopper slowly labored to lift its heavy
load up and out of the hot LZ. He really is one brave SOB! I'm
sure he was scared too, but he sure handles it in a cool way. We
all get scared, but some just seem to show it less than others. I

have been scared shitless on several occasions, and my medics would say later, "Shit, Doc, you didn't even act like you were scared at all." Well, on the inside, you are real scared. I'm just thankful for the ability to keep it on the inside. Anyway, Hack is now at 24th Evac recovering from a gunshot wound and should return to FSB Danger in a few days.

While I was gone, two of my medics were seriously wounded, and two others re-upped for three more years in order to get out of the field and into a rear-echelon job. I really can't blame them, as both had seen a lot. It's just that I am shorthanded now and will have to go out more myself until I get replacements. It used to be kinda fun and exciting, but that has worn off after seeing so many fine young men die.

I just got back from the TOC, where they are displaying the spoils of the latest operation. They captured a bunch of VC flags, like the one I sent home, and one large red flag with a yellow hammer and sickle on it. There was a picture of Ho Chi Minh pinned to it. They also captured several hundred weapons, including Chicom SKS rifles, AK-47s, a huge pile of grenades, some captured M-16s, RPGs, claymore mines, tons of ammo, machine guns, and an antiaircraft gun. They also had a bunch of pith helmets, some camouflaged with grass, as well as VC ammo pouches.

Three nights ago, the Viet Cong blew up the ammo dump at Dong Tam. The explosion was unreal. A chopper flying overhead was blown into tiny pieces, and the blast leveled buildings four to five hundred yards away. Many soldiers' bodies were never found. Our aid station, which is located on the far side of the base near the helipad, had all its light bulbs blown out, and all the supplies were knocked off the shelves from the concussion. To top it off, one of my close friends apparently had a paranoid schizophrenic break. It's so pitiful, he was such a damn fine officer who had done an outstanding job over here. He was certainly headed for a general's slot. All that is probably lost now. They said he just started babbling irrationally and thought that those closest to him were plotting against him. I had known he was tied up in knots pretty badly, like the rest of us at times, but I really didn't expect him to snap. I just feel awful about it. He was such a cool head under fire. It just reinforces in my mind the massive amount of mental pressure we are all under over here, especially those of us out in the field. I guess it's sort of like an iceberg, only a minor portion of the problem is visible on the surface.

Baby, there are some really good articles on Vietnam in the 8 February 1969 *Saturday Evening Post*. You should try to get hold of one and read it. It expresses so many of the feelings I have and am having a hard time expressing myself. We all tend to want to bury this whole damn Nam experience and forget it, and I'm not so sure that will be good for us after we get back home. Time will tell! I don't agree with their opinion about stopping all our offensive operations, but they put it so beautifully when they said that every soldier who returns from Nam alive does so with a terribly frustrating sense of bewilderment and guilt.

I'm doing OK, Baby, I just miss you so much, that's all. Our six wonderful days in Hawaii seem so very far behind me now that I am back out in the boonies at FSB Danger. They are now just a sweet and wonderful memory.

Baby, I've thought and prayed about it a lot, and I think the best thing for me to do is to try and get transferred to a hospital whenever possible. Things are getting worse in the field, and I don't know what we are proving over here. So, I'll be ready to go when my transfer comes through. I'll miss my men, but they, too, come and go, with too many of them leaving in body bags. I'm sure I will always have a real warm spot in my heart for the 4/39, but I don't feel like I can take another six months of seeing so many good friends killed and mutilated. At least at the evac hospital the casualties will be unknown to me. It hurts so much more when they are boys you have lived with, laughed with, and cried with, day and night for months on end.

2 Apr 1969

FSB Danger

Well, Baby, I'm back in the swing of things. For the past two nights I have gone flying around the Delta with a good friend, Lt. Larry Tahler, call sign Nighthunter 6. Larry was a platoon leader with Bravo Company under Capt. Bruce Hartshorn when Colonel Hart was the CO. They made a great team as both are bright, energetic, and aggressive people. Hartshorn with his pale blue eyes and bottlebrush mustache, could present a real sinister appearance when he wasn't smiling. At one point, he and I considered decapitating one of the dead Viet Cong to try to get a skull, but word of our plans got out, and our attempts were foiled. It is incredible to consider what this action called "war" will do to the minds of ordinarily civilized human beings. Hatred of the "enemy" is manifested in many different and sordid ways. Lieutenant Tahler's and Hack have devised this real neat tactic for hunting Charlie at night, which heretofore has been his time to come out and play. They figured that most of the enemy's supplies are moved at night by sampan, so they outfitted two M-60 machine guns with Starlight Scopes and mounted them in the doors of a Huey helicopter. We fly along, about 100 to 150 feet above the rivers and canals, looking through our Starlight Scopes, and when we spot a sampan, we open fire. Our machine guns are loaded with tracer rounds, so a red stream of bullets marks the target area, and then we pull up and let the two Cobra gunships, which are flying above us, swoop down on the target area to hose it down with minigun and rocket fire. It is an incredibly exciting way to destroy the enemy. You wouldn't believe the tremendous secondary explosions which occurred last night when we hit a small convoy of sampans. It lit up the whole area for a mile or so around. The concussion even shook our bird. It seems like a fairly safe way to hunt Charlie, compared to sloshing through the paddies, mud, and booby traps. The local civilians know all about the dusk-to-dawn curfew, so if we see any movement on the water, and it doesn't look like U.S. riverine craft, we let them have it. Last night, I was on one of the machine guns and spotted five sampans, and before they could fire at us, I plastered them with tracer fire, and then watched as the Cobras dropped down and rained death and destruction on them. Larry estimated the body count at thirty VC dead to zero GIs killed or wounded. That's the kind of odds we need to keep up to ever win this damn war. Hack is ecstatic about the early success of the program. We are finally outguerrillaing the guerrilla—shortened to "out-*G* the *G*" as our new slogan has become known around the AO.

Oh, I've been meaning to tell you a neat story about my jet flight back from Hawaii. After we were well on our way, the pilot announced that he was going to open the cockpit door and anyone who wanted to could come up front and sit for awhile.

Well, quite a few fellows went up, and after a while the crowd slacked off, so I went up as we were approaching the Philippine Islands. The pilot was a real John Wayne look-alike from Houston, Texas, with white hair and a real southern drawl. He was a former U.S. Marine and had fought in the Philippines during World War II. After a little while, he leaned forward and pointed to a little crescent-shaped atoll and said, "Well, boys, that little chunk of dirt was my home for over ten months, back before most of you were born. In my wildest dreams back then, I never could have imagined that thirty years later I would be flying over that tiny island twice a week, hauling young GIs to another war in this part of the world. In fact, guys, I never believed I would survive to grow up and return home, much less live long enough to become an old white-haired airline captain!" He might have had white hair, but he looked tan and lean and in real good condition, and we all had the feeling that he could have deplaned in Nam and gone off humping the boonies with us and survived again. What a small world!

I hope I never see Vietnam again after I leave here. I really hate the place and the people. It's such a dump. I had another VC die in my aid station today. Some of our grunts shot him just down the road from here, with an M-60 machine gun. He was really torn up, and his BP was 30/0, and his pupils were dilated and barely reactive. I got an angiocath started on him, and he arrested on us. He was all shot up across the groin and was almost shot completely in two. He looked terrible. I get so damn tired of seeing all this death. I'm tired of hating. I want to return to a place where people don't hate so much, but I can't help hating Charlie. He is so ruthless and has killed so many of my friends. Baby, I know I will never forget Vietnam, but I do hope I will be able to put it way back in a distant corner of my mind. All this hatred and killing have really brought out the worst in me.

6 Apr 1969

FSB Danger

Well, Baby, my transfer came back today from USARV HQ approved pending satisfactory replacement. So now begins the waiting game. It could be as early as one week or as long as six to eight weeks. I am definitely ready as Nam has taken its toll on my nervous system. So I'm kind of glad, but sad, too, in a way, to be leaving my men. But I'm ready to go into a real hospital, where I can start being a professional again, instead of a hell-raising GI!

Today is Easter Sunday, but it seems just like any other day over here. It is about 9:00 P.M., and I am sitting here in my little aid station bunker. The place is full of guys, ten in all, playing cards, smoking, and raising hell to the sounds of AFVN radio. They're all good friends, but I will welcome some privacy. This black "soul-man" DJ just started his program, and he said, "All you boys are thinking about your girls . . . she may be twenty-four thousand miles away or she may be in Memphis, Tennessee!" and in unison they all stopped what they were doing and looked at me as we all cracked up laughing!

We just got through working on a poor kid's hand. He had lost two big flaps of skin off his knuckles, and you could see all his tendons and cartilage. He really needed a skin graft, but I thought I could repair it with a primary closure, so we infiltrated it with xylocaine and undermined the edges of the flaps and stretched them until they would cover the defect, and sutured them together. We wrapped it in Vioform gauze and splinted his hand so he couldn't move his fingers for a couple of weeks, and it looked pretty good when we finished. Wintzer assisted me. These medics all make real good assistant surgeons. He probably could have done as good a job as I did, but I always give the boys the best available. I've always considered myself a good surgeon, and my experiences over here have verified that in my mind. Not bragging, but if you don't think you are good, you

152

probably aren't! It takes a certain kind of confidence to be a good surgeon, and everybody can't do it.

I saw in the Pacific *Stars & Stripes* today that you've had some real nice spring weather in the sixties and seventies recently. I know you welcome the change. I was sorry to hear that you had started to peel. Naturally, I am still brown as a berry.

Knapper still hasn't returned. He is supposed to be back in a few days, but nothing definite yet.

I wish we could have had all that extra time together too, but I'm much better off to remain healthy. I guess I'm tough as old nails or something because I never really get down bad, not since my high fever in December. I slept really well last night for the first time in ages, and it was great to wake up feeling rested.

I read recently that we have had more casualties in Vietnam than were sustained in the Korean War. We are averaging forty-nine dead GIs per day! I'm really fed up with this place. It's not worth the blood of so many Americans, and I wish they would pull all the troops out and let Charlie and the ARVNs fight it out. I would put my money on Charlie to win if and when that happens.

I'm hoping that by getting to a hospital it won't be so hard on me, as I won't know the guys they bring in and it will be less personal. It didn't take me long to get back in the groove after returning from R & R, but that same old feeling about casualties remains. Last night we dusted-off four boys from Knapper's Company. They had brought them in here about 11:00 P.M. for us to stabilize them for dust-off to 24th Evac. One of them had most of his teeth blown out and his lips all cut up from a booby trap that exploded in his face. He was so pitiful. I don't worry about getting killed like I did before coming over here. I guess I just have too much faith to worry about such things. But I do worry about the effect all this killing and dying and sorrow has had on me. I may come home without any visible scars, but I can assure you there are many scars way down deep inside me that may never heal. You can't be exposed to all that I have seen, felt, smelled, and heard and not have it affect you.

10 Apr 1969

FSB Danger

Well, Baby, I am lying around the old aid station tonight, listening to AFVN radio, and they are playing "Please Release Me" by Englebert Humperdinck. It really reminds me of you and just how much I love you and miss you. Music is such an important morale factor over here. Between mail call and the music from AFVN, I somehow manage to avoid going out of my tree. There is one real crazy DJ over here who starts off each morning show with a long-drawn-out "Good morning, Vietnam!" and then he starts cracking on the place and what a bummer it is for us to have to be over here, halfway around the world away from our loved ones. I don't know how he gets away with it, but the troops really love him. He is our answer to Hanoi Hannah, and he will frequently sign off with "and up your nose with that info, Hannah!"

Last night I had a real close call, thanks to someone else's mind not being on his business. The night started out with a 10:00 P.M. Nighthunter operation out of Firebase Danger. As we were putting on our helmets and headsets, the pilot asked Lieutenant Tahler if it would be OK with him if we just went for a joyride as it was to be his last mission, and he really didn't want to do any treetop flying this particular night. Larry came back with, "Well, it's nowhere near my last fucking night, and I want to go out and shoot some fucking gooks! Right, Doc?" "Roger that, Nighthunter!" I answered. The pilot and copilot shrugged their shoulders, and we took off for the Plain of Reeds and our usual area of operation. It was a dark night, with a sliver of a moon in the western sky, but the stars were out, with just a few puff clouds floating by. We could see the streams and canals as dimly lit silver highways crisscrossing the blackness of the uninhabited jungles and swamps gliding by below us. We flew for about an hour and a half without any contact and had turned back south towards the Mekong River, which we could see off on the horizon, when all of a sudden, the night sky was lit up by a blinding flash, which appeared to come from directly below us. Simultaneously, there was a tremendous concussion and explosion, which shook our chopper so bad it almost flipped onto its side. I was on the low side, and it felt like I was going to fall out the open door as the slick continued to shudder. The pilot had his hands full trying to keep us airborne, while the copilot was flipping frequencies on the radio. "Shit, man, we've been hit!" someone said over the net as I looked at Larry, who raised his eyebrows and turned his palms up as if to say, "Who the fuck knows what is going on?" Listening to the radio chatter, it didn't take us long to learn that we had strayed into a free-fire zone for the eight-inch guns and that one of their shells had exploded right under our bird. The pilot, a CWO (chief warrant officer), had failed to check with div arty before planning our AO for the night, and his absentmindedness had almost cost all of us our lives. When we all realized what had happened, we agreed to his request to go joyriding for the rest of the night, and we spent the next two hours flying up and down the middle of the Mekong River at an altitude of about two thousand feet. No one even looked for sampans. The reality of our close call was too fresh in our minds to want to take any chances with this mentally preoccupied short-timer of a pilot. As we descended back into Fire Base Danger, about midnight, I said a short prayer of thanksgiving for another close call survived. The pilot apologized as he dropped us off. We told him to forget it as he had been great in the past, and he, too, was allowed to be human.

11 Apr 1969

FSB Danger Giao Duc, South Vietnam

I'm OK, just bored and lonesome, that's all. This damn place is driving me batty. I'm so damn tired of being in the field. I've become a grouchy old man, and I think it's really time for a change. I resent being bothered for anything except a patient that's bleeding to death or at least sick as hell! I've been having a hard time sleeping. I sleep on an air mattress on the hard floor of our aid station bunker, affectionately known as Giao Duc General. It's pretty uncomfortable. I roll around all night and have been having some weird dreams. I'm so damn bored with this job. Maybe my transfer will come through soon, and I can get back into a real hospital environment. I really do miss hospital work. I'm just another grubby GI out here, whose life isn't worth a plugged nickle! At first it was real exciting being out in the combat zone where all the action was, but lately it's beginning to become a pain in the ass! Oh well, please forgive my bitch, bitch, bitch, but I do need to complain to somebody.

We had another man killed today. The poor fellow had only been with the battalion for one week, so I didn't really know him, but it still hurts to see a healthy young man turned into a lifeless form in a torn, bloody uniform. He had half of his chest blown away, and he really never knew what hit him. Thank God his parents couldn't see what he looked like when we got to him. It just tears your guts out. You never get used to the smell of a bloody death and that sticky feeling that comes from handling a bloody corpse. One of my medics was shot through the wrist in the same fight and another in the foot. It just seems like such a damn waste!

14 Apr 1969

Giao Duc

Well, I've got reports from two reliable sources that my transfer should come through by the end of April. So I'm kind of anxious to move on and see what lies ahead. I'm so dormant, mentally speaking, that I feel like I really need to dust the cobwebs out. I sure hope I get the kind of assignment I want, although anything would be an improvement over what I have now! I'm tired of living in a ten-by-fifteen-foot bunker with five other men! One of the most frustrating things about being over here is just seeing men all day long and not ever being able to just talk to a female. Don't get me wrong Baby, it's just that living day after day after day with eight-hundred men is just not very pleasant. I don't want any other females, but it would be nice to work around a real bonafide nurse. I wouldn't care if she weighed three-hundred pounds and wore horn-rimmed glasses! I hope you know what I mean. I'm sure you got tired of living with several hundred nursing students, it's sort of the same thing. It's like going to an all-boys school or something.

There's not too much new happening over here. Just more of the same old crap. Knapper never did come back. I really question whether he will return or not. We have tried to find out something about him, but have not been able to so far. Got to run. Dust-off coming in with two WIAs.

16 Apr 1969

FSB Danger Giao Duc

Today I'm *happy*! My replacement is in Dong Tam, undergoing orientation at the headquarter's company and will be out today. How does that grab you? I will be out of the field soon, and you can breathe a lot easier. I will hang around here for a few days, getting the new doc oriented to the 4/39, and then I will get Casey to drive me on up to the 90th Replacement Battalion at Long Binh where I first entered Nam. I can't believe it is really happening! And today makes exactly six months, *halfway home*! It's all downhill from here, baby. This will have to be short as I have a bunker full of patients, and I want to get this in the mail. I'm trying to get a MARS call through to you on the portable MARS station, which will be here for a few days. If I don't get through to you, I will call you from Long Binh.

24 Apr 1969

Long Binh

Believe it or not, between trips to Long Binh and Saigon and Dong Tam and Giao Duc, and two going-away parties, I have been going like a madman since I last wrote to you. Darling, I really lucked out. I have been assigned to 3d Field Hospital in Saigon, about one-half mile from Tan Son Nhut Airbase. It's the nicest hospital in Vietnam, and I still can't believe it's for real. You might recall my former MSC officer, Dick Alexander, is the registrar there, so through him, I know quite a few people there. That's the same place Dr. Max Mass was assigned when I ran into him last December. I'll send you some pictures soon so you can see how safe and secure it is.

I came up to Long Binh yesterday to get checked into the 68th Medical Group and spent the night in the transient BOQ. After supper, I went to see a movie, *The Young Runaways*. It was pretty good. Well, Baby, I've got to run as someone is here to take me down to Saigon. Will write more tonight.

Much later. Well, Baby, as usual, I got shafted. Instead of going to 3d Field Hospital, I am at the 218th Medical Dispensary in downtown Saigon. It's really not a bad place, but it's not OJT in ophthalmology, either! Colonel Thomas said he would try to work something out for me, but I will be surprised if he does. Down here, I have my own air-conditioned office, bedroom, and bathroom, so that's a great improvement over the boonies, but it's not what they promised me. I'm just kinda blue but I'll be OK. The dispensary is located in an old hotel, right on busy Tran Hung Dao street in downtown Saigon, and the view from the roof at night is really quite spectacular as the building is six stories tall. Nighttime covers up all the dirt and poverty, and all the lights look like a Christmas tree. Off in the distance you can see flares and occasional flashes from artillery explosions in the outlying areas.

25 Apr 1969

218th Dispensary Saigon

I have been so blue and depressed the last couple of days. I just feel like I'm in a shell and can't get out. Everybody here at the dispensary is real nice, and it's the greatest assignment a guy could ask for here in Vietnam, but I was really counting on getting some OJT in ophthalmology, and I'm afraid it won't happen now. I'm sure this will be a nice place to finish up my tour; it's just that I don't feel like I belong here now. It's hard to explain how I feel on paper, but I just go around with a lump in my throat and feel like crying. Isn't that silly? I don't think I'm flipping my lid or anything like that. I'm just very tired, and I know my nerves are pretty jangled up. I guess that a week or two in this nice environment will help me considerably. Please don't worry about me, Baby, it's just that I need to talk to you about it, and this will have to do. Please continue to pray for me, darling.

26 Apr 1969

Saigon

Dear Mom and Dad,

How are you two doing? I finally found time to listen to your entire tape. I can't tell you how much I enjoyed it. Especially the part where you two just sat there and laughed and talked and teased, just like you would do if I was sitting there with y'all. The "mass confusion" tapes are fun too, but they are kind of hard to decipher sometimes.

Dad, enclosed is my driver's license. Please see if you can get it renewed for me. Tell them I would love to do it in person if I could! The oranges arrived in fine shape along with the picture. Thank you both.

Dad, I am sitting at my desk in my air-conditioned office looking at the copy of "If" by Rudyard Kipling that you gave me to bring me luck over here. You'll never know how many times I have read that when I was depressed and thought about you, and it has picked me up. You're a great dad, and I know I have enough of you in me to make it through almost anything. I have been real blue lately but just listening to your tape and laughing along with y'all really helps. I should be real happy. I have my own air-conditioned room, my own flush commode, hot and cold running water, *and* shower. What more could a guy ask for after living out in the jungle for six months! I do miss my friends in the battalion and feel guilty living in the lap of luxury while they continue to live out in the boonies, but I'm sure that will pass with time. Only five-and-one-half months and I will be home, back in the real World. I know this has to be the longest year of my life, although one from which I will profit much, I am sure.

Mom, you asked about the monsoons. They should begin in another month or so. Thank goodness, I will be inside.

Well, I must run to make the movie in time. How's that for a switch? I love you both much more than I can express in my letters. I hope you know that. You truly are the finest parents a man could ask for, and I'll always love y'all for the way in which you have stood behind me through thick and thin.

29 Apr 1969

218th Medical Dispensary Saigon

How are you, precious? Fine, I hope, and better than me, I trust. I just can't seem to kick the blues. I have been very frustrated and depressed for several days now, and I don't know what to do about it. I don't guess there is really anything I can do about it. I really thought that getting out of the field would be great, but it's like my nerves held on until I could get out, and now they are shot. My hands shook when I was doing a simple I and D of an abscess this A.M., and it was embarrassing as hell. My hands never shook during hundreds of deliveries in medical school and internship, not to mention hundreds of operations during the past six months under very trying circumstances. I've dreamed of being an eye surgeon for years now, and it will kill me if the shakes continue. I'm sure it is just some kind of decreased-stress syndrome and that it will pass once I can get out of this place. But right now it is pretty scary. One of the medics tried to get me to take some Valium, but I have never had to rely on nerve pills, and I sure as hell don't want to start now. Please pray for me, and I'm sure it will all work out soon. I think part of it is the feeling of guilt I keep having about leaving so many of my friends out in the mud and grime of the field, while I sleep on clean white sheets in air-conditioned comfort.

I really have a thing about these "Saigon warriors" who think they have been to war and have never left the relative safety of the city. They have never had to undergo the mental and physical strain that is part of a grunt's daily existence, where the highlight of any day is mail call. Half of these REMFs have girlfriends with apartments or villas and live there with them. I don't think I am going to be very popular with them, but I have started looking into just who sleeps in their beds and who doesn't, and all hell will break loose when I put a stop to their little pillow games. They are officially AWOL if they are sleeping off army property, and if we had an offensive, we would be in big trouble. None of them even clean their weapons, so I kind of feel like Hack did when he came to the HARDCORE. They need their asses kicked, and I'm in the mood to do it.

30 Apr 1969

218th Medical Dispensary Saigon

I'm feeling OK but am still quite depressed. I really don't know why. I guess it's just a combination of things. I just want to come home so badly. I've tried praying and reading the Bible, but nothing seems to give me any peace of mind. I feel like I'm absentminded or something. Kind of like I'm held together by Scotch Tape and would fall apart if somebody shook me real hard. I know it sounds crazy. I never felt that way out in the field under fire, but now I feel so strange. I will just have to keep my chin up and try to do the best I can. I know there is no way I can come home early, so I will just have to make the best of my situation here. I just kind of go around with a lump in my throat and feel like I'm going to burst out crying over nothing, and meanwhile, I try to put on a facade of happiness and well-being, but I wonder who I'm fooling. I'm all knotted up inside and find it extremely difficult to engage in anything more than passing conversation with anyone. I just hope that my emotions don't interfere with my functions as a physician. I don't believe it has yet because, even with the shakes, I'm still a very good surgeon. Perhaps time will help. I sure hope so.

1 May 1969

218th Medical Dispensary Saigon

Psychologically I'm doing much better, but I'm sorta under the weather physically. I've got a little fever, some diarrhea, and general malaise. Am also nauseated, so I got one of my medics to pop me in the butt with 10 mg of Compazine—the old standby. Took two Fiorinal and am going to bed soon. We just got another new doc from the field, and the poor guy shakes worse than I do. He reminds me of the way I was when I first got here. I'm going to be all right, Baby. I do feel 100 percent better!

4 May 1969

Sunday Evening 218th Medical Dispensary

I'm doing real well this evening. Sunday is not just another day now like it was in the field. We shut down except for emergencies and rotate call, so I've had the entire day off to read, sleep, etc. I just got through eating a T-bone steak, tossed salad, french fries, and ice cream, topped off with a cold Budweiser, so I am content as possible under the circumstances.

Every Sunday afternoon we go to the BOQ #1, which is near Tan Son Nhut Airbase and houses majors and colonels. They have a steak house there that is really something. It's just as nice as any restaurant back in the States, and for $2.25 you can get a delicious T-bone steak cooked to order. Just walking in and sitting down inside the place is like an in-country R & R after living out in the boonies of the Mekong Delta. It's nice to just get out and have a little change of scenery.

I'm real happy at the 218th, and my CO said he thought I would be here until my DEROS in October, so I'm hoping it will be so. Last night was a bad night. I was up till 3:30 A.M. and then got called again at 6:00 A.M., so I slept in from 8:00 till 1:00 P.M. I had one fellow who had been struck over the head in a brawl in a bar on Tu Do Street and had a deep laceration through a scalp artery. I have never seen so much blood from one small cut. His front and back, from the top of his head to the top of his shoes, was covered with clotted blood, and he was still spurting like a geyser! I finally got a couple of figure eights with catgut in the area and got the flow stopped so I could then go about closing the laceration with mattress sutures. His BP had fallen to 70/0, with a rapid pulse, and he had passed

out. I was afraid he might arrest on us, so we had to give him a
unit of whole blood through one arm while I ran in a liter of
Ringer's lactate in the other. Naturally, he was stoned drunk.

Then I had two poor guys with acute bladder obstruction and
bladders as big as basketballs. I had to catherize both of them
with Foley's, with dramatic results. It's beginning to remind me
of Stateside emergency-room duty, so I am enjoying it. Thank
goodness, it's only every fourth or fifth night over here. It sure
is nice to be a doctor again in a nice environment. They even
address us as "Doctor" rather than "Captain." Well, we were
going to show a movie tonight, but something happened to the
film, so we won't see one after all. I guess I'll just read instead.
I really do have a lot of time to myself now. Just the opposite of
what I had in the 4/39th. I'm beginning to feel almost civilized
again, Baby. I still hate gooks, and I'm sure I always will . . . to
some extent anyway.

I'm in real good spirits now and I think I can do OK until I
see you on R & R in Hawaii in July. And then it will be all
downhill from there. Won't that be great to know that this whole
empty depressing year is behind us? By the way, you can bring
my medical school class ring to Hawaii in July. I think I can
wear it now without worrying about getting shot and losing it
to some Viet Cong.

Speaking of VC, they have detonated quite a few bombs
around Saigon lately, and I spent four hours the other night
digging hundreds of shrapnel fragments out of one poor civilian's back, buttocks, legs, and the back of his head. What a mess
he was!

5 May 1969

218th Medical Dispensary Saigon

There's not too much to write about. I'm keeping fairly busy
and am really beginning to feel better. I don't have as many
aggravations to put up with as I did in the 4/39. One of my
medics was killed the week I left the battalion. One can't ever

get used to that sort of thing. At least here, I am not involved personally with any of my patients and don't really treat many friends, which does make it a lot easier. Of course, here I don't have many friends at all, so this makes it much more lonely. It really seems to be every man for himself here in "REMF City"! By the way, my telephone number here in Saigon is 60041,42, or 43, extension 103 or 106. It seems strange to even have a phone number again after six months of living out in the boonies.

11 May 1969

218th Medical Dispensary Saigon

I guess I really haven't told you too much about my new surroundings. The dispensary is located on the main drag of downtown Saigon, Tran Hung Dao Street, and is located in a six-story building, which used to house the 17th Field Hospital, complete with three operating rooms. There is a five-story dormitory located directly behind the dispensary, which is connected by covered walkways at each level. I live on the 5th floor and have a suite, consisting of a bedroom, bathroom, and study. It's really quite nice. Not modern but 100 percent nicer than the boonies! At least it's cool and private. My only complaint is that, on the top floor, the pigeons and other birds make a hell of a squawking sound at night. I am still a very light sleeper, but it's still better than the boonies. I suppose I'll get used to them. I got used to sleeping through cannon fire all night, so I guess I can get used to anything.

I run the minor surgery and venereal disease clinics, and the emergency room Mondays through Fridays—8:00 A.M. to noon and 1:00 to 5:00 P.M.—and Saturdays, 8:00 A.M. to noon. I'm on call for ER every fourth or fifth night. My working quarters are in an all-green-tiled OR, converted to examining rooms. It is quite nice. I have a good X-ray department for chest and fracture diagnoses. We also have a lab and a blood bank. I have a Bovie electrocautery to treat venereal warts. Approximately two afternoons a week, I do physical exams on anywhere from twenty to sixty GIs and local civilians. What a pain! We have a little mamma-san, who cooks three meals per day for us, and she is a pretty good cook. We have breakfast at 7:30, lunch from 12:00 to 1:00 and supper from 5:00 to 6:00. Each night there is a movie shown in a large air-conditioned room converted into a theater, usually with fifty or so in attendance. They usually run from 7:30 till 9:00 or 9:30, and on Saturday and Sunday, they run the same flick both nights. Last night we saw *Skidoo* with Carol Channing and Jackie Gleason, and it wasn't very good. In fact they show very few good ones, but at least it's a safe way to pass the time away. The other night we saw *I Love You Alice B. Toklas* with Peter Sellers. It was quite funny in spots but pretty boring in lots of other places. It seems like they don't produce many good movies anymore. I'll never forget *Doctor Zhivago*. Now that was a movie! Also, *Gone With the Wind*. I guess I'm just getting old or something, but all this mod, beatnik, flower-power crap just doesn't move me one bit. I don't think I'm a square, but I'm definitely not "hip."

13 May 1969

218th Medical Dispensary Saigon

I guess you have heard or read about the increased amount of terrorist activity in and around Saigon over the past few days. We have had quite a few civilian casualties brought in here, all shot up with different types of shrapnel wounds. I really do feel sorry for the civilian population over here because I am sure they have become very confused and tired of all the years of fighting, and they, more than anyone, are the victims of all this madness called war. I hope someday they can truly know peace as we know it in America, whether it be under democratic or communist rule. It's such an ugly war, and I am so hopeful that the peace talks will become productive soon. On the other hand, I am quite pessimistic about dealing with lying, cheating Communists over a bargaining table, no matter what shape it is. I do know one thing for sure, I am fed up with our involvement in this sorry country. I have talked to Hack about it and, although he won't say it publicly yet, he believes the VC will prevail. Not because we can't defeat them on the battlefield, but because the powers in charge won't let us fight the battle the way it should be fought. After our rout of the 261 Alpha Main Force Battalion, all these generals and colonels came out to FSB Danger to see the spoils of the battle, but not one was interested in Hack's offers to sit down and let him show them why he felt we had been successful and what he felt could be done in the other battalions in the 9th Division to improve their performance. I think they all believe he was just grandstanding, but I know that he really cares, and he obviously knows his business.

15 May 1969

218th Medical Dispensary Saigon

I just got back from 3d Field Hospital, where I shot the breeze with Dick Alexander, my former MSC Officer in Dong Tam. We had a few rum and Cokes, followed by a delicious filet mignon steak dinner, and then downed a few beers afterward. I tell you, darling, I'm really out of shape as far as drinking is concerned, and I feel pretty tipsy right now. So please excuse the grammatical errors! It really is nice to have the luxury of a night off, with no responsibility, which affords the opportunity of having a few drinks with your friends without worrying about incoming choppers loaded with casualties. After dinner, I had a seven-mile taxi ride back downtown to the 218th. The cab driver, a small, funny-looking Vietnamese, had some sort of nervous disorder, and all of a sudden, without warning, he would start making all sorts of crazy involuntary movements of his head and shoulders and make strange grunting sounds. Well, if I had been cold sober, I would have been filled with pity for the poor devil, but being a little high just made it all seem hilarious, and I had a real hard time maintaining my composure. I kept thinking, It's bad enough riding through the hectic, crowded streets of Saigon at night in a tiny, blue-and-yellow cab with a normal driver, but this is really too much. If Knapp had been along, it would have been a riot. He must have had Huntington's chorea or something similar. He sure made some weird gyrations, and all the while he successfully drove his little cab through very heavy traffic composed of thousands of rickshaws, bicycles, and Honda mopeds. We didn't hit anyone, and I was real glad when the 218th came into view.

18 May 1969

218th Medical Dispensary Saigon

Today is Sunday, and we went down to the Rex Hotel and ate at the roof-top restaurant. The view from up there is really neat, and it lifts you away from the smells and sounds and dirt of the city, and it looks like any European city, with tree-lined streets and lots of large buildings of French colonial design. We are going to the Blue Diamond restaurant tonight, where they are supposed to serve delicious Vietnamese cuisine, and it is reputed to be clean and safe. There are three or four doctors who always go on Sunday evenings, and they invited me along, so we shall see.

I will have to work next Sunday, so I am really enjoying just lying around reading in bed today. I didn't get up till about ten, then showered and picked up around my suite until time for lunch. This afternoon I have been reading up on some general surgery.

Well, I just returned from a delicious dinner of Vietnamese-style sweet-and-sour pork, served over a bed of hot white rice, and wet my whistle on a small glass of sake. It is pretty potent. I just had a tiny demitasse, yet I could feel it a short time later. I ate the entire meal with chop sticks. I'm getting quite proficient with them, you know. Today is my sister Barbara's birthday. I think she turned thirty-one.

21 May 1969

218th Medical Dispensary Saigon

Well, darling, I had a real good morning. I went over to 3d Field Hospital and assisted Dr. Joe Elia, staff ophthalmologist, in surgery for a few hours, and it was really neat. We did a lateral rectus muscle resection and medial rectus recession on a Vietnamese woman with strabismus, commonly known as walleye. This is the opposite of cross-eyed, where the eyes turn in. This woman's right eye turned out toward her right ear, and after surgery it was straight. It was so much fun! Intricate as hell, and he let me do some suturing with those tiny little instruments and needles. I did fine—almost no sign of the shakes. He was quite complimentary, so now I know I will be OK to go ahead with my plans to get into ophthalmology residency when I get out of the army in 1970.

We also did a blepharoplasty or ''lid-lift'' on a lady with droopy lids, and I did quite a bit of the suturing there too. I am planning on helping him with a couple of cataract operations early in the morning, and I can hardly wait! I am planning to spend two mornings a week in surgery and one afternoon in the eye clinic, so that really gives me something to look forward to.

There's not much else to write about as I've had a nice easy day and it's almost time for the movie. Then I will probably read until about 11:00 P.M., and then call it a night. What a contrast to the job of a battalion surgeon! I occasionally pinch myself to see if it's for real. I am still having some nightmares about the VC and the horrors of the past six months, but it's getting better with each day away from it. I think being away from all the serious casualties like they have at 24th Evac helps a lot too. I know it's still going on, but since I don't see them, hear them, and smell the blood and death, it's a lot better.

22 May 1969

218th Medical Dispensary Saigon

It has rained cats and dogs here today. The monsoon season is really upon us now. Thank goodness, I'm out of the field. It's really a mess out there now, and you can't always get air support when you need it when it's so nasty. I was really lucky as it only rained for the first month or two when I was in the field. I heard from some of the guys in the 4/39 that the Knapper is stationed in Hawaii and that Lieutenant Risley is in the hospital with malaria. I guess I have really been lucky not to have gotten really sick or wounded over here. I have been plagued with diarrhea since moving to Saigon, but I continue to gain weight in spite of the runs.

You asked what DEROS meant. That is the day I go home, October 16. It stands for *D*ate (of) *E*stimated *R*otation *O*f *Ser*vice. That's the day everyone lives for, 365 days per year, here in the Nam. You mentioned how pretty Saigon looked from the air in the postcard. Well, it may look beautiful from the air, but it's a filthy, stinking place. No photograph could ever capture the stench—seriously, it's nauseating!

1 Jun 1969

218th Medical Dispensary Saigon

Well, here I am working in the dispensary ER, complete with surgical scrub suit just like I wore back in the real World at Baptist Memorial Hospital in Memphis. All I need is my old white lab coat—and you—and I would feel right at home. Also, I've had the usual Saturday night crocks!

Today I had a surprise visit from some of my old buddies from the HARDCORE Battalion. They were in Saigon enroute to an R & R in Australia. They brought some sad news that one of my medics was killed last week. He was a hell of a fine kid, big handsome boy about twenty-three, with a pretty wife and two sweet little children. He had been a conscientious objector (CO) when he first came to Nam, but had not been here long before he had asked me to show him how to shoot a rifle, and I had gotten him an M-16 of his own. I am very sad to learn of his death. He was quite a nice guy, and I remember telling him less than two weeks ago that his chances of getting killed over here were almost nil if he would just keep his head down. Oh, darling, this whole thing is such a waste of good American lives. I'll never get used to hearing about friends of mine getting killed over here. Why do we have to be here? It seems like it should be enough to send financial aid. These young kids shouldn't have to come over here to die for this lousy, stinking country. I do hope President Nixon will get some backbone soon and pull the troops out. It's the only sensible thing to do, I sincerely believe.

Baby, there's not too much new happening to tell you about. I am in much better spirits than I was a few days ago. I was laid up in bed for a few days with severe diarrhea, nausea, and vomiting, but I feel almost well now. If I didn't know better, I would think I had typhoid fever or cholera, but I'm supposed to be protected against those diseases, which are quite common over here in paradise!

2 Jun 1969

218th Medical Dispensary Saigon

Enclosed you will find a few pictures of me and Toby Hager on an Eagle Flight together. Did I tell you he caught a frag in his chest from a booby trap and will be coming home to Mountain

Home, Arkansas. He will be all right. He only had forty-five days left in the field—damn good soldier! One of the best I had the privilege to serve with.

3 Jun 1969

218th Medical Dispensary Saigon

Note to Mom and Dad:

My spirits are up considerably now. Thank you for the card, Dad. I carry it in my wallet, and I think it is a very beautiful psalm. I really feel very little danger now. I used to feel that I might get hit out in the field, but I don't feel that way anymore. Dad, I hope you had a nice birthday. I guess you are fifty-seven now. That's not really so old is it? Especially when I'm pushing thirty!

4 Jun 1969

218th Medical Dispensary Saigon

I have enclosed an article from the Pacific *Stars and Stripes* about Hack. Please save it for me. He is really quite a guy. I really miss working with him as he is one of the few people I've met in the army that I really respect.

5 Jun 1969

218th Medical Dispensary Saigon

How are you? I'm kind of puny, so this won't be very long. I've been feeling pretty crummy over the past several days, and it looks like I just continue to feel worse. I feel real tired all over, and my throat is sore, and I stay feeling nauseated. I guess it's just a virus. I just know I wish I had my pretty blonde nurse here to pamper me and nurse me back to good health! Dream on! I have been grouchy with everybody the past few days. I hate to feel so bad and will be happy when I get over whatever it is that has a hold of me! I'm sitting at my desk now, and I feel like I could just lay my head down and fall asleep right here, and I've gone to bed at 9:00 P.M. the last three nights.

Two years ago tonight I graduated from medical school. Who would have dreamed that I would end up here. I think I told you about my classmate, Bob Fields, who was recently killed over here. He was a brilliant guy, and I'll always think of my first gross anatomy exam when I think of him. Dr. Paff had tagged various nerves, arteries, and veins on our cadavers, and we had two minutes to identify them all, and then the bell would ring, and we would rotate (run) to the next table and its cadaver, with a new area marked. We all were writing like mad to get it down in such a short time. Bob was so afraid he might miss something that he would still be at the last station and I would have to literally push him out of my way. At first it pissed him off, but after three or four stops he started laughing about it. We remained friends throughout our four years of medical school. He went to South America with Perry Dunnick, another good friend, on a clinical clerkship. It seems that Bob was in a dust-off chopper, going to help evacuate casualties from two other choppers that had been shot down, when his bird got hit and went down. All on board bought the farm. He was a fine fellow and a good doctor, and I was very saddened to learn of his death.

I guess I have been very fortunate over here. I really feel quite

173

aware of all the prayers being said daily for me. So many of my friends and of course you, Sondra, mention in their letters that they are praying daily for me, and that means so much.

I have enclosed some samples of the type of money I carry over here: a $.05 MPC or Military Payment Certificate, also South Vietnamese VN $.20 and VN $.50 pieces. You can save them for our scrapbook. I don't know when or if I will want to put all this stuff into a scrapbook, but I should probably do it not too long after I return home and then try to forget the place. I know that will be impossible as many experiences over here are engraved indelibly on my mind. But it's actually history and should be recorded in some fashion.

6 Jun 1969

229th General Dispensary

I've been quite busy and just haven't felt too well either. Mainly depression, I guess. As you might have guessed from my return address, I have been transferred again, this time to the 229th General Dispensary at Tan Son Nhut Airbase. I will move over here in the A.M. I am kind of pissed off about having to move, just when I was getting good and settled over here at the 218th. The only consolation is that Troy Williams is stationed over there, although I haven't seen him yet. You will remember meeting him in San Antonio. It seems that I am to become the new commanding officer of the joint, which sounds like a real pain in the butt! It's also puzzling since they have a major there who should be the CO. Oh well, Murphy's Law and army reasoning. That's how it goes!

So Baby, you see I'm a little depressed again, as it seems like something is always happening to bug me. I'll just be so glad to get back home. At least there I will have you to come home to, and that will help 100 percent! So, you'd better start mailing letters to my new address.

I just met a very interesting guy today. His name is Danny Abella, and he served with Hack in Korea, so he must be about thirty-five years old. He is from Hawaii and is one of the nicest guys

I've ever met, with his ever-present grin. He is a lifer (career soldier) so he really knows the ropes. Word is, if you need something or want to get something done without the usual red tape, call Abella, as he really has the connections around Saigon.

I went down to the Saigon USO and waited several hours trying to get a line to call you about my new assignment. The line was so long, and they only had one circuit open, so I wasn't able to get through to you. I know I should be getting some orders soon for R & R and will be calling you then, if not sooner. I know I've been pretty poor about writing lately. I must confess I have been pretty blue and have been going out beer drinking with some of my men, so when I get back home I don't feel like writing—just sleeping. Don't worry, Baby, I don't get drunk, and I didn't mess around with any women. Just drank to escape from the boredom of this damn place. I'm like you, darling, I have good days and bad days. It seems like I've had more than my share of bad days lately, especially with this transfer. I will be in charge of the MACV (Military Assistance Command Vietnam) General Dispensary located at MACV HQ at Tan Son Nhut Airbase. That's where all the commanding generals, like Abrams, are located, and that is where they get their shots, physicals, etc. Maybe I can fix up the right one and get him to arrange a big drop in my DEROS! Fat chance!

10 Jun 1969

229th General Dispensary
Tan Son Nhut Air Base

Well, here I am, moved again, and finally getting settled down, for the last time before October, *I hope*! I think I will be OK over here. I have a private, second story bedroom with air-conditioning, a desk and a chair, single bed and bedside table, lavatory and mirror, but no bathroom. I will have to go downstairs for my showers, etc.

Troy looks real good and seemed happy to see an old familiar face. He spent his first six months as a battalion surgeon with the Big Red One, the 1st Infantry Division. He asked all about you and sends his best regards.

They just played the theme from *Gone With the Wind*, and it really brought back some great memories of time spent with you. God knows, I miss you so much that I feel like I'm going crazy sometimes, Baby, but it won't be long until we are together again in Oahu. I should get my R & R orders this week and will try to call you with the flight number and time of arrival in Hawaii. I will definitely want you to meet me at the R & R Center at Fort DeRussey. I sure don't want you to have to ride on the bus with a load of horny GIs!

13 Jun 1969

229th General Dispensary

After I finished talking to you tonight, I went to see *Guess Who's Coming To Dinner* with Sidney Poitier. It was really a very good picture, and the acting was superb. I think you would have enjoyed it, too. Every time I go to the theater, it reminds me of you and makes me miss you even more. We have two nice air-conditioned theaters here, complete with plush upholstered seats and popcorn machines, just like back in the real World! There is also a nice gymnasium nearby, with tennis courts and a swimming pool, so I shouldn't have any trouble finding something to do. It at least helps to pass the time.

Troy popped his head in the door and said he just heard over AFVN radio that two brigades of the 9th Infantry Division will be among the first twenty-five thousand troops withdrawn. The 4/39 is one of three battalions in the 1st Brigade, so I imagine they will be included in that group. Knowing the army as I do, if I had stayed with the battalion, I would probably have been transferred to a hospital, as I'm sure they want to get their money's worth out of me. Oh well, I'll be happy for my friends if they can get out of the boonies early. I'm fairly well off now.

Baby, I'm going to cut this short as I have to get up early, and

I am on call tomorrow night, and that can get hairy sometimes, so I need to get my rest.

14 Jun 1969

229th General Dispensary

How are you, baby? I'm doing OK. I had some company from Dong Tam today, Dave Risley and Sergeant Slater. Dave is getting kinda short now, only fifty-eight days left, and Slater is being transferred to MACV HQ, so I will be his doctor again. Sergeant Slater and I went through quite a bit of rough crap together, and I have always thought a lot of him. I can't help but feel kind of frustrated that my old battalion is going home. If I had stayed with them, I might be coming home late July or August. That would have been so great. God, I miss you so much! If I had known this would happen, I would have never put in for a transfer, but like dad always said, "If a cow had wings, it could fly!" I really was suffering from combat fatigue or burnout, so it's just as well I left when I did. Besides, for the past two months, I have been living in relative luxury compared to conditions in the field, so I really don't have a legitimate beef with anybody. You just can't help thinking, What if? But I won't cry over spilled milk. My personal disappointment is overshadowed by my joy that the 4/39 will finally be out of Nam, and no more of my friends will be victims of this absurd military operation.

There's really not too much new to tell you now. Each day just sort of begins and ends, and I mark off another date from my calendar. I try to stay busy so the time will pass faster. There are lots of little loose ends I have to tie up around this dispensary. Apparently my predecessor didn't give a damn, and he let things go pretty far. I'm getting pretty hard nosed, and I am getting a reputation as a real SOB. The other night I pulled a surprise bed check, and over half of my men were nowhere to be found at 0300 hours. The next morning, I was waiting for them as they straggled in, most of them drunk or hungover. As they arrived, I had them go to the general holding area where I had a real scorcher of a meeting with them en masse. I told them all about the Torpies and the Rollinses and told them there wasn't a man in the room who was fit to carry a real soldier's weapon. I told them they were a bunch of sorry no-good REMFs (rear echelon motherfuckers), and if I had the authority to do so, I would ship their asses out to the field, so they could begin to appreciate all the luxuries they took for granted, not to mention the danger. I had put on my Colt .45, and I honestly believe I would have shot the first one to give me any grief over the speech. I believe George Patton would have been proud of my speech, even if these candy-asses weren't. One of them had the audacity to come to my office later that morning and tell me I really didn't have the right to talk to them like that because it wasn't their fault they hadn't been sent to the field. "And I'm sure you all volunteered to go but were turned down!" I replied. Someone turned in a report to Colonel Thomas, and he called me and said, "You should have shot the room up and then they really would have something to complain about!" and laughed.

Well, precious, this is short, but I'm not in a writing mood. I'm in a talking mood and would give anything to be sitting in your big easychair, with you sitting on my lap, and then we could really talk the night away!

15 Jun 1969

Sunday A.M. 229th General Dispensary

I forgot to tell you the other day that I have a car now. They furnish the CO with a black, standard-government-issue, four-door 1965 Plymouth sedan. No big deal, but it comes in handy in bartering for supplies when somebody with goodies we have on back order needs to borrow the wheels for a weekend of fun and games. I have learned a lot about wheeling and dealing from Nighthunter 6 and Danny Abella, the "Smiling Pineapple." So this morning I will drive over to the 218th and see some of my old friends from the 4/39 who are staying with Dick Alexander.

We will go have a steak dinner atop the Rex Hotel, overlooking the ''beautiful city of Saigon.'' I will think of you and will miss you.

I got some news today that made me feel better. They are only going to send home early those GIs whose DEROS is from now until 10 October 1969. The rest of the guys will be transferred to other infantry units while the 9th moves to Hawaii. I would have been screwed by the system again. So, I'm much better off to stay put right where I am in my boring-but-safe little medical clinic.

I saw a good movie tonight, *House of Cards* with George Peppard. Remember, we saw him in *The Carpetbaggers* in Memphis. I don't think I will want to go to any more drive-in movies after this year of sitting outdoors with the mosquitoes and occasional mortar attacks. Give me some air-conditioned comfort.

16 Jun 1969

229th General Dispensary

You'll never guess who came bopping into my office this A.M. The Knapper! I could hardly believe my eyes! He just returned yesterday on an R & R flight from Hawaii. He had been stationed there on TDY (temporary duty) while recovering from his weird febrile tropical illness, which they were never able to diagnose. Two important things happened during his stay there. First, Stinky became pregnant; second, he was promoted to captain, so he is very pleased on both counts. And now he will probably be transferred to the States with the battalion as his DEROS was 22 September 1969. He looks real good and relaxed and has gained about twenty-five pounds. He sends his warmest regards to you.

I just got back from the movies. We saw Paul Newman in *The Secret War of Harry Frigg*. It was pretty cute but it certainly wasn't one of his best.

Well darling, only thirty-seven more days till I see you in Hawaii. It seems like all I'm living for now is July 24. I remember back in March we talked about how when we were down to four months, I would start feeling short. Well, it ain't so. I hope I feel shorter with two-and-one-half months to go after our week in Hawaii, but I guess I won't really feel short until I call you from Travis Air Force Base after arriving home in October. Like you said in your letter, slowly but surely the time is going by. Thank God a year has only twelve months in it.

Well, everything is pretty quiet on the home front here. In fact, last night we had a rocket attack here on Tan Son Nhut Airbase, and the place is so huge that I didn't even hear it. Now that's a plush way to go through the war. I've been sleeping a lot better lately, although I usually wake up every night between 3:00 and 4:00 A.M. and then go back to sleep pretty quickly. I always think of you immediately on awaking and wonder what you are doing back in the World. I just miss you so much.

18 Jun 1969

229th General Dispensary

I just got back from the movies with Troy. We saw *Better a Widow* with Virna Lisi. It was a real cute picture and made me miss you as she is also a cute blonde with green eyes. I just never can find the words to tell you just how much I need you and miss you, Sondra. Somehow, I feel that you know.

20 Jun 1969

229th General Hospital

Just heard today that my old unit, the 9th Division, will be heading out for assignment to Hawaii in either late July or August. So I still would have been a long way from home, and might have had to stay there until September of 1970, so everything works out for the best, as I want to come all the way home when I do come home!

You asked about the circumstances surrounding my transfer out to MACV headquarters. Well, they needed a commanding officer for this dispensary, and we had one extra at the 218th. We had all served our time in the field, so in order to be as fair as possible, our CO spread a deck of cards out on the operating table and said, "Low man goes!" I drew the two of diamonds. So here I am! It's really not too bad, I have my own car since becoming commanding officer of the dispensary, and of course, it is air-conditioned. Naturally, I do have my share of headaches too!

22 Jun 1969

229th General Dispensary

Well, today is truly a "blue" Sunday as it's been gray and overcast and rainy all day long. The monsoons have arrived, and I've never seen such huge raindrops. I know that sounds crazy, but sometimes it looks like it's raining grapes, and it's not hail, just huge raindrops, and lot's of times it comes down in buckets.

Believe me when I tell you it's a different type of rain than I've ever experienced anywhere else in the world.

I have been reading and have finished a novel this afternoon. Troy and I are going to see *Gone With the Wind* tonight at the MACV HQ theater. I enjoyed seeing it so much with you that I am sure I will enjoy it again.

I got a real sweet letter from my sister Barbara today and a good letter from Dapper Dan McCue. He has been so faithful with his letter writing and always sends his latest copy of *Flying* magazine. He and Anease really are enjoying their new son, Eric Wayne. I do get an occasional letter from my brother Bruce, but he is not much of a letter writer. Mom and Dad, and you, Sondra Jean, are the ones who keep me going. I do get an occasional letter from Don Jennings, and I believe he really wishes he was over here with me. Donnie would have made a hell of a fine infantry soldier, of that I am certain.

24 Jun 1969

229th General Dispensary

I took an interesting trip today. We drove up to Long Binh, where I spent my first few days in Nam last October. We visited the 90th Replacement Battalion. That's where I spent my first night in country, and the typhoon blew the roof off the hooch. Well, I can tell you it was quite a morale boost to go there today, with three months and three weeks left on my tour of duty. Troy and Chris Rivera and I went to the officers club and had a few beers and sat around reminiscing about how we had felt back in October, and looked at all the new guys in khakis who had just arrived here from the World. They look so scared and pitiful. I do feel sorry for them, and I know that some of them will be going home in body bags, and that bothers the hell out of me! After R & R, I will have at the most two months and two weeks left over here, and then we will be back up there processing out of country.

I'm finally beginning to feel short, Baby, and it's such a great feeling. I just can't tell you just how much I am looking forward to coming *home*!

There's not too much new happening here, just the same old headaches of being CO and seeing lots of patients, but that helps time to pass quicker, so I don't complain about it.

26 Jun 1969

229th General Dispensary

I feel so good tonight. For one thing, hearing from you and seeing your sweet face in so many poses in the proofs you sent has really cheered me up. And I just got back from seeing a good movie, *100 Rifles*, and then took a good hot shower and shampoo. So, all I need is *you*!

Darling, I am so sorry to hear about your friend from Walnut Ridge, Johnny Frank Davis, getting killed over here. It's such a terrible waste and this whole damn country isn't worth the life of one GI, much less those of thousands. I can't really blame the antiwar demonstrators for their actions, although I think their methods are wrong. Nobody wants to die at a young age. Especially for no apparent worthwhile cause.

27 Jun 1969

229th General Dispensary

How are you tonight? I'm doing OK. As well as possible without you, I guess. There's really not too much new to write about. Everything I do is practically the same as the day before. I work here at the 229th Dispensary and at the MACV HQ dispensary on alternate days. We usually see patients from 0800 hours until

1100 hours and then take two hours for lunch and a snooze. Then we start back at 1300 hours and work till 1500 hours. We have evening hours at MACV HQ only from 1800 hours till 1900 hours. Most evenings I either go to a movie, am on call, or go to one of the nearby officer clubs or stay here and write letters and read.

There is one really neat bar at the USO which is quite secure and has the neatest atmosphere. It is very cool, even in the hot afternoons after 3:00 P.M. when we usually go there. It is decorated quite colorfully with red plush wallpaper, and the bar is of solid mahogany from the Philippines. We have gotten to know the bartender quite well, and he is really a very intelligent and interesting person. He was born in Hanoi in 1937, and all of his family still lives there. At age seventeen, he fought with the Viet Minh in their defeat of the French and afterward came south with the huge exodus which was allowed at that time under the Geneva Convention. He is an articulate, neat person, and I would be comfortable having him in my home anytime. We ask him how he feels about our airplanes bombing his former home and the present home of his sisters and brothers and parents, and he says he understands that we believe we are doing it in the name of freedom so he can accept it. He wouldn't say whether he stays in touch with his family or not, but we suspect he is probably a spy for the North Vietnamese. He is such a likeable guy that I can't really hold that against him. After all, this is his home, not mine. He does see a big difference between the North and the South, and he says that no matter who wins the war he plans to go to Hanoi and round up his family and bring them to Saigon to live. He says that life in the South is so much more laid-back, and the people are more friendly and outgoing. Also, he said the winters are pretty severe in Hanoi, and he really loves it down South. He has been tending bar at the USO for five years, so whatever he is, he is dependable. He has a gorgeous oil painting of a nude woman, probably Oriental but with quite Occidental eyes, long black hair, and beautiful breasts. Believe it or not, it is done in such good taste that you could hang it in the halls of the White House and no one would be offended. It is such a wonderful place to go to escape the heat, dirt, humidity, and boredom of life in Saigon. And Joe the bartender is always glad to see us.

29 Jun 1969

229th General Dispensary

I have had lots of company from the 4/39 lately. They are real good about coming by to see me when they are in the Saigon area. We always have so much to talk about—war stories, etc.—and I always enjoy seeing them. Experiencing war together builds a unique bond between people. I feel like some of these fellows will be friends for life.

I just got back from the movies. We saw *The Wrecking Crew* with Dean Martin. It was pretty funny, kind of slapstick humor. We laughed a lot. As usual, he was surrounded by lots of voluptuous women, and it really got me to missing you.

30 Jun 1969

229th General Dispensary

I've got some real good news for a change. I've just received a copy of a request for orders, typed in Atlanta, Georgia, at Fort McPherson. I will be assigned to the U.S. Army Hospital at Fort Mac located near downtown Atlanta, *and*, in the space where it says "date eligible for return from overseas" it says September 1969! So, *perhaps* I will be coming home in September. They were requesting orders for me to begin work there in October, so they would have to let me come home thirty days before that so I could have my thirty-day leave. Now, Baby, this is *not* definite, so don't count on it too much, but I have a hunch I might be *home* in September. Wouldn't that be fabulous? September 1 is only sixty-two days away, so I might be much shorter than I realized. Once you are assigned to a hospital, if they need you early, they can take you anytime after you have completed ten months over here. That point will be 16 August for me. I'm excited as hell, but I won't count on the drop until I see it in writing on my orders. But at least now we know I will be assigned in the good old South, and we can start making our plans accordingly. Baby, I can't tell you how happy I am about the possibility of getting out of this hellhole early. You'll just love Atlanta. The winters are cold, and spring is as beautiful as it can be, with dogwoods and redbuds blooming all over the hills, and the summers are hot like they are everywhere else, but it will be like heaven after a year in Nam.

I think this will be my best Christmas since I was twelve years old. My grandmother was dying with lung cancer during that Christmas season, and she died on December 30, and I never really enjoyed Christmas season much after that. But, this year we will have so much to be thankful for that it will be a Christmas to remember! So, I'm as excited as a little kid, just thinking about us getting a tree and all the trimmings. In case you can't tell, I'm so excited I could just bust!

I was talking to a friend of mine who was stationed at Fort Mac, and he said it has a beautiful officers country club with a huge pool, golf course, and the whole works. They also have a flying club, so I should be able to get my private pilot's license fairly cheap there. Also, it's close enough to the Great Smoky Mountains that we can drive up there for long weekends in the mountains in the spring and fall when the leaves are so pretty. Sounds great, huh? Well, I've got to run over to MACV for evening sick call, so I will finish it later tonight.

6 Jul 1969

229th General Dispensary

Colonel Hackworth was down from Pleiku, where he is now the II Corps G-3 advisor to the ARVN G-3 operations officer. It is really a waste of time from what he says, but they had to get him out of the field before he got himself killed. He is being groomed for general and is supposed to go to the War College when he finishes here in six months. However, I get the distinct impression that he is as fed up with this situation over here as I am. He is on his fifth tour now, and he doesn't see it getting any better. His biggest disappointment is the fact that even after he turned the 4/39 losers into fighting HARDCORE Recondos, he still couldn't get the brass to listen to him concerning training other units to "out-*G* the *G*" the way we did in the 4/39. It seems that every move on the part of the brass has to do with their individual promotions up the military ladder; little concern is shown toward the ongoing slaughter of fine young Americans, in what most of us who have been here see as a losing effort. I only have to be here for a year, but I can understand his frustration since the army has been his whole life, and now he is feeling that the system is heading for a self-destructing mode as far as Southeast Asia is concerned. He is also concerned that the "Ira Hunts" of the army will be the commanding generals in a really big confrontation some day, and that could be disastrous. I don't really know how to advise him, but we discussed it over a few cold Budweisers and I know he is in a real state of unrest about it. He is on his way to R & R in Hawaii and is planning to drop by and spend a night or two on his way back. He is really a class act, and it was a real pleasure seeing him again. He is truly a soldier's soldier. I'm really glad to see him out of the boonies because he took too many chances with his own life. I hope you can meet him someday. He was really the highlight of my tour with the 4/39.

Well, it's time to get some shut-eye. Seeing Hack in civilian clothes reminded me to tell you not to look for me in khakis, as they are too uncomfortable to travel in, so I will be in something loose, casual, and comfortable.

8 Jul 1969

229th General Dispensary

I am bushed so this will be short. I had a very interesting but nerve-racking day. I was the only physician in attendance at the departure ceremony for the 9th Infantry Division. My old unit, strange coincidence, huh? My medics and I were responsible for providing all medical coverage for troops and dignitaries. We set up a large tent with cots and lots of ice-cold drinks and a few IVs because of the extreme heat. In my care were President Thieu, Vice-President Ky, General Abrams (commanding general of all Allied Forces), General Truong (commanding general of all ARVN forces), U.S. Ambassador Bunker, and all the generals and ambassadors for the armies of Australia, South Korea, and Thailand. I was very concerned about the possibility of a terrorist attack but felt it probably wouldn't happen because this ceremony marks the beginning of the end of foreign intervention. I believe that Charlie knows that once we are all gone, he will be able to drive into Saigon undisturbed. So why try to screw it up now?

Well, my hunch was right and the only casualties I had were several GIs who suffered from heat exhaustion. I wasn't introduced formally to any of the brass, but General Abrams knows me from MACV dispensary, so he included me in the initial briefing with all the brass. I stood around in a circle composed of some of the most newsworthy men of our times. They all smiled and nodded my way when he told them I was their doctor for the event if anyone felt ill. President Thieu seemed quite tense and reserved, and Marshal Ky seemed quite cocky and unconcerned. Needless to say, I was very relieved when the ceremony ended without a hitch. That's a lot of responsibility to put on the shoulders of one young doctor.

I saw about twenty-five of my buddies from the 4/39 who had been transferred to the 3/60 in order to leave earlier than the planned departure of the HARDCORE. They were very surprised and happy to see old Doc Holley there, and the feelings were mutual. Well, as of tomorrow I will officially become a "Two Digit Midget," with only ninety-nine days remaining until DEROS! Praise the Lord, I'm getting short!

17 Aug 1969

229th General Dispensary

This is really a year I will try to forget as soon as possible, but will never be able to forget completely, I am sure. I'm just finishing up a book I want you to read, if possible, before I get home. It will help you to understand much of what I feel and will have to say, and to help me cope with the bitterness I know this experience has instilled deep in my inner parts. It's title is *The Betrayal* written by William R. Corson, retired U.S. Marine Corps, and it really tells it like it is. He confirms so much of what I have witnessed over here firsthand as well as much of what I have suspected was wrong with our military effort in Vietnam. He echoes, almost to the word, Colonel Hackworth's sentiments about our war effort over here. Suffice it to say, I will *not* be interested in accepting any invitations to speak to any groups about my wasted year in Vietnam. I am afraid that much of what I would have to say would sound treasonous to some patriots, and Lord knows I am patriotic and love America as much as anybody, but this fiasco has nothing to do with patriotism, believe me. If anyone other than very close friends or family wants to know how I feel about our role in Southeast Asia, I will refer them to Corson's book.

Troy and I went downtown shopping for some art and found a local Vietnamese artist selling original oil paintings in nice frames for the grand price of twelve hundred piasters or about ten dollars American currency. I bought two and will package them up and get them in the mail to you soon.

27 Aug 1969

229th General Dispensary

I have enclosed several items. One, a photograph taken at my going-away party at Dong Tam. The other, a photo of a little Vietnamese boy. So typical. He reminds me of hundreds of little fellows I have seen out in the hamlets and villages. So cute, sad, and pitiful in a way. They seem very grown-up and wear hats similar to the one in the picture. In fact, the first thing the picture reminded me of was that morning back in February when the post-Tet offensive began and the old village chief brought me all those ammo boxes full of body parts. There was one little fellow about that size, and he still had his little hat on. I was so calloused by then that I doubt if I showed any outward sign of being emotionally affected, but it branded that sight and stench forever in my mind. War really is hell on earth, and I'd go through another ten years in Vietnam if it would prevent you and my other family members from having to live one day in that kind of hell! Thank God for our beautiful America! Even though She is having her own problems now, She's still the *best*! I'll stand a little taller and a little straighter when the national anthem is played or the flag goes by. Please excuse my sentimental journey, I just get that way sometimes, it seems.

I also enclosed a picture of a cute little mutt. There are stray pups everywhere, and they all seem to grow up to become big, ugly mutts. Of course, a lot of them end up at the end of a rope tied to a shanty where they are fattened up, slaughtered, and wind up as dog stew, dog-burgers, or whatever. It's just kind of hard to identify with people who eat rats and dogs on a regular basis.

28 Aug 1969

229th General Dispensary

Things are really hopping around here. I have gotten a new first sergeant to help me straighten out this damn place, and I think he is really going to work out well. I've gotten absolutely no help in the past from my other ones, so I'm real glad to finally have some decent help.

I also got the word that my relief for CO of the 229th is due here on October 11. If Troy and Chris get drops before that date and I don't, I will raise hell like they have never heard before, because we all three came over on the same airplane and should go home together. That's the way I see it. If that happens, 3d Field can just lend this place one of their extra docs to fill in as temporary CO until the real thing comes along!

1 Sep 1969

229th General Dispensary

I sure am getting a short-timer's attitude. I don't feel like doing anything but eat, sleep, and drink. I wish I could just go to sleep and wake up one day before DEROS. But it's really best to keep busy, which I am doing with all the troubles at this dump. Things are improving, but my popularity with my men is at an all-time low. The work is getting done, and people are sleeping in their designated beds at night, and I almost believe we could pass an inspection for the first time since I've been here. The place really is spic-and-span, but it has been a drain on me emotionally. I'll really be glad to get it off my shoulders.

7 Sep 1969

229th General Dispensary

I have been running day and night straightening out all kinds of problems at this damn dispensary. I hate the place. I've had nothing but trouble with this bunch of duds who work under me. They are all lazy and live like a bunch of pigs! So 3d Field Hospital came down hard on us, and it's been hell. My new first sergeant finally joined me in kicking ass, and we have gotten the place neat enough to pass inspection yesterday. But, in the process, I am just about worn out from fighting so many people. I never had this type of problem in the field. I guess because we depended on each other for survival.

All these assholes care about is getting stoned and screwing gooks, seven nights a week! I have issued more Article 15s in the past three months than were issued by all the COs over the past one-and one-half years. They really seem to hate my guts, and I have gone back to sleeping with my door locked and my .45 under my pillow. I don't think any of them have the guts to try anything, but I'm getting too short to take any chances. I'm learning that in the army's scheme of things, nice guys finish last! I'm currently a very unpopular person here, but I really don't give a damn. They're a bunch of bums. I'm not having any trouble with the doctors, just the enlisted men, and even a few of the regular army types.

16 Sep 1969

229th General Dispensary

Dear Mom and Dad:

The tape and the fudge arrived in good shape. Thank you for both. I must confess I sat here and listened to those sweet kids and couldn't keep the tears back. I love them all so very much. I sure do miss them. Robert was so cute when he said, "I hit a grand slam, Uncle Byron!" And Rhonda talking about being on the Safety Patrol, and Robin just being her silly self. Little Bruce really is growing up isn't he?

I'm doing all right, just anxious to come home. I'm hoping that the troop withdrawal might help us all to get home a little early. At worst, I have only thirty days—*one month*—and I will have this unbelievable year behind me, and I can get on with the rest of my life. I've already started packing my trunk of books and heavy items, so all I will have will be my duffel bag and my camera to keep up with on the return flight. Well, someone just called from downstairs with a sick patient, so I will have to go for now.

20 Sep 1969

229th General Dispensary

I had a patient almost die from an anaphylactic reaction to streptomycin this A.M. Scared the hell out of everybody! He responded to my triple whammy of steroids intravenously, with Adrenalin subcutaneously, and Benadryl intramuscularly. Those three together have never failed yet to save one I thought would die without treatment. It reminded me of how I constantly lived through death and near-death situations out in the field. Now I'm getting spoiled with routine patient care, and I don't miss all the horror of the frequent deaths I encountered in the field.

24 Sep 1969

229th General Dispensary

This sorry job is about to drive me crazy. I have never hated a job so much. I have the biggest bunch of duds working for me, and it seems like I'm always having to kick somebody's ass. No one has any pride in their work or takes any initiative. It's really disgusting!

I had a patient have one hell of a reaction to a Kantrex injection today. His BP dropped to 40/0, and his pulse fell to thirty, and he was barely breathing when I got to him. I really thought he was going to die. His chest sounded awful, with real tight wheezes, but he responded to my good ole "triple whammy" treatment. Danny Abella just stuck his head in the door and sends you his best.

28 Sep 1969

229th General Dispensary

I am sitting here all alone, looking out the window, thinking about you, and watching it rain. It's coming down in buckets, and I really feel sorry for the grunts all over this land who have to slosh around and sleep in this mess. Larry Tahler, Nighthunter 6 from the 4/39, is down from Pleiku, scrounging supplies for Hack. He usually gets a lot of help from

Danny Abella, the Smiling Pineapple. Danny is going home on R & R to Hawaii next Sunday, and Larry's DEROS is 11 Oct, so I will really be glad to put him on his freedom bird! They are both great guys, and I will miss them both.

Hack was telling us the other night how he had fought the Koreans with Danny and his brother, Eddie Abella, in the 27th Infantry Regiment, known as the Wolfhounds. Both brothers were damn good fighters, and I think it's neat for Hack to have contact with Danny over here, twenty years later on a different Asian peninsula. They have both seen a lot of action. Abella told me about one night the Chinese and North Koreans overran one of their rifle companies, and the bodies were piled up six feet deep. He and Hack were up on a hilltop, overlooking the valley where it occurred. War really is hell, no matter when or where it is fought. And, if you are anywhere near the action, it leaves an incredible impression on you and changes you forever. This past year has taught me much about life, living, and death. I truly believe I will get so much more out of every day than I used to.

30 Sep 1969

229th General Dispensary

I'm doing pretty well, just tired. Troy, Chris, and I have been keeping some pretty late hours the past few nights, like 2:00 to 3:00 A.M. just horsing around like college kids. We are so happy about leaving that we are acting like teenagers.

Al Taylor, a former medical school classmate of mine who interned with Troy, is down from the 101st Airborne. He just got transferred to the 68th Group and is hoping to be stationed at the 229th. He is already slated for transfer to Fort McPherson in January, so you will get to meet him then. He is a real neat guy, kind of quiet, but very nice and polite. This will be short as I have a splitting headache.

10 Oct 1969

229th General Dispensary

My Dearest Sondra,

Well, precious, this will be my *last letter* to you from Vietnam! I can hardly believe it! This will be mailed tomorrow and should arrive in Memphis on the fifteenth or sixteenth, about the same time I arrive there. My replacement got in today, but I still can't leave until the fifteenth. At any rate, I will be with you in Memphis in five days. Troy and I are booked standby on a flight out of Tan Son Nhut Airbase at noon on Wednesday the fifteenth. If we aren't able to get out on that one, we will leave on the 8:00 P.M. flight, so we should be in California by early in the A.M. of the sixteenth.

Baby, I really don't know how to begin to thank you for your faithfulness in writing such good, sweet letters to me as often as you did over this past year. Your letters literally kept me going on many occasions. Just knowing that you cared and had taken the time to write and tell me how much you cared was so very important to me. I'll never be able to tell you just how much I did appreciate them, but I have saved every one of them and will keep them for posterity. They are enroute to Memphis in my large trunk loaded with books, etc. Maybe someday our letters will form the nucleus for a book on this past year's experience. I know you got tired of writing, as I did, too, but just a note from you meant so much more than no mail at all. So many times out in the field, I would feel so sorry for so many of my men who would go day after day without hearing from their loved ones, while I would rarely go more than a day without hearing from you or my mom and dad. Please never forget how very deeply I love you, admire you, respect you, and need you. See you soon!

Byron

14 Oct 1969

My Final Night in Vietnam

Well, we finally were told we could leave on the noon flight on the fifteenth and had our bags packed and ready to go, and then, out of the blue, we got a surprise visit from Hack. He had heard from Abella that I was leaving and wanted one last chance to go out for a fine Vietnamese dinner, down a few beers, and swap a few war stories. We started the evening sipping a few cold Buds and smoking Hav-a-Tampa cigars in my room, where we were joined by Troy, who was to accompany me on the flight home the next day. We then headed out to a fine Vietnamese restaurant, run by one of Hack's old Korean War buddies. We were there for hours, during which time we consumed a lot of beer and sake and more beer. Finally, Hack decided I just couldn't leave Nam without meeting one of his old friends who had a villa near the Cholon district, so off we went, with Troy doing the driving, as Hack and I were drunk as coots by then! Well, few people know it, but Colonel Hackworth has a terrible sense of direction, and in his present state it was worse than usual. After an hour and a half of cruising up and down numerous dark and filthy alleys, he finally decided that this was the place. He dragged me out of the car and we staggered up to a wall-enclosure with a fancy wrought-iron gate, and he started screaming at the top of his lungs for his friend to come out. I looked at my watch and saw it was almost 4:00 A.M. and told Hack, "Damn it, Hack, don't get me shot in a filthy Saigon alley on my last night in country. Let's get the hell out of here before somebody shoots us!" I finally persuaded him to return to the car and we made a short but blurry trip back to the 229th, where we helped each other up the stairs and plopped in the sack at 5:00 A.M. I remember setting the alarm for 6:30 A.M. as we were supposed to be at Tan Son Nhut at 0900 hours.

I crashed and the next thing I knew it was twelve noon! *"Damn it to hell! I've missed my flight!"* I hollered, as I stumbled out of bed and went next door to look for Hack. His bed was empty, neatly made up, with a note on the spread. "Doc, tried to wake you up, but you were like a wild man. See Abella, and he will get you on the next flight out. Keep in touch! Hack." I found the first sergeant just coming upstairs from morning clinic. "What time did Colonel Hackworth leave, Sarge," I asked.

"He was up bright-eyed and bushy-tailed at 0700 hours, and tried to wake you up, but there was no way, sir! I ran him out to the terminal for an 8:00 A.M. flight to Pleiku."

Well, that old SOB had drunk me under the table, and was already back in Pleiku, and here I was just stumbling out of bed, and with one hell of a hangover, I might add. He really is one tough old warrior, and I will miss him.

Well, as Hack promised, Danny Abella had us out on the 6:00 P.M. flight from Tan Son Nhut. I still felt lousy, and when I looked in the mirror at the terminal, I was surprised to see how green my face was. That sake was strong stuff, and I sure didn't want to get sick in the plane, so I went to the restroom and had little difficulty vomiting and soon felt and looked better. I was irritated at myself for missing my flight after waiting for 365 days and now at feeling so poorly on a day I had thought about for so long. But the wild, crazy night with Troy and Hack had been worth it, and we would laugh about it later—me being the klutz who slept through his DEROS flight!

I couldn't believe the excitement I felt as I climbed aboard the Flying Tigers DC-8 that would take me home. There were no FNGs exiting this plane as it had flown down from Da Nang where it had dropped its load of new guys, so we missed the opportunity of razzing them as we had been razzed at Bien Hoa airfield so long ago! There were, however, the cold, gray metal coffins, waiting to be loaded in the baggage hold of our freedom bird, about twenty-five of them this trip. How grateful I felt not to be in one, as I said a quiet prayer of thanksgiving.

After one final glance at the country I had come to loathe, I entered the refreshing coolness of my freedom bird and settled down in a seat next to the window. As the large silver jet began to roll down the runway, my heart raced with joy. As we lifted off the ground, a thunderous cheer and ovation sounded throughout the cabin. The stewardess smiled knowingly. After one last glance at the coastline of Vietnam as it faded into the distance behind us, I settled down for a nice nap and didn't wake up until we were landing at Guam for a refueling stop.

I was impressed with the vast assortment of military aircraft scattered all over the airfield, and I knew the B-52s had spent lots of time over the country I was now so happy to be leaving. Only difference, they would return to Nam, and I would never have to again.

A shiny World Airways flight, bound for Vietnam, loaded up its cargo of FNGs and took off into the western sky as we waited to reload our bird. My heart ached for these young kids and what lay ahead of them. Some would return in a year, changed for life, and others would not return alive. The twenty-five coffins in the hold of our aircraft held twenty-five young kids who made the same trip, with the same uncertain, frightened looks on their faces. Now their faces were still.

It was nighttime when Troy woke me and said, "Look out the window, Doc. Those lights are on the coast of California! We are back in the World!" I couldn't believe how ecstatic I felt at finally being back home. Don't crash this plane, mister, I've got lot's of people waiting to see me back here! I remember thinking. When we touched down at Travis Air Force Base we had a few cheers, but more subdued than those heard on our departure from Nam. As we stepped down on the tarmac, I found a relatively dry spot between the puddles and dropped down on my hands and knees and kissed the grimy surface. The night of my first firefight, I had promised myself I would kiss the good old ground if God would just let me return home. I sure wasn't going to let a few rain puddles and airplane grease stop me, not after all my Lord had pulled me through. Troy laughed at the grease ring on my face and the water marks on my knees, but I knew that I had kept my end of the deal and just grinned and said, "God Bless America! We are home!"

After a very brief debriefing, we picked up our luggage and headed for the long row of telephone booths, where we had made our tearful good-byes one year ago. This time it was me hollering into the phone "Hi! It's me! I'm back home from the war zone!" I couldn't help but wonder if the fellow in the next booth was on his way to Vietnam, and if so, I knew exactly how he felt.

After a seemingly endless taxi ride, we finally arrived at San Francisco. As we approached the Bay area, we saw the Golden Gate Bridge, all lit up and engulfed in a shroud of fog. As the fog rolled in, I was suddenly filled with an eerie feeling of ghosts of past warriors who had sailed under that same bridge on the way to the Pacific theater of World War II, many never to return. The more things change, the more they stay the same, I remember thinking.

We went directly to San Francisco International Airport where I was booked on an early red-eye flight to Memphis. As Troy and I bade each other farewell, I was suddenly aware of how overstuffed all the people in the terminal were. They all looked like different versions of the Pillsbury Doughboy! It suddenly dawned on me that for the past year I had lived around short, thin people and had seen very few truly fat people. Wow, these folks could use a little starvation and poverty! I mused. How spoiled and lucky they are, and most of them don't even appreciate it, I thought. Very few have ever seen poverty like I witnessed firsthand in Vietnam, and hopefully never will.

As I sat in the boarding area waiting for my long-anticipated flight to Memphis and Sondra, I thought how lucky I was to be coming home without having earned a Purple Heart. Well, I may not have a Purple Heart to display on my chest, but I am coming home with a bruised and broken heart from what I have experienced. I'm sure time will do much to heal these wounds, but the memories will remain forever.

As I boarded my nearly empty 3:00 A.M. flight and tried to get comfortable, I suddenly realized it was freezing cold in the cabin and rang for a stewardess to get me a blanket. She took one look at my chest full of medals and said, "You're a big war hero. Find one yourself," and walked toward the rear of the cabin. I was shocked, I was hurt, I was mad. As I sat there alone in the now darkened cabin, tears welled up in my eyes. *Welcome home, GI!* Is this how it will be? Well, it was not my war. I had just done what my country had asked me to do. After all, John F. Kennedy had said it all:

> Ask not what your country can do for you,
> but what you can do for your country.

Well, I have just given my country one of the most incredible years of my young life. Thank God, I didn't have to give it all. Lots of fine young men did, and I had the privilege of living and fighting with some of them, of saving some of them, of bleeding and crying with some of them, and mine were the last eyes some of them looked into as they laid down their young lives. My life will never be the same because of them. May God rest their young souls!

Conclusions

Brandon, Florida

As I sit here twenty-two years later and reflect on all the events recorded in the letters which have led to the writing of this book, I feel obligated to draw some conclusions based on my experiences in South Vietnam. The comments made in the book were made by a twenty-seven-year-old physician-soldier who was older than most of the men in his charge, but was still awfully young in the overall scheme of life. The following comments are made by a middle-aged doctor, husband, and father of three, and of necessity will reflect some of what I have read or heard since my days in the Mekong Delta. If it's not original, and it's reported here, it's because I agree with it. I will not knowingly copy anyone else's quotes without their permission.

Conclusion 1:

I was right in the initial feeling, soon after arriving in country, that we shouldn't have been there in the first place. It was, and still is, an internal affair and should have been settled without our involvement. Harry S Truman dropped the ball when he rejected Ho Chi Minh's proposed Declaration of Independence, fashioned almost to the letter from our own, in deference to taking the side of our ally, France. All that Ho and his followers were trying to do was to rid their country of foreign influence and form one independent nation. If we had just reflected on our own history in our efforts to escape the rule of the English Crown, we surely would have sided with their cause. But no, it was a purely political decision which set the stage for the final years of French rule and eventual fall at Dien Bien Phu as well as the ensuing quagmire we found ourselves involved in during the sixties and early seventies. All those lives were lost in vain, and the whole debacle could have been avoided if those in positions of responsibility would have had the courage to say, "We were wrong to side with the French and we will not interfere any further in the internal affairs of these struggling people." I consider presidents Kennedy and Johnson to be the most responsible for sending our troops over there, and I don't think former President Richard Nixon has been given enough credit for his successful efforts in finally extricating us from the quagmire.

Conclusion 2:

I disagree totally and completely with many former military men who say the war was winable. The North Vietnamese and Viet Cong soldiers knew why they were there and what they were fighting for. They were acclimated to the physical elements that made their homeland such a difficult battleground for us Americans. We made a very gallant and stubborn effort, but we really did not have a burning justification for being over there in the first place. We were all told by various South Vietnamese soldiers that they couldn't understand why we would come over there to risk our lives when they would not do the same for us.

Conclusion 3:

The lives of their soldiers were definitely more expendable than ours. We Americans have always placed a very high value on human life, whereas the average Southeast Asian doesn't expect much out of life. They have traditionally accepted such hardships for generation after generation—first at the hands of the invading Chinese and later from the French. With millions of people to help feed their army, they knew they could outlast us, despite our superior military hardware, technology, etc.

Conclusion 4:

"Gook" is really an awful name to attach to a group of people. Same thing with "Dink" or "Slope." We tried to convince ourselves that the enemy were some sort of subhuman species. This was not the case at all. They were scared young boys who would have preferred not to be there. Just like us. They each had mothers, fathers, sisters, and brothers, just as we had—families who missed them and mourned their loss just as we had. These slang names and feelings were largely our way of justifying our continual attempt to eliminate them, by whatever means available. We had to rationalize our existence in their country as well as our actions.

Conclusion 5:

Self Survival was the force which drove many of us to do things we would ordinarily find disgusting and appalling. The country of Vietnam is really not a hellhole as I describe it so many places in the book. War is a hellhole, no matter where it is fought. Vietnam is actually one of the most beautiful places I have ever been. The conditions which make it offensive, the odors of sewage and the numerous insects used to be prevalent right here in my home state of Florida, and in the future will probably not always be present in Vietnam.

Conclusion 6:

There are just too many poor people in Southeast Asia. Most of them can't help it, and therein lies the problem, What to do with them all? The Khmer Rouge tried extinction in Cambodia, but that obviously wasn't the answer. The country contains one of the most fertile agricultural regions on earth, and surely that asset has to be managed to its potential.

Conclusion 7:

It's time to extend the hand of friendship, just as we have done with Japan and Germany. Not only did we kill hundreds of thousands of their finest young people, we also changed the face of their homeland with our bombing and our use of defoliants. True, we paid dearly in loss of human life, but then, we really shouldn't have been there in the first place. It's time for us, the greatest free nation in the world, to help this struggling nation get up on its feet again. Let political bygones be bygones. By recognizing them as a nation and establishing normal economic and diplomatic relations with them, the final chapter in this war story can be written: The resolution of the MIA-POW ISSUE.

Conclusion 8:

Both sides committed atrocities against their enemy. But *war itself is an atrocity.*

It is my fervent hope and prayer that the American government has learned a valuable lesson from our experience in Vietnam. If not, then all those young men truly died in vain.

Index

Abella, Danny, 174–175, 178, 194–195, 198
Abella, Eddie, 195
About Face (Hackworth), 3
Abrams, General, 188
Aid station, 53, 63–64, 76–77, 91, 98, 103, 148
Air ambulance, 5, 6, 25, 40, 112–113
Airborne medics, 13
Air Medals, 128
AK-47 assault rifles, 54, 55, 61, 79, 87, 97, 106, 108, 138
Alamo, 4
Alexander, Richard, 29, 31, 158, 167, 178
Allison, Jack, 89, 119
Ambulance, air, 5, 6, 25, 40, 112–113
Anaphylactic reaction, 61, 193–194
Ann-Margret, 94
Antiwar demonstrations, 183
ARVNs, 18, 48, 52, 53, 54, 64, 107, 138, 186, 188
Ashley, Sergeant, 36, 43, 50, 73, 82, 84, 96, 100, 101, 113, 116, 117, 118
Austin, Colonel, 86

Australian shower, 65
AWOL, 42, 47, 82, 161

Baptist Memorial Hospital, Tennessee, 1, 11
Battalion, 21
Ben Luc, 24
  bridge, 67, 68, 101
Ben Tranh airfield, 103, 104, 132
Betrayal, The (Corson), 189
Bien Ho, 17
Binh Phuoc, 24
Binh Sohn rubber plantation, 25
Black soldiers, 91, 99–100
Booby-trap casualties, 66, 91, 98, 140
Boots, combat, 28
Bridges, 67, 68, 101, 102, 103
Brigade, 21
Brown, Les, 94
Bunker, Ambassador, 188
By Valour and Arms (Streeter), 114

Cai Be, 48, 49, 51
Cai Lai, 129
Cai Lay, 24
Cambodia, 25, 75, 119, 120,

Cambodia, *(cont)*
    121, 122, 126, 127, 137, 203
Camp Bullis, Texas, 10–13,
    14–16
Can Tho, 99
Caribou, 26–27
Casey, Bill, 82
Casualties, 58, 81–82, 95, 98,
    109–111, 112, 114, 115–116, 153
    categories of, 8–9
    medics, 5, 67, 82–83, 104,
    148, 164–165, 171
Chancroid, 39, 44
Chaplain, 29, 58
Children, Vietnamese, 33–34,
    47, 57–58, 81, 190
Chinooks, 25, 62, 63, 68, 71,
    113, 119, 127
Christmas, 75, 90, 93, 94, 96–
    97, 186
Clearing stations, 7
Climate, 23, 27
Cobras, 25, 70, 105, 106, 108,
    118, 142
Colt .45, 41, 43, 48, 68, 69–
    70, 81
Combat Medical Badge
    (CMB), 52, 83, 88
Company, 21
Corson, William R., 189
Court-martial, 42–43, 47, 82
Cradle cap, 33–34
C rations, 122, 126, 127

Davis, Johnny Frank, 183
Defenbaugh, Sergeant, 43
DEROS (Date (of) Estimated
    Rotation Of Service), 82,
    100, 170, 179, 189, 191
Diarrhea, 102, 170
Dobbs, Sondra. *See* Holley,
    Sondra Dobbs

Dong Tam, 20, 25, 26–27, 28,
    29–31, 39, 42, 46, 48, 56,
    57, 58, 71, 73–75, 81–82,
    84, 89, 92, 94, 96–104, 111,
    113, 124, 128, 132, 141, 143,
    148, 190
Dooly, Ken, 78
Drug use, 74, 91, 96
Dunnick, Perry, 173

Eagle Flight, 119, 132, 171
Eastwood, Clint, 89
Elephantiasis, 45
Elia, Joe, 86, 169
Ewell, General, 127–128,
    132
Eye surgery, 86, 169

Field hospitals, 8
Field, Leon, 87–88
Fields, Bob, 1, 173
Fire Support Base Moore, 128,
    130, 132
1st Infantry Division, 176
Flores, Bob, 4
Fontenot, Benny, 137
Fort Benning, Georgia, 13
Fort Bragg, North Carolina, 13
Fort McPherson, Georgia,
    185–186, 195
Fort Sam Houston, Texas, 3–9,
    13, 16
4/39th Infantry Battalion, 20,
    21–22, 29, 127–128, 176,
    177, 185, 187, 188

Gas mask, 11
General hospitals, 8
Geneva Convention, 131, 184
Geraci, John P., 71–72
Giao Duc, 137–141
Gonorrhea (GC), 45

"Good morning, Vietnam," 154

Granuloma inguinale (GI), 44, 45

Green Berets, 64

Greer, Rosie, 94

Groves, Lieutenant, 76

Hackworth, David, 3, 128, 133, 137, 141, 142, 150, 161, 172, 189, 195
  in hot LZ, 147
  ignored by brass, 167, 187
  last night in Vietnam, 197–198
  leadership of, 130–131, 138–139
  and morale, 125
  new battalion commander, 114–115, 116
  physical appearance of, 115
  as real soldier, 117–118, 124–125
  reputation of, 119–120, 139, 144
  transfer from field, 186–187

Hager, Toby, 105, 106, 107, 119, 132, 171–172

Hanoi, 184

Hart, Franklin, 34, 149

Hartshorn, Bruce, 87, 88, 149–150

Hawaii, 128, 139, 140, 146, 150, 176, 179, 180

Heart massage, 126–127

Helicopters, 62, 70, 71, 81, 99, 115, 116, 117, 127, 128, 155
  ambulance, 5, 6, 25, 40
  light observation (LOH), 37–38, 107, 120, 138, 142

in search-and-destroy mission, 105–109

Helmets, 74

Heroin, 91, 96

Ho Chi Minh, 201

Ho Chi Minh trail, 137

Holley, Sondra Dobbs, 1, 2, 3, 88, 90

Hope, Bob, 90, 93, 94, 132

Hornfeck, Sergeant, 56, 69

Hueys, 70, 105, 106, 116, 117, 150

Hunt, Ira "Mickey Mouse," 131, 142

Immersion foot, 27–28, 39, 50, 111

Impetigo, 41

Influenza epidemic, 85–86

Jennings, Don, 120, 182

Johnson, Lyndon B., 4

Kennedy, John F., 200

Khe Sanh, 68

Khmer Rouge, 203

Knapp, Bob, 119–120, 125, 128, 139, 144, 145, 146, 147, 153, 157, 170, 179

Ky, Vice-President, 188

LAW (light antitank weapon), 69, 102

Leech bites, 27, 32, 114

LOH (light observation helicopter), 37–38, 107, 120, 138, 142

Long Binh, 18–19, 86, 113, 157, 158, 182

Long Dinh bridge, 101, 102, 103

Long Truong, 32–42, 43

LRRPS (Long Range
Reconnaissance Patrol
Subsistence), 122, 126
Lymphogranuloma venereum
(LGV), 39, 44
LZ (landing zone), hot, 105–
107, 147

M-16, 35, 36, 43, 48, 53, 54,
68, 69, 92, 102, 105, 138
wounds from, 4–5
M-60 20, 54
M-79 grenade launcher, 35,
55, 69, 89, 96, 102, 107,
108, 138
McBurney, Ronnie, 2
McCue, Dan, 102, 182
McDonald, Charles B., 144–
145
MACV (Military Assistance
Command Vietnam) General
Dispensary, 175, 181, 183–
184, 188
Mail call, 115, 125, 154
Malaria, 23, 40–41, 72, 84,
86, 88, 102, 128, 146
MARS network, 28, 30, 83,
84, 86, 157
Martin, Phil, 104
MASH (Mobile Army Surgical
Hospital), 6, 7, 25, 39
Mass, Max, 87, 158
MEDical Civil Action Program
(MEDCAP), 21
Medical service corps (MSC)
officer, 22
Medical treatment
in aid stations, 53, 63–64,
76–77, 91, 98, 103, 148
of booby-trap injuries, 91,
98, 140
eye surgery, 86, 169

heroin withdrawal, 91, 96
influenza, 85–86
levels of care, 6–9
malaria, 40–41, 86
minefield explosions, 109–
111, 116–117
priorities of, 9
shrapnel removal, 73–74, 80
sick calls, 50–51, 93, 98
skin disease, 27–28, 39, 41,
50
venereal disease, 41, 43–45,
50
of Vietnamese, 59–62, 72,
81, 84, 86, 88–89, 131, 136,
151
Medics
Airborne, 13
AWOL, 82
bravery of, viii–ix
casualties, 5, 67, 82–83,
104, 148, 164–165, 171
drafting of, 1–2
duties of battalion surgeon,
22–23
supplies for, 50
training of, 4–5, 10–13
transfers, 86, 152, 157–58
uniform of, 41
Mekong Delta, 23, 24, 25–26,
52
Mekong River, 25, 59, 101,
154, 155
Merlin, Paul, 56–57, 58
Military organization chart, 21
Miller, Lieutenant, 100
Mitchell, Larry, 38, 43, 92,
46, 59
Mobile Army Surgical Hospital
(MASH), 6, 7, 25, 39
Mobile Riverine Force (MRF),
24, 94

Monsoons, 23, 160, 170
Morale, 115, 125, 130–131, 154
Mosquitoes, 123, 125, 126
Muc Hoa, 114, 120, 121
My Diem, 119
My Phuoc Tay, 29, 42, 63–72, 142
My Tho, 24, 25, 59, 77–78, 103, 135
  orphanage at, 57–58

Napalm, 66
Nha Be, 42, 47, 49
Night ambush patrol, 78–79
Night map course training, 13, 14–16
9th Aviation Battalion, 25
9th Infantry Division, 20, 21, 24, 114, 117, 127, 144, 167, 176, 179, 181, 188
9th Medical Battalion, 78
90th Replacement Battalion, 157, 182
Nixon, Richard, 202

Obstacle course training, 12
101st Airborne, 195
Orphanage, 57–58

Paff, Dr., 173
Palmetto Medical Clinic, 2
Pelvic inflammatory disease (PID), 45
Penicillin reaction, 51, 61, 193–194
Plain of Reeds, 20, 24, 26, 29, 52, 73, 105, 113, 121, 145
Platoon, 21
Poverty, 34
Priorities of treatment, 9
Prisoners of war (POWs), 67–68, 70, 131–132, 141

Punji-stake wounds, 27
Purple Heart, 146

R & R, 144–146, 147, 176
Radio communications, MARS network, 28, 30, 83, 84, 86, 157
Radiotelephone, 40
Redfearn, 101
Ringworm, 39, 41
Risley, Dave, 139, 144, 145, 147, 170, 177
Rivera, Chris, 182
Roads, 95
Roberson, John, 142–143
Rodriguez, Jose, 105
Rollins, Corporal, 79, 107, 108, 109–111
RPG (rocket propelled grenade), 95, 100
Rung Sat, 26

Saigon, 47, 62, 68, 86–87, 95, 113, 144–146, 158–174, 175, 184
Sampans, 40, 59, 61
  ambush of, 35–36, 78–79, 97, 150
Sanitation, 22–24, 34
Saturday Evening Post, 149
Saxton, David E., 2
Saxton, Jesse J., 2
Schizophrenia, 148
Schwartz, Captain, 146
Search-and-destroy mission, 104–109
Seeker, John, 97, 99
Shit detail, 18–19
Showers, 65, 101
Shrapnel, removal of, 73–74, 80
Sick call, 50–51, 93, 98

Sinclair, Mike, 129
Sinclair, Spec Four, 97
68th Medical Group, 158
Skin disease, 27–28, 39, 41, 50
Slater, Sergeant, 177
Sleeping quarters, 68, 71
Southerland, Harold, 11–12
Special Forces camp, 64
Starlight Scopes, 53, 55, 150
Stars and Stripes, 62, 153, 172
Streeter, James, 114
Stress syndrome, 161–163
Summers, Harry, viii
Syphilis, 44, 45

Tactical operations center
    (TOC), 76
Tahler, Larry, 87, 149–150,
    154–155, 194–195
Tan An, 24, 71, 75, 76, 78,
    80, 101
Tan Son Nhut Air Base, 95,
    128, 140, 146, 158, 163,
    174, 180, 196, 198
Tan Tru, 24
Taylor, Al, 195
Tear gas, 11, 97
Templeton, Jeff, 81
Tet offensive, 101, 190
Thanh Phu, 142
Thanksgiving, 72, 75
Thieu, President, 188
3d Field Hospital, Saigon, 86–
    87, 146, 158, 167, 169, 192
3d Surgical Hospital, Dong
    Tam, 24, 81, 100, 109–111,
    112, 116
Thomas, Colonel, 86, 158, 178
3/5th Armored Cav., 24–25
3/17th Air Cav., 72
Thu Thua, 66–67, 76, 80–81

Tiger Scouts, 59, 84, 86, 88–
    89, 106, 112
Torpie, William, 144, 147
Travis Air Force Base,
    California, 3, 16, 49, 199
Triage, 8
Tripler Army Hospital, Hawaii,
    146, 147
Truman, Harry S, 201
Truong, General, 188
24th Evacuation Hospital, 112–
    113, 143, 148, 153, 169
27th Infantry Regiment, 195
29th Evacuation Hospital, 99
Twigg, Louis, 24
2/60th Infantry, 72
218th Medical Dispensary,
    Saigon, 158, 159, 165–166,
    170–171
229th General Dispensary, Tan
    Son Nhut Airbase, 174, 177–
    178, 183–184, 191–192, 194
Typhoons, 18, 23, 182

Uniform
    medics, 41
    peasant, 33
U.S. Army Medical Corps.
    See Medical treatment;
    Medics
USO, 184

Vam Co Tay River, 68
Venereal disease (VD), 41, 43–
    45, 50, 70
Viet Cong, 5, 6–7, 20, 24, 26,
    34, 46, 51, 66, 76, 77, 91,
    92, 95 99, 118, 119, 124,
    126, 127, 129, 130, 148, 167
    bus bombing by, 135–136
    hatred of, 150, 151

Viet Cong, *(cont)*
  medical treatment of, 59–62,
    84, 86, 88–89, 131, 151
  prisoners of war (POWs),
    67–68, 70, 131–132, 141
  propaganda of, 84–85
  in sampan ambush, 35–36,
    78–79, 150
  search-and-destroy mission
    against, 106–109
  as Tiger Scouts, 88–89
  white phosphorous artillery
    round of, 133–135

Viet Minh, 184
Vinh Long, 24, 137

Wagon Wheel, 51–52, 101,
  104, 113, 114–115, 116
Westmoreland, William, viii, 67
White phosphorous ("willy
  peter") burns, 133–135
Williams, Troy, 174, 175–176,
  180, 182, 189, 195, 196,
  197, 199, 200
Wintzer, Charlie, 113, 134,
  135, 137, 142, 143, 152

About the Author

Byron Edward Holley was born in Tampa, Florida and is a graduate of the University of Miami School of Medicine. He also holds a Bachelor of Science degree in Biology from the University of Tampa. Dr. Holley was drafted into the U.S. Army in 1968 at the height of the U.S. involvement in Southeast Asia. Following a two-year tour in the service, he entered Tulane University, where he completed a three-year residency in ophthalmology. He then completed a clinical fellowship in diseases and surgery of the retina and has been in the private practice of ophthalmology in Tampa since 1975.

While serving in the U.S. Army Medical Corps, he was awarded the Combat Medical Badge; the Bronze Star for meritorious achievement, with two oak-leaf clusters; the Army Commendation Medal for Valor, with two oak-leaf clusters; the Air Medal; the Republic of Vietnam Service Medal; and the National Defense Medal. He is listed in *Who's Who in the South and Southwest* and is a member of the American Medical Association as well as numerous other professional organizations. He is married to Sondra Dobbs Holley and is the father of two sons, Charles Edward and John Byron, and one daughter, Allison Miriam.